They Came for the Schools

THEY CAME FOR THE SCHOOLS

One Town's Fight Over Race and Identity, and the New War for America's Classrooms

MIKE HIXENBAUGH

MARINER BOOKS
New York Boston

HarperCollins books may be purchased for educational, business, or sales promotional use. For information, please email the Special Markets Department at SPsales@harpercollins.com.

FIRST EDITION

Designed by Chloe Foster

Library of Congress Cataloging-in-Publication Data has been applied for.

ISBN 978-0-06-330724-7

24 25 26 27 28 LBC 5 4 3 2 1

For Ezra, Eleanor, Milo, and Fifi,
whose kindness and curiosity give me hope

Contents

Prologue

FORGET EVERYTHING YOU'VE BEEN taught to believe about America's suburbs, land of quarter-acre lots, cul-de-sacs, and two-car garages. They are not, broadly speaking, lily-white, close-knit, or sleepy. Some suburbs in some places might have started out that way, but those of 2024 are now more diverse than the nation overall—and just as bitterly divided.

Maybe you noticed the trend a few years ago when outraged parents started packing into suburban school board meetings, convinced that someone somewhere was trying to teach white kindergarteners that they should be ashamed of their skin color. Or when librarians began pulling picture books from shelves because they were afraid someone might see an illustration of two dads holding hands and call the police. Or when white nationalist extremist groups pivoted from amplifying false claims about a stolen presidential election and started focusing on public school curriculum in places like Downers Grove, Illinois, and New Hanover County, North Carolina.

For me, the first hint that these political winds were blowing into the suburbs came late on the night of July 3, 2020.

I had just finished brushing my teeth.

"Look at this," my wife said, handing me her phone as I climbed into bed. A friend from down the street had texted a link to a post in our neighborhood Facebook group—a page where, up until this moment, people had typically gone to upload pictures of lost pets or to ask about changes to the trash pickup schedule.

On this summer night, the middle-aged white guy who lived behind us had logged on, instead, to sound an alarm. He wrote that he'd seen what looked to him like members of Antifa—a highly decentralized anti-fascist militant group that had attained a foreboding status in the psyche of many American conservatives—buying ammo at a nearby sporting goods store. It wasn't clear what about their appearance triggered his suspicion, other than the fact that they were dressed in black, but my neighbor warned in his post that his sighting meant that our little tree-lined subdivision, located more than twenty-five miles from downtown Houston, could be a target for a violent attack.

"What the hell is this?" I said to my wife, as I began scrolling through the comments.

Three years earlier, in 2017, we'd moved to the suburbs for many of the same reasons you hear from other parents. We could afford a little more house out that way, and a little more yard, which is helpful when you're raising four young kids on one journalism salary. Plus, everyone said the schools were good.

Timberlake Estates, a mostly white but diversifying subdivision, was the kind of place where children rode bikes unsupervised on sleepy streets and met up on weekends to cast fishing lines into a man-made lake at the center of the neighborhood. We liked our new house, but it was a major disaster that made the neighborhood really start to feel like home. Three months after moving in, Hurricane Harvey dumped a year's worth of rain across the Houston region in the span of a few days, pushing Cypress Creek over its banks and flooding thousands of surrounding homes. In the weeks that followed, as front yards filled with debris piles, we watched neighbors show up to swing sledgehammers and deliver plates of barbecue. The shared trauma and communal recovery made us feel deeply connected to our new community, and to our new neighbors.

But something had begun to change by the time my wife showed me that Facebook post three years later, and not just in our subdivision. The country was in the grips of a nationwide shared trauma, and America's response had been anything but communal. Rather than bringing neighbors together, the COVID-19 pandemic had been driving them apart, forcing people inside and online, deeper into their own echo chambers and, in some instances, planting seeds of suspicion and resentment—

feelings that only grew more intense following George Floyd's murder under the knee of a white police officer in Minneapolis in May 2020. That spring and summer, people were taking in a constant stream of footage from protests and riots that, depending on which cable news network they preferred, were being framed as either a historic opportunity to address centuries of racial injustice, or a lawless attack on cities by anti-American extremists.

Now it seemed all that anger and angst and uncertainty had found a landing spot on my neighborhood's Facebook page. In a separate comment on the same post, another neighbor shared her fear that Antifa and other groups might be strategically planning their assault on Timberlake Estates for the night of July Fourth, with the shooting masked under the cover of fireworks.

"We need to be on alert for sure!" she wrote.

In a follow-up post, the neighbor who'd written the initial warning about Antifa offered a tip for what to do if activists showed up and swarmed anyone's cars: "Once they block you, they are no longer protesters but a threat," he wrote, and then posted a copy of a Texas statute that he said gives motorists the right to shoot to kill in that situation.

"Yup!" someone else responded. "We are locked and loaded all the time!"

That last comment made my breath catch in my throat. Why were the people of Timberlake Estates preparing for combat?

A few of my neighbors, it seemed, had latched on to a viral conspiracy theory that was rearing its head in suburbs and small towns all over the country in 2020, fueled largely by the man whose presidency had already done so much to expose and exploit Americans' primal distrust of one another. All summer and through the fall, Donald Trump had been warning supporters that Black Lives Matter activists and Antifa were on a mission to destroy suburbia. And he didn't mean figuratively.

"Does anybody want to have somebody from Antifa as a member and as a resident of your suburb?" Trump, campaigning for a second presidential term, asked a crowd in Freeland, Michigan, later that September. "I don't think so too much." Then he did a bit where he pretended to be a married couple discussing their new neighbors. "'Say, darling, who moved in next door?' 'Oh, it's a resident of Antifa.' 'No, thank you. Let's get out of here. Let's get the hell out of here, darling. Let's leave our suburbs. I wish Trump were president. He wouldn't have allowed that to happen.'"

Two days later, Trump's campaign sent a text message warning millions of supporters that members of Antifa would "attack your homes" if Biden was elected.

The fact that some of our neighbors were gearing up to face that imagined threat was almost comical—until we realized they were serious.

My wife, Bethany, the biracial daughter of a Black police officer, had always been burdened by fears that her dad might be killed in the line of duty, or while out on a run in his overwhelmingly white neighborhood in Ohio, where a neighbor had once called the cops on him for jogging past their house. Another time, someone vandalized my father-in-law's car with the N-word. We'd intentionally chosen to raise our kids somewhere more diverse, and yet, here we were, sharing a fence with someone who was stocking up on ammo in response to disinformation and assumptions he'd made about strangers based on their appearance.

The next day, I sat our kids down and instructed them not to ride their bikes past that neighbor's house.

A few weeks later, partially in response to the Facebook fearmongering, Bethany decided to plant a Black Lives Matter sign in our front yard, a small gesture that nonetheless felt like a big one. Because of my line of work as a journalist, we'd always refrained from displaying political messages on our car or around our home. Reporters, after all, are trained to appear objective. But that summer the words "Black Lives Matter" had, for a short time at least, seemed close to ubiquitous, accepted across mainstream American culture—a collective acknowledgment and repudiation of systemic racism. The phrase was showing up in anti-racism resolutions approved by nonpartisan school boards and city councils all over the country, and in new corporate mission statements. NBCUniversal, my newsroom's parent company, tweeted out its support for the cause: "We stand with our Black employees, colleagues, partners, and creators in outrage at acts of racism. Black Lives Matter." A few days later, Republican senator Mitt Romney tweeted out the three-word slogan along with a photo of himself marching with anti-racism activists.

For those reasons, our family's black-and-white cardboard yard sign felt like an even-handed, nonpartisan way to take a stand for human rights. But many Americans, especially white conservatives, viewed signs like ours as an attack on law enforcement, or worse, an attack on America. That might explain why, every weekend for two months after my wife put the sign up, someone drove their four-wheeler into our yard and did donuts in it, churning up deep divots in the grass.

I didn't know it at the time, but similar acts of anti–Black Lives Matter aggression were quietly popping up all over the country. Yard signs were stolen, set on fire, and desecrated with swastikas and slurs. In one case, a white man in a Detroit suburb admitted to shooting at a Black family's home, slashing their car tires, and writing racist graffiti on their truck because he didn't like the BLM sign posted in their home's front window.

As a white man who grew up in a nearly all-white town in a rural stretch of Northeast Ohio, where racism was rarely discussed in any meaningful way—and not at all in school—I wasn't prepared for the backlash. I never got used to the rush of anger and fear each time we heard the roar of that four-wheeler engine in our yard. It felt so personal and threatening, having someone come onto our property week after week while our kids slept. For Bethany, who'd dealt with subtle and overt acts of racism her entire life, it stirred more familiar and distressing questions about identity, safety, and belonging.

I found her one morning sobbing in our living room, apparently overwhelmed by the sudden realization that she no longer felt welcome in the neighborhood where we'd planned to watch our kids grow up. "I don't want to live here," she told me, her voice cracking.

I put my arm over her shoulder and told her I was sorry, and that we would figure something out. But as I sat with her, trying to process the gravity of her words, another thought hit me: She can't be the only one feeling this way. I realized that what we were seeing and experiencing that summer—intense acrimony among neighbors over race and politics in a diversifying community—probably wasn't unique to our little suburb. This, I imagined, was likely a defining struggle of American life in 2020. So, while my wife searched Houston real estate listings, I did what I almost always do when confronted with personal trauma: I turned it into a journalism project.

That's how, in early September 2020, I ended up on the phone with then Texas GOP chairman Allen West, a Black army veteran and former Florida congressman who'd risen to prominence in far-right circles during the Tea Party movement a decade earlier. I called him up because I wanted to know what he thought of Trump's message about defending the suburbs from Black Lives Matter, and about the impact the president's claims were having on the lives of regular people.

At first, West fed me what would turn out to be a false statistic about a surge of white women getting permits to carry guns, apparently trying to make the case that white suburban voters shared Trump's concerns about growing lawlessness. But when I pressed West on whether he thought voters truly believed the president's claim about Democrats wanting to "abolish the suburbs," he pivoted, telling me, "Well, I will give you anecdotal evidence."

West told me about a "very nice, well-to-do, affluent community" between Dallas and Fort Worth that had been "receiving threats from Black Lives Matter." He said these threats had led to serious problems in the town's high-achieving suburban school system, and that parents there had decided to fight back, setting an example of grassroots activism that West said should be copied in communities all over Texas.

At the time, I didn't know what he was talking about. But his words would prove remarkably prescient.

The parent-versus-parent fight just beginning to simmer in that North Texas suburb would intensify and spread in the months and years that followed, becoming a model—or cautionary tale, depending on who you ask—not just in Texas, but for suburban school districts all over the country. In hindsight, we should have seen it coming. America's public schools, since their very creation, repeatedly have become ground zero for this country's most divisive battles over politics and civil rights—from the fights over evolution and segregation to those over sex ed and school prayer. After all, it's in our schools—in social studies curricula and civics lessons and mandatory reading lists—that America is grappling with how to tell its story to new generations, how to teach kids what's right and wrong, what's true and what's false. And this grappling has gotten ugly.

After I got off the phone with West, I scribbled a reminder to myself. Six words on a pink Post-it note that would shape the next four years of my life, leading me to discover that the anger, fear, and animosity splashing onto my neighborhood Facebook page and into my front lawn that summer was nothing compared to the political tsunami that was about to crash into America's schools.

"What," I wrote, "is going on in Southlake?"

Part I

SUBURBAN DREAMLAND

1

Perfect City, U.S.A.

EARLY ONE MORNING IN February 2006, Amy Rolle loaded her three children into her Chevy Suburban and set out from Los Angeles on a cross-country road trip in pursuit of a quintessentially American ideal: a good school for her kids.

She pulled out before sunrise, hoping to escape the city before the morning rush, and headed east on Interstate 10. Five-year-old Raven rode in a booster seat in back, watching movies on a portable DVD player as a blur of desert flashed by the side window. In exchange for pacifying her eighteen-month-old baby brother, Roman, with an unlimited supply of Goldfish crackers and gummy worms, Jasmine, the twelve-year-old, was given control of the car stereo. She sang along to "Unwritten" by Natasha Bedingfield and "Bring Me to Life" by Evanescence as her mother—fueled by coffee, Diet Coke, and a sense of purpose—kept an eye on the directions she'd printed off MapQuest to guide their path from California to Texas.

Rolle and her husband, Reggie, had for several years been raising the children in Studio City, a ritzy neighborhood just over the hill from Hollywood, where they'd both pursued acting careers. In an only-in-L.A. romance, they'd met in 1998 on the set of *Power Rangers Lost Galaxy,* the seventh season of the wildly popular children's superhero fantasy series. Reggie, who's Black, had been cast as the iconic Green Ranger. Amy, who's white, starred opposite him as the evil alien insect queen, Trakeena. Despite their campy costumes—he wore green spandex; she had huge purple antennae protruding from her forehead—the attraction was instant.

Seven years later, the show was in syndication, Reggie had gone to work managing a chain of upscale clothing stores, and the Rolles—by then a family of five—had traded their pursuit of Hollywood fame for more domestic ambitions. "Every parent wants their children to have more and better opportunities than they had," Amy recalled. "That's the dream, isn't it?"

Increasingly, however, the Rolles's attempts at achieving that dream in Los Angeles had begun to feel like a high-stakes shell game. They loved their house, a modern stucco a short walk from upscale restaurants, winding hiking trails, and gorgeous views of the San Fernando Valley. But the middle and high schools the Rolle children were zoned to in the Los Angeles Unified School District were far from elite, at least according to standardized test scores and other metrics that tend to measure student demographics and the wealth of their parents as much as they do academic achievement. The Rolles at first considered buying a home in a different L.A. neighborhood, but in most instances switching to a more highly rated middle school for Jasmine meant a worse elementary school for Raven, who would soon be entering kindergarten.

Amy, having grown up in small-town Kentucky, and Reggie, who graduated from a public school outside Minneapolis, were willing to move for something better. After Reggie's employer agreed to consider transferring him to a location outside California, the Rolles spent months researching the best places in America to raise a family, relying on websites such as GreatSchools.org to guide them. Initially they thought about moving to an affluent suburb in Minnesota, near where Reggie grew up, but Amy worried about how she and the kids would adjust to the long winters.

Then, in late 2005, a friend of Amy's mentioned a fast-growing suburb in Texas that neither she nor Reggie had heard of before. "And she starts telling me that Southlake is a town near where her mom and dad live, and that it's got some of the best schools in the whole nation," Amy said. "The more I looked into it, the more I thought, 'We need to check this out.'"

A last-minute work obligation prevented Reggie from coming on the initial visit, but having spent weeks planning the road trip, Amy was determined to see it through.

After more than twenty-two hours in the car—and a short stay at a roadside motel in New Mexico—she and the kids arrived after dark in North Texas and spent the night with a friend in a town outside Fort Worth, less than a half hour from Southlake. Rolle was immediately impressed heading into town the next morning, and not only because it was eighty-five-degree tank top weather in mid-February.

She met their realtor at Town Square, a master-planned downtown that developers had carved into the middle of the suburb a half decade earlier, transforming 133 acres of pastureland into a high-end shopping and dining district. Two things Amy noticed first were how meticulously the town had branded itself, and how proud everyone seemed of their local schools. The banners hanging from decorative light posts were bright green to match the colors of the school district's dragon mascot. Many of the women coming in and out of Williams Sonoma and Pottery Barn were wearing T-shirts of the same color, each emblazoned with phrases like "Expect Excellence" and "Dragon Pride." Even the *S* emblems on Southlake street signs were in the shape of curvy little dragons.

After grabbing breakfast at a coffee shop, Amy and the kids got back in the car and cruised down Southlake Boulevard, trailing the realtor as she guided them through neighborhoods with names like Diamond Circle Estates and Lakes of La Paloma, each with a decorative fountain blasting water into the air from the center of a retention pond. Amy couldn't believe how smooth the roads were or the size of the houses—or that they could afford a four-thousand-square-foot home on a half acre of land for less than the price of a three-bedroom bungalow in L.A.

"I couldn't get over how clean everything was," Amy said. "There were sidewalks everywhere, and people out jogging and walking their dogs and kids out riding bikes."

And then there was Southlake's crown jewel. The institution that had been attracting upper-middle-class families here for decades: the Carroll Independent School District, where the Dragons football team is a perennial state championship contender and average SAT scores are good enough to get most students into top-tier universities. Amy drove past the campuses of the schools her kids would attend and pictured her little ones with the other children in the bus line.

By the time Reggie called to check in that evening, Amy had already made up her mind. She rattled off everything Southlake had going for it. The acres of green space. Gorgeous houses. Top-rated schools. She remembered joking with him, "What's the catch? What's the catch?"

From the start, this town seemed almost too good to be true.

A half century before Amy Rolle's road trip, the U.S. Army Corps of Engineers dug a seven-thousand-acre reservoir in northeast Tarrant County and named it Lake Grapevine, triggering a rush of residential construction on the surrounding farmland. Not everyone welcomed these developments. On September 22, 1956, a few dozen people filtered through the Carroll Hill School, a six-room schoolhouse that served as a central gathering place for residents in the unincorporated area south of Lake Grapevine that would soon become known as Southlake. In those days, residents could on occasion pay twenty-five cents to see white actors put on blackface and perform old-time Negro minstrels at Carroll Hill, with the proceeds going to the school's Parent-Teacher Association. On that Saturday, however, they'd gathered for a different purpose: to prevent change from coming to their rural, nearly all-white community.

White settlers had begun arriving a century earlier to this slice of North Texas, wooed by generous land grants and by the rolling prairie and thick timber forest that had once been occupied by members of the Comanches, Kiowa, and Wichita tribes. Families came from Missouri and other southern slave states and built log homes and churches. In 1919, local white men voted to raise their property taxes to build a school, and named it after B. E. Carroll, Tarrant County's superintendent of public instruction—a revered country educator who, according to newspaper clippings, had ties to the Ku Klux Klan. A year later, a freed slave and wealthy rancher named Bob Jones built a school of his own to educate his grandchildren and other Black and mixed-race students who were not welcome at Carroll.

By 1956, word was spreading that the nearby city of Hurst was planning to annex thousands of acres of farmland and forest surrounding Carroll Hill as part of its rapid expansion in northeast Tarrant County. Hurst's growth coincided with an explosion of new suburban development nationally, spurred in part by *Brown v. Board of Education*, the U.S. Supreme Court's landmark 1954 decision striking down America's tradition of racially segregated schools. Fear of integration had begun fueling an exodus of white residents from cities. Now the people at Carroll Hill had a decision to make. They could let Hurst city officials come in and impose new zoning rules and taxes and watch their land get scooped up by developers and paved over with new subdivisions, or they could establish their own municipality—one where they could make the rules.

The vote was set against a backdrop of tectonic social and political change, in Texas and across America. Elvis Presley had a few weeks earlier made his first appearance on the *The Ed Sullivan Show*, shattering TV ratings records and outraging parents who saw his hip-gyrating as a sign of the nation's moral decline. As part of a conservative campaign to expand the influence of Christianity in America, Congress that summer had voted to make "In God We Trust" the nation's official motto and encouraged schools and other government facilities to display it with pride. Texas lawmakers, meanwhile, had begun debating legislation to pay private school tuition for any white students who otherwise might be forced to attend a racially integrated public school—an explicitly racist forebearer of the contemporary school choice movement. And just thirty miles south of Carroll Hill, in another small Tarrant County community, a federal judge's order to desegregate the all-white Mansfield High School had led to an ugly and widely publicized showdown.

When three Black teens arrived at Mansfield High on the first day of school that August 30, 1956, they'd been met by a white mob of about three hundred. The demonstrators had strung nooses around the necks of three black effigies—one dummy for each new student—and hung them above the school's front entry, a visceral warning to any Black student who dared to step inside. A full year before President Dwight D. Eisenhower famously sent federal troops to assist with the integration of a high school in Little Rock, Arkansas, Texas governor Allan Shivers sent Texas Rangers to "keep the peace" at Mansfield—which in this instance meant blocking the three Black students from attending.

One month later, the residents at Carroll Hill decided by a vote of 30–24 to incorporate as the town of Southlake—not as part of a grand vision to establish one of the most desirable suburban communities in Texas, but to prevent a rush of new development. As the town's first mayor, Gail Eubanks told the *Fort Worth Star-Telegram*, "We heard about Hurst's proposed action, and we incorporated for protection."

For the next half century, that word—"protection"—would define the governing philosophy of Southlake and suburban communities like it across America. Years later, it would be enshrined in the Carroll school district's official motto: "Protect the Tradition." The town's early leaders adopted rules to protect against growing too quickly, including zoning policies requiring any new homes to be built on at least one acre of land, and prohibiting the construction of apartments and other multifamily housing units. But those restrictions couldn't completely stop the march of progress. Southlake's location just northwest of the new Dallas/Fort Worth International Airport, which opened in 1974, made the area a prime target for developers, causing land values to skyrocket and creating a tension that would influence town politics for decades.

In the years after the civil rights movement of the 1960s, the conflict between economic growth and the desire to prevent too many people—or, perhaps, the wrong people—from moving to town shaped suburban development across the country. In an era when cities and neighborhoods could no longer explicitly keep residents out based on their race, the debate in places like Southlake was usually framed around a coded set of phrases. Residents who opposed growth said they were determined to protect the town's "rural atmosphere" from "high-density housing," which they feared would lead to crime, overcrowded schools, and other "urban" problems.

"We came out here to get away from high-density living, and we don't appreciate having it pushed down our throats," a Southlake resident complained to the city council in 1971, when the town was considering a modest zoning exemption to allow a developer to build homes on lots smaller than a half acre. "You're asking us to give up all these rights we came out here and fought for before there even was a Southlake."

Opposition to affordable housing became a litmus test for anyone seeking elected office in Southlake, even after the city started attracting major corporate development. IBM's decision in 1982 to open a new regional office in town helped propel Southlake's population to more than 4,700 by the middle of that decade—a surge that coincided with rapid residential development in the neighboring towns of Keller, Grapevine, and Colleyville. Among them, Southlake earned a reputation as an ideal bedroom community for oil and gas bosses and senior managers at American Airlines, which had recently moved its corporate headquarters to Fort Worth. As the town and surrounding communities grew, both in size and reputation, so did the Carroll Independent School District. The town's economic boom ensured the district was flush with resources. But many of the educators brought in to teach the children of wealthy business executives soon discovered a reality that remains true today: It's hard to find an affordable home in Southlake on a teacher's salary.

Then again, that may have been by design.

In 1985, after a local business owner complained that the city's prohibition against apartments and smaller residential lots had the effect of blocking lower- and middle-income families from moving to Southlake, the city's mayor, Lloyd Latta, acknowledged as much in an interview with the *Star-Telegram*. "I guess that it seems to be the will of the people," Latta told the newspaper, "and I don't find any fault in it."

A few years later, Southlake's city attorney warned town leaders that their blanket opposition to multifamily housing left them vulnerable to a potential federal lawsuit under the U.S. Fair Housing Act, which prohibits exclusionary zoning policies. One such lawsuit already had been filed that year against the town of Sunnyvale, another Dallas suburb with similarly restrictive zoning rules, where a councilman once bluntly confided to a developer that he liked the one-acre minimum because it kept "n——rs" from moving to town. Ultimately, members of the Southlake City Council rejected their lawyer's advice to allow multifamily housing. They were far more concerned, it seemed, about the blowback they would get from voters if they ever let developers build apartments. The outrage would be so severe, one member of the city's zoning board said, "we might as well just bring our own rope."

What none of them acknowledged at the time—at least not publicly—was that, in America, income is often a proxy for race, and that by keeping Southlake wealthy, its leaders were, in effect, keeping it white.

While exclusionary zoning policies like those in Southlake had the effect of walling off most Black families from moving to the suburbs, a lesser-known U.S. Supreme Court decision from the mid-1970s, *Milliken v. Bradley*, ensured that those invisible barriers would block most Black children from crossing them to attend highly desirable suburban schools.

Two decades after *Brown v. Board*, white flight and racist housing policies had led to a regime of de facto segregation across America. In cities all over the nation, predominantly Black—and chronically underfunded—urban school systems were increasingly surrounded by virtually all-white suburban districts, which reaped the benefits of higher property values.

In 1974, the Supreme Court had an opportunity to upend that system after the NAACP sued the state of Michigan in an attempt to desegregate schools in Detroit. At the time, about two-thirds of the students in Detroit were Black, while dozens of fast-growing suburban districts surrounding the city were almost exclusively white. As a result, the plaintiffs in *Milliken v. Bradley* argued, the only way to truly integrate the area's schools would be to require the state to bus Black and white children across city lines—effectively breaking down the barriers to equitable school access created by zoning restrictions, racist neighborhood covenants, and redlining policies that blocked Black families from getting housing loans.

The case had the potential to finally fulfill Brown's promise of school integration in America. But by the time *Milliken v. Bradley* reached the Supreme Court, President Richard Nixon—whose strategy to win support among Southern whites included opposition to forced integration—had appointed four conservative justices to the court. One of them, future chief justice William Rehnquist, had written a memo only a few years earlier, while serving as an assistant attorney general in the Nixon administration, urging his boss to push for a constitutional amendment to put an end to court-ordered school desegregation efforts. Rehnquist's vote proved pivotal in the Detroit case.

In a 5-to-4 decision, the court sided with the suburbs, whose lawyers had argued that they bore no responsibility for desegregating Detroit's schools. Rehnquist and others in the majority reasoned that local school systems—even those that were nearly all-white and located a short drive from majority-Black schools—could not be forced to participate in a regional desegregation plan unless it could be proven that district lines were drawn with explicitly racist intent. Another justice, Potter Stewart, wrote in his concurring opinion that the rampant and accelerating segregation in greater Detroit was "caused by unknown and perhaps unknowable factors," and therefore there was no constitutional remedy to address it.

In a scathing dissent read from the bench, Justice Thurgood Marshall, who had been the lead counsel for the NAACP when the *Brown* case was brought to the court two decades earlier, predicted that his colleagues' decision in *Milliken* would cement racial segregation in America: "The very evil that *Brown* was aimed at will not be cured, but will be perpetuated." Then, in a line that seemed to foreshadow the conflicts over race sweeping the nation's suburban schools today, Marshall added, "For unless our children begin to learn together, there is little hope that our people will ever learn to live together and understand each other."

Just as Marshall had feared, most desegregation efforts collapsed in the ensuing years. After a federal judge ordered Boston to desegregate its schools through a busing program that would affect only students within city lines—affluent suburbs were not involved—thousands of parents in the largely poor white enclaves of Southie and Charlestown protested, waving signs with handwritten messages like "Whites have rights" and "We are not 'racists,' 'pigs,' 'animals,' we are 'parents.'" The first week of school, buses carrying Black children home from these neighborhoods were pelted with rocks—the beginning of years of violent protests over the integration program. One anti-busing mother warned a reporter that the program was ruining white neighborhoods. "Busing," she said, "has torn the fabric that linked us." Similar scenes repeated in major cities all over America. When a busing plan was coming up for a vote in Philadelphia in 1975, hundreds of irate white parents crammed inside a public meeting hall to pressure the city's board of education to reverse course. After the board killed the plan, one school board member confided to a *New York Times* reporter, "Desegregation in Philadelphia is not possible."

In the few metros where integration initially seemed to succeed, progress was undermined by a surge of new private Christian schools that catered exclusively to white students. These segregation academies flourished across the country even after the Supreme Court ruled that they could not exclude students based on race. One Dallas-area school, Trinity Christian Academy, found a way to put up less explicit obstacles to keep Black children out. "We have had some Blacks apply from the area," Trinity's headmaster David Coterill told the *Associated Press* in 1972, "but the pathetic situation is that they cannot make the preliminary testing." The school's tuition was another barrier for Black children, and Trinity, Coterill said, did not offer scholarships.

In wealthy suburban communities like Southlake, meanwhile, public schools thrived. By the mid-1980s, the fast-growing Carroll Independent School District was drawing regional praise for its students' exceptional test scores. The *Fort Worth Star-Telegram* began running annual articles comparing the above-average SAT results at Carroll and other suburban school districts in the region with the lower scores in urban districts such as Fort Worth and Arlington that served large numbers of Black students, helping create and perpetuate the perception that suburban schools were simply better run.

In a 1983 newspaper interview, Carroll's longtime superintendent Jack Johnson seemed to acknowledge that the district's SAT scores were in large part a measure of Southlake's demographics. "In districts where you find parents well educated, the expectations are greater," Johnson said. "This community is probably quite a bit above the average as far as number of years of education per parent." Having accomplished and well-off parents wasn't the only thing that differentiated Southlake students from those at nearby urban districts; flipping through Carroll's high school yearbook from that year revealed page after page of virtually all-white faces—a reality that no doubt helped shape the district's culture. In one photo, two female members of the school's 4-H Club appeared to be performing a skit for their classmates while dressed in blackface—a tradition steeped in centuries of racism.

Three decades after *Brown*, America's schools had effectively resegregated, perhaps not explicitly based on race, but according to wealth, geography, and social status.

Around that same time, a new niche field of study was emerging among a group of Black legal scholars at Harvard University that was intended to help people understand the way race-neutral policies like those upheld in *Milliken* had the effect of perpetuating racism. This new academic framework would challenge the notion that systemic racism had ended with the passage of the Civil Rights Act. It would encourage legal scholars, activists, and historians to connect modern racial disparities—in housing, in wealth, in education—with the explicit racism of America's past. By the late 1980s, these scholars had come up with a name to describe their work: critical race theory.

But more than three decades would pass before most Americans became aware of that phrase.

White parents weren't the only ones reading headlines about superior test scores in Southlake and other suburbs and concluding that those places held the ticket to giving their children the best possible education. Beginning in the 1990s, a growing number of middle- and upper-class Black families had begun to leave cities in pursuit of better-performing schools—a new, smaller Great Migration that would, slowly, over the course of decades, help change the demographic face of suburbia. By 2020, nearly half of all residents residing in America's suburbs were non-white, although in many suburban communities—especially exclusive, strictly zoned enclaves like Southlake—change came more slowly.

After Frank Cornish signed a free agent contract with the Dallas Cowboys in 1992, he and his fiancée, Robin, went in search of a place to put down roots. Both Black natives of Chicago, they'd met a few years earlier while attending college in Los Angeles, where Frank had been a star on campus as a towering All-American offensive lineman for the UCLA Bruins. Now, in their mid-twenties, they were ready to get married and start a family. Several of Frank's teammates were living in Coppell and Plano and other affluent north Dallas suburbs, but their realtor said she wanted to show them an up-and-coming community a little farther out.

Frank fell in love with Southlake the moment they pulled into town.

By then, the city and its schools had started to attract statewide media attention, thanks mostly to the upstart Dragons high school football program, which under the direction of legendary coach Bob Ledbetter was in the middle of a state-record-setting seventy-two-game winning streak. Recently dubbed "the city of the 90s" by a Dallas developer, the town of about seven thousand was on the cusp of explosive growth that would see its population triple by the end of the decade. The city's decision to run water and sewer lines through the southern half of town had unleashed a boom of new home construction. Yet the place still had a rural feel, with new luxury subdivisions popping up alongside acres of horse pasture.

Frank, who'd spent many summers at his grandfather's farm in rural Louisiana, told Robin on that first visit, "We're moving to Southlake." Robin was having a different reaction as they rumbled down a two-lane dirt road leading into a neighborhood that was still partially under construction: "I was like, 'If you're happy, I'm happy,'" she recalled telling him. "I'm a city girl, I'm from Chicago. But this is my husband and what he wanted, so I wanted to compromise."

In time, Southlake worked its magic on her, too. The people were friendly, she said, and after she and Frank brought home Frankie Jr. from the hospital in 1994—the first of their five babies—Robin struggled to imagine a better place to raise a family.

Back then, it didn't bother her that they were one of only a few dozen Black families in Southlake, making up less than 1 percent of the population. They'd made good friends, and it didn't hurt that Frank was revered in the community, having won a pair of Super Bowl rings with the Cowboys before injuries forced him to retire from the NFL in 1995. Robin was too busy shuttling kids to playdates and library visits to notice that, even then, racial tension was simmering in their newly adopted hometown.

Those issues, usually discussed privately among a small group of Black parents, exploded into public view on a warm Saturday afternoon in October 1996, when nearly ten thousand fans jammed into a Tarrant County stadium for the first-ever meeting of two powerhouse football programs. In the end, the Grapevine Mustangs were led by a pair of standout Black players to defeat the all-white Southlake Carroll Dragons, 28–14. But all anyone was talking about afterward was the homemade sign that a white Carroll sophomore had been waving from the sidelines.

In large print, he'd written five letters: *T.A.N.H.O.*—short for "tear a n——r's head off." In another incident before the game, school officials had discovered the same acronym scrawled in shoe polish on three cars in the Carroll High parking lot. Years later, Grapevine's star wide receiver, Jack Brewer, who is Black and went on to play in the NFL, said white Carroll students had also dangled a dummy from the stands wearing his jersey number and a noose around its neck.

Carroll's superintendent at the time downplayed the issue after it made headlines in Dallas and Fort Worth, telling reporters that the incidents were isolated and did not reflect the attitudes of all Carroll High School students. But once Black parents learned that the student who'd made the sign was given what they viewed as a lenient punishment—a few thirty-minute detentions and two weeks without extracurricular activities—they were outraged.

Judy Gilmore, a white Carroll school board member, told a reporter that the incident should be a wake-up call for the city. "We have to start dealing with the diversity in our community," Gilmore said. "We're located between two airports and we're attracting a more diverse population. We're not isolated anymore, and people need to understand that."

On a Monday night three weeks later, on the eve of President Bill Clinton's reelection, parents of Black and Latino Carroll students lined up to speak at a special school board meeting. One by one, they shared accounts of racist insults they said their children had endured while attending school in a district where, at the time, about nineteen out of every twenty students were white. "There's no mechanism in the school district for these kids to get some relief from acts of prejudice," one Black parent told the board. "There are a whole lot of things going on that aren't as noticeable as a sign at a football game."

Afterward, the Carroll school board directed an existing volunteer committee called Bridging Differences—formed after a Southlake mother complained in 1994 that her child was coming home from school in tears over being called racial slurs—to come up with ways to promote cultural awareness. The district brought in guest speakers to talk to students and teachers about diversity, empathy, and kindness. District leaders pledged to hire a Black teacher for the first time in Carroll's history—though it would take a few years before they finally delivered on that promise.

In an era when color blindness was being promoted as the preferred answer to racism in America, the 1996 episode may have felt like a turning point to some in Southlake. But in fact, in the decades-long tale of the town's transformation from a remote farming community into an elite world-class suburb, the letters *T.A.N.H.O.* barely register as a footnote.

The following school year, in the spring of 1998, when an area magazine ranked Carroll High School as one of the five best in the Dallas–Fort Worth region, the principal credited the town's traditional values for its success, calling his school—seemingly without a hint of self-awareness—"a throwback to the 1950s." Because at Southlake Carroll, he said, "doing the right thing is the popular thing to do." The principal's rosy description of an era when anti-Black racism was enshrined in Texas law went unchallenged in the magazine.

As for the district's pledge to make the school climate more welcoming, a collective amnesia seemed to set in afterward. The school board's volunteer Bridging Differences committee completed its work—quietly, out of the public spotlight—and the town seemed to move on.

By the time Amy and Reggie Rolle moved their kids across the country for better schools, Southlake's reputation in North Texas as a sort of high-end suburban utopia had been cemented, and nothing made this clearer than the release of the September 2007 issue of *D Magazine*, which featured an article about the city's "otherworldly success."

The cover of the Dallas-based glossy magazine showed three white Carroll High School students with their arms crossed, chins up, smirking at the camera. One was Carroll's student body president; another, the head cheerleader. Between them, wearing a green letterman's jacket with his collar popped, was the star quarterback. Below the students, in bold yellow font, the headline screamed, "WHY YOU SHOULD HATE SOUTHLAKE."

The subheading provided the in-your-face explanation: "Because the Kids Are Smarter, Stronger and Better Looking Than Yours." If the cover was meant to be provocative, the article itself—titled "Welcome to Perfect City, U.S.A."—didn't show significantly more restraint.

"They're good at everything in Southlake," the magazine declared, noting that, in addition to football, Carroll had won state championships in cross-country, swimming, baseball, soccer, theater, accounting, and robotics. "If you've never been, there's something a little Pleasantville about it. The streets are cleaner than your streets, the downtown more vibrant, the students more courteous, their parents more prosperous. Everyone is beautiful in Southlake. Everyone smiles in Southlake. Everyone is a Dragon in Southlake."

The magazine article caused an uproar, with some longtime residents misinterpreting the tongue-in-cheek cover headline as an attack on their city. But others embraced it. "I've lived here twenty-five years," then mayor Andy Wambsganss told a reporter afterward. "The article is right on the money." More than anything, the story seemed to make official what had been true for some time: Southlake had become the

"It" suburb of the Dallas–Fort Worth metroplex, a designation that tends to inspire strong feelings among outsiders.

It didn't take long for the Rolle family to get swept up in Dragon pride. They'd never lived someplace with such a strong collective identity—virtually all of it tied to schools and sports. "At Carroll," Amy said, "you start out as a Dragon in kindergarten, and you graduate as a Dragon from the senior high." It felt almost like a family, and they loved it.

Soon, the Rolle kids had amassed drawers full of green T-shirts to wear on Carroll spirit days each Friday. "That's the mom uniform in Southlake," Amy said. "A tennis skirt, and a shirt with a Southlake Dragons something on it." Amy and Reggie even got in on the fun, though they stopped short of buying one of the shirts with Southlake's 76092 zip code spelled out in shimmering rhinestones.

Initially, the town—its people, its schools, its culture, all of it—met or exceeded the Rolle family's every expectation. Six-year-old Raven had just one complaint: She wished people at school would stop calling her Iris. In the span of a few days, the school nurse, a teacher, and a few classmates had all mistakenly called her by that name, and she could not figure out why. Raven finally solved the mystery a few weeks later at recess when a group of girls dragged her by the arm to meet the only other Black girl at Rockenbaugh Elementary. Her name was Iris—Iris Maryland, the daughter of Russell Maryland, a former number-one NFL draft pick and star defensive lineman for the Cowboys, whose family had followed Frank Cornish to town years earlier. It turns out, Iris said, people had been calling her Raven—a trend of mistaken identities that would follow the girls all the way through high school, even though they don't look very much alike.

There would be other annoyances in those early years. The white classmates who constantly touched Raven's hair and commented on its texture. The two girls on the playground who said they couldn't play with her because her skin was brown. The initially bewildering question that Carroll kids constantly asked her at school: What number does your daddy wear? In a town where the median household income now surpasses $250,000, and where the typical home goes for more than

$1 million, the attitude, according to Amy, was, "Oh, you're Black, so your dad must be a Dallas Cowboy, or on one of the professional teams."

There was one other thing. Amy and Reggie's move to Southlake had coincided with the emergence of Barack Obama as a national political figure. And while his presidential run was seen as an inspiration to most Black Americans—with his eventual election ushering in what some (usually white) commenters declared America's "post-racial era"—many of the Rolles' white neighbors seemed to view Obama's rise in a harsher light.

The Rolles knew before moving that Southlake was mostly Republican—certainly more conservative than their neighborhood in L.A.—but to Amy, the intensity of some people's opposition to the nation's first Black president seemed to go beyond the typical left-right political divide. In one incident that made headlines in Dallas, a Black Southlake resident reported to police that someone had come into his yard overnight and set his Obama campaign sign on fire. Later, when the newly elected president Obama gave a video address to the nation's schoolchildren focused on the importance of education, Carroll school leaders declined to play his remarks, bowing to pressure from parents who'd accused the president of trying to indoctrinate children.

Amy and Reggie tried not to read too much into any of this. Overall, they felt great about their decision to raise their children in Southlake. These types of things could happen anywhere, they reasoned, and when you added it all up, they seemed like a small price to pay to get their kids a top-notch education.

Back then, Raven loved Southlake, too.

2

You've Got to Change

CHRISTINA CATLIN COULD NOT stop smiling as she stepped inside her classroom and flipped on the lights on the first day of school in August 2018. She was thrilled to be starting a new school year, a major change in her outlook from a few months earlier.

A couple days shy of her twenty-fifth birthday and entering her fourth year as a teacher, Catlin had been feeling burned out after three years at a charter school in southwest Dallas County, where—in a reflection of America's failed desegregation efforts—an overwhelming majority of her third-grade students were Black or Hispanic and came from poor homes.

Catlin, who's white, had gotten into education because she saw it as a calling, a way of living out her Christian faith by loving, nurturing, and educating children. That's why she'd signed up after college with the nonprofit Teach for America—a program that places educators at under-resourced schools—and went to work at Uplift Hampton Preparatory, a free public charter. Each morning before work, she would remind herself of the Bible verse she'd written on her college graduation cap, 1 Corinthians 15:58: "Therefore, my beloved brothers, be steadfast, immovable, always abounding in the work of the Lord, knowing that in the Lord your labor is not in vain."

But at Uplift, Catlin felt like most of her labor was spent putting out fires rather than making a lasting difference in the lives of children. She was writing her own curriculum and coming up with daily strategies for redirecting kids who were lashing out at school because of trauma at home. She tutored students for free after hours because too many weren't getting the services they needed to learn during the day.

The challenges seemed too big, and the resources too few.

Catlin had felt guilty that spring when she took the interview at Johnson Elementary in Southlake—as if she was turning her back on vulnerable kids. Later, after she officially accepted the job in the Carroll district school, Catlin said one of her Black charter school colleagues called her a traitor. "She said, 'You want to go work with all these white kids when you could actually make a difference here.'" Reflecting on those words, Catlin said, "I'll never forget her saying that."

It hadn't taken long for her feelings of contrition to fade. At the orientation for new teachers that summer, administrators handed out green T-shirts that read, "There's No Place Like Carroll," and soon Catlin began to believe it. Her new gig, teaching fourth grade, came with a $10,000 pay increase and plenty of other perks, including a guarantee that she would have no more than twenty-two students in her class and access to the best and newest classroom technology. She would be teaching the children of highly engaged parents who were eager to help in class—generous, it would seem, both in terms of time and money. (Catlin would be stunned that first year by the lavishness of the gifts teachers received at Carroll; before winter break, a child walked up to her desk holding a "money tree"—a plastic desk plant with $200 worth of twenty-dollar bills clipped to it.)

As her new students filtered into class on the first day, Ms. Catlin greeted each with a smile before showing them to their desks. After the morning announcements featuring a video message from the principal and an interactive workout routine to help the children wake up, Catlin loaded up an introductory slideshow. She clicked through photos of herself growing up in Sarasota, Florida, graduating from a private Christian college near Tampa, and teaching African children in a one-room, dirt-floor schoolhouse in Uganda during a summer abroad—using the last slide as an opportunity to highlight the privilege of growing up in America and going to school someplace like Carroll.

As Catlin scanned her new classroom, she was struck by the diversity of the faces staring back at her. This wasn't just a bunch of white kids, as her former colleague had suggested. Driven largely by an influx of affluent South Asian professionals, Southlake and Carroll had grown more racially and ethnically diverse in the twelve years since the Rolle family moved to town, with non-white children now making up about 33 percent of the district's student population. Although only one of her students was Black—still just 2 percent of the overall population in Southlake was Black—Catlin was comforted by the idea that she'd landed in a suburb that attracted people from a wide array of ethnic and cultural backgrounds.

As the children were getting ready for dismissal, she snapped a photo of herself with her students and texted it to her boyfriend along with the caption "Best first day ever!" All day long, she told him later, the kids had been energetic and engaged. There hadn't been a single disciplinary issue. No fights at recess or drama in the bus line. And all the parents had been so kind.

"I felt like I was in a dream," Catlin would say four years later, after a group of those parents had led a campaign to have her run out of Southlake. "It was a perfect Carroll dreamland."

Two months later, in October 2018, the dance floor at the Hilton in Southlake's Town Square was packed as Raven Rolle, now a high school senior, stepped inside the ballroom, looking glamorous in a red long-sleeved dress and gold heels. It was Carroll's 2018 homecoming dance and, like most things in Southlake, the scene was probably a little fancier than what you remember from your high school days. Many of the kids had rolled up in huge party buses that they'd rented with twenty or thirty of their friends, with the dance itself serving as just one stop in a daylong party.

Raven was hoping for a more low-key night with a few friends. She surveyed the room: girls in designer dresses, sweaty boys in half-unbuttoned dress shirts, all of them crowded up around the stage, hands in the air under flashing lights, shouting every lyric as the DJ stood onstage behind turntables.

Mia Mariani, a queer student who uses both female and gender-neutral ("they/them") pronouns, was a Carroll freshman that year and, for the first time, feeling bold enough to come to a school function dressed as her authentic self. That meant wearing a crisp black suit with a pink undershirt and a pair of black-and-white saddle shoes. Mia was feeling good—until she noticed some of the boys staring and pointing. "Look at that little girl in a boy's suit," one of them blurted out, a harsh preview of the types of taunts she would hear over her next four years at Carroll.

Jack Tucker, a white senior and student body president, had helped plan the dance. He and his friends had spent hours decorating that morning, filling the dance hall with balloons and streamers, excited for one last homecoming together. The student council had voted to decorate with a circus theme that year, a fitting metaphor for the political chaos that would be unleashed that night—the unofficial start of Southlake's racial reckoning.

Raven, Mia, and Jack—as well as a half dozen other Carroll students—all remembered the moment when the mood in the room shifted. It happened when the DJ, a Black man, cranked up one of the most popular hip-hop tracks from 2018: "Mo Bamba" by Sheck Wes. The song, released a year earlier, had become a hit that summer, particularly among a certain class of white hip-hop fans. Although the DJ was playing radio edits of songs, the uncensored version of "Mo Bamba" includes a whole bunch of words that administrators wouldn't want students screaming at an official school function, most notably, the N-word.

In the version of "Mo Bamba" that played that night, the word "brother" is dubbed in for the N-word:

I be ballin' like my brother Mo (Bamba)
Sheck Wes, I ain't a joke (haha, hahahahaha)

But the clean version didn't stop members of Carroll's mostly white student body from shouting the uncensored lyrics from the dance floor—lyrics they clearly had heard before arriving that night.

When she noticed, Raven whipped around to make eye contact with a friend. "Are you hearing this?" she shouted over the music. "Listen to all these white people using the N-word!" They both rolled their eyes, annoyed but unsurprised. Raven and her friends ducked out not long after that, ditching their final homecoming dance to get slushies at Sonic.

For Mia, who's white, two moments stood out from her first homecoming: crying in the bathroom after hearing yet another boy making fun of her outfit and, later, hearing "all these white kids just jumping up and down screaming slurs." Things didn't calm down after "Mo Bamba," Mia said. From that moment onward, students were shouting uncensored lyrics of nearly every song, and growing increasingly rowdy. At one point, after a boy jumped onstage, Mia and other students said the DJ briefly cut off the music and admonished the teens to be respectful.

Jack was annoyed that some of his classmates were wrecking all the work the student council had put into planning a memorable dance. "There were times where it was extremely uncomfortable," he said. "A song would be playing, and you just hear a horde of white, privileged teenagers, you just hear the N-word, and you can't single it out because it's everyone there."

Many months later, what did or did not happen at homecoming would become central to a growing political fight in Southlake, as adults looked for almost anyone to blame besides the students themselves—with some parents even falsely accusing the DJ of openly encouraging students to say the N-word and other explicit lyrics.

If those parents had asked around, Carroll students probably would have told them what Raven, Mia, Jack, and others told me: Hearing the N-word on the dance floor wasn't surprising. In fact, you could hear white students using that word at most Carroll dances, and even more often in the halls of the high school. As one district leader would later tell me, teachers and administrators in Southlake had gotten used to dealing with these types of issues on a case-by-case basis, and doing it quietly.

But there was no way of quietly dealing with what happened after the dance.

That evening, a group of Carroll students—white students, mostly underclassmen—headed to a friend's house for a homecoming afterparty. At some point, eight of them gathered around a cell phone and recorded themselves gleefully chanting the same slur that so many Carroll kids had been shouting from the dance floor that night.

Only this time, they weren't repeating a rap lyric.

Donald Trump's rise to power had a profound impact inside America's public schools. Adults weren't the only ones watching as the real estate magnate and reality television star rode down an escalator in 2015 and launched his presidential campaign by depicting immigrants from Mexico as rapists and criminals. Children heard the recording of the Republican nominee bragging about the ease with which celebrities such as himself could sexually assault women. They heard his promise to ban Muslims from entering the country, his promise to empower evangelical Christians who were outraged by the legalization of same-sex marriage, his promise to defeat the so-called "globalist" conspiracy against working people that registered in the ears of many Jews as an anti-Semitic dog whistle. It's not that teenagers didn't make racist comments or carve slurs onto bathroom stalls prior to 2016, but Trump's ascent to the most revered office in the country seemed to embolden some to openly embrace divisive, hateful language, just as it had some adults.

A day after Trump's election, middle school students in the mostly white Detroit suburb of Royal Oak—one of the school districts that would have been forced to integrate under the policy rejected four decades earlier in *Milliken v. Bradley*—were filmed chanting "Build the wall! Build the wall!" during their lunch period, while some Latino students reportedly cried at their cafeteria tables. That same day, in a predominantly white suburb outside Minneapolis, someone vandalized a bathroom stall at Maple Grove Senior High School with the words "Go back to Africa," "Make America great again," and "fuck n——rs." In Redding, California, a student at Shasta High School filmed himself handing out fake deportation notices to non-white classmates, then posted the video on social media. And in Florida, a white teacher at a suburban high school outside of Tampa was placed on leave after reportedly telling a group of Black students, "Don't make me call Donald Trump to get you sent back to Africa."

Between 2014 and 2018, the Government Accountability Office

documented a doubling of hate crimes in America's schools and an increase in reports of racist taunts. In total, according to agency estimates, about 5.8 million middle and high school students were exposed to derogatory words or symbols during the 2018 school year, including racial and homophobic slurs, anti-Semitic symbols, and references to lynching. At the same time, a growing body of research had begun connecting discriminatory harassment with serious health problems. Children who faced frequent taunts related to their race, gender, or national origin were more likely to be diagnosed with a mental disorder and twice as likely to develop severe psychological distress, increasing risk for suicide.

As these incidents grew more prevalent, they also became easier to document, with most students carrying high-definition cell phone cameras. Stories about teenagers behaving badly at school are now so common, they've become an entire subgenre of news articles on the internet, with a new story posting every few days across the country. After noticing another spike in these types of reports after the deadly Unite the Right rally in Charlottesville, Virginia, in August 2017—when white nationalist supporters of Trump marched with torches chanting "You will not replace us!"—the group Teaching Tolerance, a project of the nonprofit Southern Poverty Law Center, decided to spend a month tracking them.

In October 2017 alone, Teaching Tolerance said it found credible news reports of more than ninety "episodes of hate" spread across thirty states, mainly involving high school students. In more than a third of these incidents, abhorrent messages surfaced on social media. In one, an Alabama high schooler produced and posted a video of himself rapping about committing genocide against LGBTQ people, calling on Trump to "protect the white race" by imposing his Muslim ban, and mused that Martin Luther King's Jr.'s "only dream" should have been "picking cotton." In another, five white students in a Utah suburb north of Salt Lake City posted a video of themselves appearing to chant "fuck n——rs" while laughing. Most of the incidents documented by Teaching Tolerance targeted Black people by using racial slurs and references to slavery. About a fifth of the news reports documented anti-Semitic acts, including swastikas painted on a school building and a note left in a locker that read "Jews will burn." The group also identified a number of reports of discrimination against Muslim and LGBTQ students.

Maureen Costello, the former executive director of Teaching Tolerance, argued that people too often think of these incidents as simply "pranks or misbehavior," when really each one is something far more serious, providing a window into the everyday bigotry that permeates America's schools. "Let's be clear: They are poisonous expressions of hate," Costello wrote in an essay announcing the October 2017 findings. "These acts should move school leaders to act decisively to restore the school community. Sadly, that isn't the usual response."

Now, one year later, it was Southlake's turn in the spotlight.

The Carroll students who filmed themselves at a homecoming afterparty probably didn't mean for the world to see the clip. Initially, they'd only shared it with friends on Snapchat, where messages automatically disappear. But one of the students must have made a copy, because the following week, the video showed up on Twitter, a far more public platform, and within hours the post had been viewed tens of thousands of times.

Eventually that number grew into the millions.

The video is kind of grainy, but you can make out faces. It shows eight white Carroll students crammed onto a bed. One girl shouts, "I say n——, you say g——!" What follows is a sort of call and response, with the girl leading the chant yelling the first half of the N-word, and her friends screaming the rest. After the group shouts the slur twice, the girl leading the chant says, "Ay, we up on that Black shit, ay?" while the students laugh.

Word of the video spread rapidly in Southlake. Robin Cornish opened a link to the tweet that someone had texted to her and immediately recognized the girl leading the chant. It was the sister of her youngest son's former best friend. Robin sent a message to the girl's mother, letting her know that she'd seen the video and was upset by it. Raven Rolle's group texts were blowing up that weekend. A couple of her volleyball teammates had appeared in the video. What an embarrassment, she thought.

School leaders, meanwhile, were being bombarded with messages from parents wanting to know what the district was going to do, not only in terms of disciplining the students, but to make sure nothing like this happened again.

Carroll administrators sent a statement to parents and the media expressing extreme disappointment in the teens in the video and acknowledged that this wasn't the first time administrators had been forced to deal with students using a racial slur. But the administrators, seemingly unaware of the episode at a football game two decades earlier, said this *was* the first time the district was having to do so in such a public way. The district pledged to discipline the students as appropriate under the student code of conduct while simultaneously casting the teens themselves as victims of technology.

"It's a tough social media world out there for our kids, for sure," the statement said. "But as Dragons, we are better than this."

The Dallas ABC affiliate, WFAA, broke the news on the night of October 29, 2018. "Controversy in Southlake tonight after teens posted a racist video online," the anchor intoned. "Tomorrow, Carroll ISD will meet with the students and their parents as it considers possible punishments." By the next day, every major news outlet in the Dallas region had picked up the story, and a reporter from *Newsweek* was working on an article—a flurry of embarrassing headlines for a city accustomed to praise.

Rumors about the video spread through the halls of the high school, home to Carroll's underclassmen, and at the senior high, the campus where juniors and seniors attend. Students whispered the names of the teens who'd been at the infamous party and speculated about how much alcohol they'd been drinking.

Liv Ferguson was a sophomore that year, like most of the students in the video. As one of only about twenty Black students in her class of seven hundred, Liv remembered getting lots of stares that week from white classmates, who seemed to be wondering how she and the other Black kids were going to react. If they'd asked, Liv would have told them: She was pissed. One of the girls in the video had been a friend of hers.

Liv remembers confronting the student that week, first over text message and later at school. "I was, like, 'I've seen this video. What the heck is wrong with you?'" At first the girl denied it, Liv said. "And then eventually, me just continuously being, like, 'I know it's you, I know it's you,' she was, like, 'Yeah, it's me.' Then she profusely apologized."

It was painful to have that kind of conversation with someone she considered a friend. Liv couldn't understand how her white classmates had made it all the way to high school without learning the N-word's complex and ugly history. Did they not know how the slur was used to dehumanize enslaved people, or how it was deployed as a rhetorical weapon against Black civil rights activists as they marched for basic human rights? Did they not realize that rappers and other Black people who use the word today—usually with an *a* at the end rather than a hard *r*—do so in a spirit of protest, repurposing an oppressive slur as a term of brotherly endearment and an acknowledgment of a shared struggle? Did her classmates really not realize how it sounds when white people say it?

Or did they just not care?

At volleyball practice that week, Raven's coach, a white woman, held a meeting to discuss the incident. She talked about the harsh backlash the players in the video were now facing and advised that nobody on the team—including the Black students—should ever use the N-word. To Raven, it was another example of how adults at Carroll seemed more concerned about the negative attention the girls in the video were getting than the pain their actions had caused.

Liv noticed, too.

She shared a Spanish class with three girls who had participated in the video and vividly remembers the day they returned to school after their suspensions. They'd all missed a pop quiz while they were gone, Liv says. Rather than giving the girls zeros for the missed work or requiring them to take a makeup test, Liv said the teacher told them, "Oh, I'll just put in hundreds for you guys. Don't even worry about the quiz."

Liv felt her head spin when she overheard the comment. "My teacher has a Black person in this class, and then in front of everyone, she's going to tell the girls who are in trouble for saying a racial slur that they can get a free one hundred on the quiz that they missed because they were suspended?" Afterward, Liv asked to be excused. She hurried down the hall to the bathroom, then stepped into a stall.

She didn't want anyone to see her cry.

Five days after the video made the news, the Carroll school board called a special meeting to provide a forum for members of the community to express their feelings. Although it was scheduled early on a Friday during work hours, the meeting room was already packed when Michelle Moore, the board's vice president, arrived. She hadn't seen this much interest in a Carroll board meeting since earlier that year when they were debating whether to suspend a beloved Dragons football coach based on allegations that he'd fostered a toxic environment for assistant coaches and players.

Moore figured this new controversy would blow over just as quickly.

She wasn't naive about the history of racism in America. As the daughter of Cuban immigrants, Moore was the only non-white Carroll school board member. Because of her Anglo surname and light complexion, though, most people didn't realize she was Latina. As the national director of corporate relations for the United Negro College Fund, she'd dedicated her career to helping combat systemic discrimination. She just didn't see it as a major problem in Southlake.

"I really thought of it more as a poor choice than immediately jumping to 'Here are some racist kids,'" Moore said of her initial reaction to seeing the N-word video. "I was just thinking, 'They're being stupid, and they've made a poor choice.'"

She knew from her emails that week, however, that many parents were having a much stronger reaction. Now she was about to find out why.

Nearly all fifty seats in the audience were filled, and several parents stood along the walls as school board president Sheri Mills called the meeting to order. She opened by acknowledging the pain caused by the video and promising that the district would take steps to better educate students on how to show kindness and respect to their peers.

"Our core values do mean something here at Carroll ISD," Mills said. "As Dragons, we expect excellence, and that begins with how we treat each other."

Then she opened the floor to public comments: "The first speaker is Robin Cornish."

Cornish, whose youngest child had graduated from Carroll that year, had been in Southlake the first time Carroll school leaders promised to impose changes to address racism two decades earlier. But like many longtime residents, she didn't recall being aware of the incident involving a white student and his racist sign at a football game, and she certainly didn't remember the district actually implementing meaningful reforms afterward. Now, with a growing awareness two years into Trump's presidency that America, like her adopted hometown, had never fully grappled with its racist past, Cornish was determined to make sure this time was different.

She strode to the lectern, adjusted the microphone, and did her best to keep her composure. "I am incredibly hurt, disappointed, and angry," she began. Cornish had come to make one thing clear to the board: This wasn't just about one video or a handful of kids. This was about the price that parents pay to raise Black children in mostly white suburbs like Southlake—Carroll's hidden cost of admission for students of color.

This was the school district where, on the day after Rosa Parks died in 2005, elementary school children told her four oldest kids, "Now you have to sit in the back of the bus," Cornish told the board. It's where a sixth-grade boy once joked with her son: "How do you get a Black out of a tree? You cut the rope." It's where, weeks after her husband, Frank, died suddenly of a heart condition in 2008, a white boy on the football team told her oldest child, "Your mom is only voting for Obama because your dad is dead and she's going to need welfare." This is the city where, only a year earlier, in 2017, someone had vandalized the plaque erected in Frank's memory at Southlake Town Square, carving six words into bronze: "KKK will get you black people."

The N-word video had reopened all those wounds, Cornish told the board. "You've got to understand," she said. "You've got to change this curriculum. You've got to change the tone in this town. If you want us to be known as Southlake Carroll Dragons and be inclusive, take action now."

The audience burst into applause as Cornish returned to her seat. Moore felt a lump start to form in her throat.

Cornish's testimony was just the beginning. One after another that morning, parents of Black students came forward with painful stories of their own—like a dam had broken under the weight of decades' worth of unaddressed grievances.

The next speaker, a Black mother who'd spent sixteen years in Southlake, recalled a white student telling her son in fifth grade, "Hey, Brandon, why are you even here? Why don't you just go back to Africa?"

Lorrie Hill, the white wife of former Texas Rangers pitcher Ken Hill, who's Black, told the story of when her biracial son was working on a group project in middle school. A white girl kept poking him with a pencil, saying, "You can't feel this because you've got that tough Black skin." The girl continued poking, Lorrie said, "until the pencil lead broke into his skin."

Another mom of biracial children said her youngest daughter had been struggling since the day after the 2016 election, when a student in the marching band called her the N-word. "We are just trying to get through this year to see her graduate," she said.

One Black Southlake mother said a constant stream of insensitive comments and racist jokes at school had left her daughter struggling with depression after she graduated, something she was continuing to work through with a therapist. "If you see a Black family in this community, or a mixed family," the mother said, "trust me when I say, they are struggling with the decision to keep their kids in this district."

Ronell Smith, a Black father who would go on to serve on the city council, confessed that these issues had him and his wife, a white woman, questioning whether they should leave Southlake or send their biracial daughters to a private school. He then motioned to three words glowing on a computer monitor in front of him: "Protect the Tradition." That phrase, Carroll's school motto, appears all over in Southlake, on T-shirts and on banners at the football stadium. It's meant to honor the history of excellence that made the town into one of the nation's hottest suburbs, and Carroll into one of the top public school systems in Texas. Smith told the board he was still proud to call Southlake home, but at some point, he said, adults in the community needed to think hard about that motto and consider exactly what tradition they were protecting.

By the end of the meeting, many in attendance were in tears, including some white parents. One white dad said this moment should be a wake-up call for the community—echoing comments by a former Carroll school board member from more than twenty years earlier, in response to the young Dragons football fan and his racist sign.

From her seat overlooking the room, Michelle Moore remembered feeling a mix of anger and shame. She was angry that nobody in the district administration had told the board that so many children felt they'd been bullied based on their race, and ashamed that she, as the only non-white board member, had herself been blind to it.

These stories didn't match the version of Southlake she'd fallen in love with after her family moved from Northern Virginia in 2005. When folks asked what brought them to town, Moore and her husband gave the same answer as most transplants: They came for the schools. It hadn't taken long before they and their two kids were decked out in Dragon green and cheering from the stands on Friday nights. It seemed like the kind of community where everyone was welcome, and where neighbors became family. That's why, when Moore heard from a friend about a surprise opening on Carroll's school board in 2015, she'd walked away from a dream job opportunity in California to stay and serve.

At the time, she'd taken the vacancy as a sign that God had a purpose for her in Southlake. He wanted her on the school board for a reason. Now, as Moore headed to her car after hearing the distressing accounts of Black parents, a new thought entered her mind: "This," she said to herself, "is not how it's going to be under my watch."

After the meeting, Moore called Cornish and some of the other parents who'd shared stories, and she promised she was going to try to make it better. So did lots of other Southlake leaders. It seemed to Cornish that her adopted hometown might finally be ready to change.

3

Not Just a Word

ZANETA OGUNMOLA HAD ATTENDED Carroll schools her entire life, but as the daughter of Nigerian immigrants she never felt she belonged. She was a junior the year of the N-word video, which was the same year that President Trump infamously denounced immigrants like her parents as having come from "shithole countries." It wasn't long before she heard that line parroted by a white classmate. "If you don't like it here," the boy told another student of color, "go back to your shithole country." Zaneta wasn't surprised by her classmates' behavior, or by the president's, for that matter, but after the viral video she felt for the first time that she needed to speak up about the racism she'd witnessed at Carroll. After discussing it with a community-college professor whose government course she was taking that semester—part of a program that allowed Carroll students to obtain college credits in high school—Zaneta took the professor's advice and wrote an email to Southlake's mayor.

She wasn't expecting to hear back so quickly.

Mayor Laura Hill, a local politician with ambitions for higher office, responded to Zaneta's message with an invitation to meet at town hall. The following week, Zaneta found herself sitting in a conference room with a half dozen other female students of color, all summoned by the mayor, including Liv Ferguson, the girl who'd overheard a teacher giving out perfect test scores to her suspended classmates. Hill, who's white, had been elected Southlake's first female mayor in 2015 after serving a decade on the city council. After the racist video, Hill had immediately gotten in touch with members of the Carroll school board to warn them about the damage the clip could inflict on Southlake's reputation, and to urge the district to take swift action.

At town hall, Hill opened by telling Zaneta and the other students that she was outraged by the video. Hill said she wanted to hear about their experiences with racism in Southlake, as well as their ideas for addressing the problem.

For the next hour, the girls took turns sharing stories about racist jokes and ignorant comments they'd dealt with at school. A Muslim girl shared how white classmates routinely called her a terrorist. When it was her turn, Zaneta talked about the time a white student called her a "Medusa-headed" N-word in middle school, and about the assumptions white students and even some teachers made about her Black family. Yes, she'd had to say again and again over the years, of course she knew who her father was. And no, he wasn't a professional athlete; he was a gastroenterologist at a children's hospital.

Afterward, Zaneta handed Hill a two-page letter she'd written about her experiences in Southlake, including her reaction when a boy used the same slur against her that the students had been giggling about in the viral video: "I never knew a single word could reduce me to feeling like gum on the bottom of someone's shoe, like nothing," she wrote. "Everything moved so fast I don't even remember how it happened, but I was on top of him asking him to say it again, and I can still picture his face laughing at me—at my pain."

The mayor seemed horrified by the girls' stories. "She listened to everything, and you could tell that some of the things affected her," Zaneta said. "You could see it on her face." Hill took down the students' phone numbers and promised to stay in touch. A few days later, she texted the group with an idea. Hill told them she wanted to record a video that would make clear that Southlake would not tolerate discrimination, and she wanted Zaneta and the other girls to star in it.

They met at a small studio in town in early December. Someone from the mayor's office handed scripts to Zaneta, one white boy, and the six other students of color who were to appear in the spot. It wasn't a complicated shoot; the filming took only about thirty minutes, Zaneta said.

A week later, the two-minute commercial appeared on the city's social media feeds.

The video opens with a single, haunting piano note. "Racism," a Black girl says, staring into the camera in front of a blank white canvas. "Discrimination," says another student. "Intolerance," the third girl says. "Exclusion," says the fourth. Then Hill appears alongside Zaneta and the other students wearing a black dress and pearls: "These things don't have a place in Southlake," she says. As Hill lays out plans for a new city-led initiative to promote cultural awareness and unity, images flash across the screen showing the range of people who call Southlake home. There's Hill in a green sari, snapping a selfie with children at the city's Diwali festival. There's Robin Cornish at the park in Town Square, where vandals once carved "KKK will get you black people" onto her husband's memorial plaque. There's a little girl in colorful face paint at the city's Hispanic heritage celebration. There's a group of white men in suits, bowing their heads in prayer. "Creating meaningful change is not a short-term effort, and it starts with you and me," Hill says, as the music builds to a hopeful crescendo. The advertisement ends with a few of the students taking turns saying, "I believe in Southlake," and then all together, "We believe in Southlake!"

The video's release was part of a weeks-long blitz by Southlake leaders to bring the community together.

Coffee and Conversation, a public forum at a local banquet hall, drew Mayor Hill, school board president Sheri Mills and vice president Michelle Moore, and dozens of Southlake moms. "Racism exists," a white woman said during the forum. "Racism exists, and we have to name it. We have to give it a name so that we can fight it." Two weeks later, Brews with Dads took place at a local pub called The Ginger Man. NBC's Dallas affiliate was invited to record as the men of Southlake sipped beer and attempted to bridge the racial divide. "Racism is real," Southlake city councilman John Huffman told the station. "It's around us and sweeping it under the rug is not gonna help."

Back then, it seemed as if most everyone in Southlake was on the same page. As Hill said in a December 2018 press release announcing the formation of her new Mayor's Alliance for Unity and Culture,

"We must hold true to our values and not tolerate racism, discrimination, exclusion or intolerance. We must do this even when it is hard."

At first, Zaneta was proud to be playing a small part in helping inspire changes in her hometown. Now, when she looks back on Hill's commercial and all that's happened since then, she feels something very different.

"I think they used us," she told me. "And I feel ashamed to be a part of that video."

While Hill and other city officials worked to defend Southlake's image, school board vice president Michelle Moore and other members of the Carroll school board were promising to make more substantive changes. It was the job of the seven elected trustees to manage Carroll's $120 million budget, to set district priorities, and to hire senior administrators to run day-to-day operations. After the viral video, a new goal rocketed to the top of the board's list of priorities: finding a way to make the district's culture more welcoming. The board directed administrators that November to form a special committee made up of parents, teachers, students, and other community members to study the cultural and racial climate at Carroll, and to come up with proposals to make the district more inclusive.

Moore said she was committed to making sure the District Diversity Council, or DDC, as it would come to be known, was more than just a symbolic gesture. "This was our genuine effort to drive change and to drive the district to be better," she said.

The school board put out an open call for volunteers, while some trustees set out to recruit respected community members for the cause.

Back then, it would have been difficult to find a Southlake resident more respected than Russell Maryland. At six-foot-one and over three hundred pounds, and with a booming voice that has a way of carrying across a room, the former Cowboys defensive lineman and three-time Super Bowl champion tended to get noticed around town. After he retired from the NFL in 2001, he and his wife, Rose, had come to Southlake for the same reasons as most folks: They wanted a big yard, and they wanted to send their three children to a top-tier public school, hoping to give them academic opportunities that Maryland never dreamed of while growing up in Chicago.

Over the years, Maryland had gotten used to being asked to volunteer his time in town, whether it was coaching youth football or speaking at the chamber of commerce. Yet he was somewhat surprised when he got a call from Carroll school board member Matt Bryant a few weeks after the N-word video came out. The men had gotten to know each other while their sons played on the same youth football team, but they weren't particularly close, and they'd certainly never had a conversation about racism. Bryant, a white real estate investor in his first year on the school board, asked to get coffee with the Marylands.

They met a few days later at a Starbucks tucked inside a Tom Thumb grocery store. According to Maryland's retelling, Bryant was emotional nearly from the moment they sat down. "With tears in his eyes, he said three things. He said, 'Russell, I can't imagine that my son would have a different experience in this school district than your son.' And he said, 'Russell, I know that Black lives matter.' I'm, like, 'OK, I'm glad you understand that.' With tears coming down his face, he said, 'I know we need to hire more minority teachers.' I'm, like, 'OK, I agree with you on that, too.' So we were all on the same level at that point."

Bryant told Maryland about the DDC, and he asked the former football star if he would be willing to lend his name and credibility to the effort. For Maryland, the decision was a no-brainer. He was aware, based on the stories his own children told, of the racist slurs and insults that too often passed for jokes at Carroll. And he believed Bryant and other Southlake leaders genuinely wanted to make things better.

As Maryland put it later, "Anything to protect our kids, I'm all on board. And I was on board."

But Rose Maryland, a Black woman who has a reputation in Southlake for saying exactly what she thinks the moment she thinks it, had some doubts. She leaned across the table at Starbucks and asked Bryant, "Are you ready for what's going to happen after we try to get this done?"

Russell Maryland said Bryant nodded. "Of course," he responded. "What could go wrong?"

• • •

Southlake was just one of countless majority-white suburbs charting a new course on diversity and inclusion in 2019. Nearly three years after Trump's election emboldened white nationalists and ushered in an era of renewed national awareness about racism, xenophobia, anti-LGBTQ bigotry, and sexism, communities across the country had begun taking action to make their schools more welcoming.

In Northern Virginia, Loudoun County Public Schools became the target of embarrassing national headlines that February after a gym teacher—in a ham-fisted attempt at celebrating Black History Month—made third-, fourth-, and fifth-grade students run through a hula-hoop obstacle course meant to simulate the journey of enslaved people navigating the Underground Railroad. The exercise, which seemed to make light of Black people's desperate attempts to escape the horrors of forced labor, family separations, beatings, and rape, was called out by parents of color as a symptom of deeper troubles in the sprawling and fast-diversifying Washington, D.C., suburb.

In response, the Loudoun County school board hired a California-based consulting firm called The Equity Collaborative to study the racial climate at its schools. The firm's June 2019 report found that Black, Hispanic, and Muslim students had been the frequent targets of racial slurs, and that Black students, in particular, were disciplined more frequently than others—mirroring disparities nationally. Just as in Southlake, leaders in Loudoun County pledged to confront racism and enact reforms. "We can and we should and we must do better," the school district's superintendent told the *Washington Post*.

It was a similar story that spring in Portland, Oregon, where high school students staged a walkout and wrote an open letter to school leaders after a series of incidents in which Black students reported being called the N-word by classmates. "We don't feel safe in a place where everywhere we go we are a minority, facing hate and ignorance at every corner, with only a select group of teachers to support us," they wrote. Afterward, Portland Public Schools pledged to move ahead with a comprehensive racial equity plan.

In March, a school system in Cheyenne, Wyoming, said it would hire a diversity and cultural awareness counselor after a group of middle school students handed out fliers that read, "Join the KKK," and "It's not OK to be gay."

In Cobb County, a suburb outside Atlanta, a community group called on the school district that summer to hire an equity officer and to implement diversity training after a series of racist incidents, including one involving a teacher who was accused of threatening to hang Black students if they didn't stop talking in class.

And school officials in the Chicago suburb of Naperville pledged to confront what they acknowledged was a pattern of racism in the district and promised changes in response to bigoted student comments. This came after a white high school freshman in Naperville posted a photo of a Black classmate on Craigslist with the heading "Slave for sale" and a description of the student as a "Hardworkin thick n——a slave."

Afterward, in an interview with WBEZ, Chicago's NPR affiliate, a Black Naperville parent named Keri King described the majority-white suburban school district as a powder keg and said the racist Craigslist post had been the spark that finally caused an explosion. Now district administrators and town leaders could no longer ignore the problem.

"We have been asking for that level of accountability for some time," King told the radio station, in comments that could have applied to any number of suburban school districts that year.

"Now they're in a position where they're going to have to show some level of accountability, because all eyes are watching."

Across the country, administrators were getting a crash course in the budding world of school-based anti-racism initiatives. They were learning about concepts like "implicit bias," an acknowledgment of the unconscious assumptions people make about one another; "microaggressions," a way of categorizing the routine indignities experienced by people of color and other marginalized groups; and "white fragility," a reflexive defensiveness on the part of many white people any time they're confronted with information about racial inequality. These terms had been coined years and sometimes decades earlier. But, unless they'd taken a sociology class in college, most Americans at this point had probably never heard of them. That was changing, though, in the era of Trump, particularly among progressives and some disillusioned conservatives who, to appropriate a phrase popularized years earlier by Black Lives Matter activists, were working to "stay woke."

To feed the growing thirst for knowledge in places like Portland and Cobb County and Naperville, media outlets and the publishing industry were flooding the marketplace with op-eds and books on deconstructing white supremacy and reexamining America's racist history. In August 2019, historian Ibram X. Kendi published *How to Be an Antiracist*, which argued that the only way to truly stand against racial injustice was to enact race-conscious policies to actively counter the effects of past injustice. One day after Kendi's treatise hit bookshelves, the *New York Times Magazine* published the 1619 Project, a special issue conceived and spearheaded by veteran education journalist Nikole Hannah-Jones that sought, as the *Times* put it, "to reframe the country's history by placing the consequences of slavery and the contributions of black Americans at the very center of our national narrative." To assist the growing number of school districts working to address America's origins, the collection of articles, named for the year that the first ship of enslaved Africans arrived in the American colonies, was also adapted into a high school curriculum.

The 1619 Project's framing, a radical departure from the way schools had traditionally presented this country's history, was bound to ruffle some feathers. For generations, schoolchildren across the South and elsewhere were fed a false narrative about white supremacy and the mistreatment of Black people in America. This Lost Cause mythology—which claimed that the mission of the Confederates during the Civil War was righteous, heroic, and not primarily about slavery (which wasn't really so bad for enslaved people anyway)—could be found in textbooks through the 1980s in parts of the country and continued to reverberate in the decades that followed. In 2010, Texas, whose massive population gives the state outsized influence over what gets published in textbooks nationally, adopted new social studies standards that framed slavery as a secondary cause of the Civil War, while failing to make even a single mention of Jim Crow, the Ku Klux Klan, or school segregation. The standards that would govern the history taught to children in Southlake and everywhere in

Texas for the next decade were so skewed that the conservative Fordham Institute think tank panned them as "unwieldy and troubling, avoiding clear historical explanation while offering misrepresentations at every turn."

This whitewashing could also be seen in one of the Carroll school district's long-standing traditions: Colonial Day, an educational celebration in which fifth graders dressed up like characters from the 1600 and 1700s, was popular with many white families. But little thought seemed to go into what such a celebration meant for Black children.

The oversight became all too clear when a classmate told one of Robin Cornish's daughters that she couldn't dress up like a Revolutionary War–era nurse; she would have been a slave.

Southlake's journey toward racial accountability began, officially, on the evening of January 30, 2019, with the first meeting of Carroll's new District Diversity Council. Russell Maryland was impressed when he walked into a conference room at Carroll's administrative building and got a look at his fellow volunteers. The sixty-three members who'd been selected from 180 applicants appeared to represent a broad cross section of the community, a mix of Black, white, Latino, and Asian American parents, students, and district staff members. Many of them were leaders in their fields, including lawyers, corporate executives, a retired ICE special agent, former pro athletes, and a member of the city council.

With the support of Carroll's longtime superintendent, David Faltys, a pair of senior district administrators—one white and one Black—briefed the volunteers on their mission. Over the next year, they were to study the district's student code of conduct, its hiring practices, the ways educators were trained on diversity, and how different cultures were represented in the curriculum. Then they were to propose changes to make Carroll more welcoming and inclusive. The district was hungry for suggestions, the officials said, and no idea was off the table.

Pam Francis, a lawyer and white mother of biracial children who later would be appointed to serve as cochair of the diversity council, remembers feeling hopeful after that initial gathering. The district was empowering the committee to propose real changes, rather than simply hosting a series of cultural celebrations and town forums. "I think it's great to have conversations," Francis said later, "but at the end of the day, you want to see action. You want results. And I felt like we were on a path to do exactly that."

But the volunteers were about to get a harsh reminder of why the committee was formed in the first place.

One week after the initial DDC meeting, before the group had even a chance to form subcommittees, another video of Carroll students shouting the N-word made the news. This one showed three white teens—two of whom were Carroll students—filming themselves while riding in a car. With a hip-hop track blaring, one of the girls yells, "Oh my God, yes, I can say n——a more!" Then she repeatedly shouts the slur while the other students laugh. Afterward, someone posted the video on Snapchat, it began to spread, and the cycle of shock and outrage began anew, once again followed by strong words from school and city leaders.

The district released a statement on social media condemning the students' actions and promising swift consequences, while referring to racism as "a heart problem" that must be addressed by the entire community. "We choose hope, love and acceptance and will concentrate on those goals moving forward."

Mayor Hill was more blunt. She told a TV reporter that the new video—posted less than four months after the first one—made her want to hit her head against a wall. In a blistering statement shared to her Facebook page, Hill pointed the finger back at her constituents and called on parents to "wake the heck up."

"I will not allow this to become a beat down on Southlake again," Hill wrote. "As parents, we constantly demand the district fix problems when we obviously haven't been able to fix them ourselves. This ugly thinking can't be 'fixed' by some magical punishment from Carroll ISD. Parents, at some point we need to be as hard on ourselves as we are on them." After reasserting her support for the work of the fledgling District Diversity Council, Hill ended her note with a warning: "Parents," she wrote, "get on the boat, or we do the future a huge disservice."

Despite all the bad press and the bold proclamations—and notwithstanding the future reforms promised by the DDC—not much seemed to change at the senior high school that spring.

Raven Rolle was no more surprised by the release of the second N-word video than she was by the first one. She'd been hearing white students, many of whom seemed to her to be "obsessed" with Black culture, using that word at school since at least middle school, often delivered as a misguided term of endearment, emulating the pronunciation and cadence of their favorite hip-hop artists. "Kids will just walk up to anyone and use that word," Raven said. "They're extremely comfortable with it. And then, sometimes, there are situations when they're doing it to hurt your feelings."

That culture didn't suddenly disappear after the viral videos. If anything, Raven said, it grew more prevalent. There were no school assemblies to discuss the N-word's racist history, no lessons on why the word can sting when it rolls off the tongues of white people, regardless of pronunciation or intent. While the viral videos may have embarrassed a lot of adults in Southlake, some white students at Carroll saw the whole thing as evidence of a different kind of injustice. The argument went something like this: If Black people can say the N-word, especially the version that they heard in rap songs, why were white students being punished for it? In fact, they'd say, punishing white students for saying the word was the *real* racism.

In March 2019, less than a month after the second N-word video, Raven says she was sitting in math class when she overheard one of her white classmates saying the slur while making that very argument. She didn't even bother confronting him. Raven got up from her desk and headed straight to Principal Shawn Duhon's office. "I told Duhon, 'This just happened, go do something about it.'"

Duhon, who is white, had been principal at Carroll Senior High since 2012, and this wasn't the first time he'd had to deal with a report of white kids using racial slurs at school. It wasn't even the first time he'd heard that complaint from Raven. This time, he called both Raven and the white student down to his office.

As she walked into the principal's office, Raven, doubting that Duhon would take her complaint seriously and wanting proof in case he didn't, secretly hit record on her cell phone.

"Come on in," Duhon told her and the boy. "Have a seat."

After laying out the facts as he understood them, Duhon told the white student he wanted to hear his side of the story. At first, the boy denied saying the N-word. "I don't use that word regularly," he said. "That's not, like, in my vocabulary."

Raven, seventeen at the time, wasn't having it.

"You're lying. I heard you say it." She described how the boy had walked into class. How she'd overheard him telling another white student that he thought it was racist that only Black people are allowed to use the N-word. How this wasn't even the first time she'd heard him using the word at school.

The boy conceded that was, in fact, his opinion about the word, but he continued to deny saying it that day. Raven pounced, like a lawyer cross-examining a hostile witness: "If that's your opinion on the word, which you did use in the sentence when you were explaining it, then why would you lie about saying it today? . . . How are you looking at me in my face and telling me that you didn't do that? Are you calling me crazy?"

Duhon, perhaps noticing the tension rising in Raven's voice, tried to mediate. It didn't matter, he told the boy, whether he'd said the word on that day, or a week earlier. It didn't matter whether he'd said the word while making an argument, or while quoting a rap lyric. Words that are "hateful, demeaning, and derogatory" have no place in class, Duhon said. Then he offered up some examples that made Raven cringe.

"It doesn't matter if it's, and excuse me for using these words, 'gay,' 'homo,' anything—it doesn't matter what the word is. Those types of words are not safe for this educational setting. . . . I'm not going to sit here and talk at my table and call people 'gay' when I got three of my teachers in my office that I know are homo . . ." Duhon stopped himself before completing the word "homosexual," seemingly unsure if it was appropriate for him to say it out loud. "That's the most disrespectful thing," he continued.

At one point, Duhon suggested that in the future, when the boy heard friends using the N-word, regardless of the context, he should ask them not to say it around him. That's what Duhon did, he said, when he heard people say the "G-D word," referring to "goddamn."

"I can't stand that word," Duhon said. "I don't accept that word. I don't tolerate it. And I'm going to tell them, 'Hey, guys, I don't like that. I appreciate it if you wouldn't say it, because I think it's totally disrespectful.'" (Raven didn't say it in the meeting, but to her, Duhon comparing the N-word to "goddamn" was insulting.)

The boy pushed back. "Well, isn't there an option where you just don't use that word, and you don't tell somebody else what they can and can't say?"

"This happens way too often in school," Raven responded. "Am I supposed to get up and leave every time I hear someone say that?"

"Well, to me," the boy said, "it's just a word."

"It's not just a word," Raven fired back, raising her voice. "Don't even say that. Do you know what that means? Do you know how disrespectful that is?"

The boy doubled down. "To me," he said, smirking slightly, "it's just a word."

That's when Raven lost her cool.

"No, it's not just a word, that is a racial slur," she said, her voice cracking as tears formed in her eyes. "I can't even believe you would just say that to me." From behind his desk, Duhon kept repeating to Raven, "Just relax, just relax," like a hostage negotiator desperate to turn down the temperature. Instead, the boy pressed on.

"There's no words that offend me."

Now Raven was screaming: "Because you're white! That's why. I'm Black, and I have to go to school in this white school and listen to y'all say that, and you're going to tell me it's just a word? It's not just a word!"

Duhon, eyes wide, motioned for the white student to leave his office. The boy rose from his seat and walked out the door without saying another word. Alone now, Raven and her principal sat in silence for several seconds.

Duhon at first tried to comfort her. "You see the word ignorance, you said it. That's what we're dealing with," he said softly, with the cadence of a man carefully measuring each word. "I'm not sure, Raven, I'm not sure if that kid will ever change."

"He's not going to," Raven said, sniffling.

Then Duhon offered her some advice.

"When you see ignorance like that, you can't let them take your joy, girl. You can't. You're too good of a girl, you're too good of a person for somebody like that." Duhon continued, talking in a hushed, soothing tone, "You're too pretty, you're too nice, everything you got going for you, you can't let something like that take your joy, right, take your peace. Don't let him see you get frustrated because of his ignorance."

Duhon reminded Raven that she only had to make it through three more months of school, seeming to imply that her emotional reaction to a classmate's racist comments could jeopardize her graduation. "You don't want to do something or say something to where he takes your joy and gets you frustrated and upset."

Before sending her away, Duhon offered to change Raven's schedule so she wouldn't have to see the boy in class. Raven has no idea if he was ever disciplined. Years later, she doubts that either the boy or Duhon had spent much time dwelling on the incident. They probably moved on, she figures.

If only she'd been able to do the same.

4

Everything Imploded

CHRISTINA CATLIN STILL FELT as though she was living in a "perfect Carroll dreamland" as she entered her second year teaching fourth grade at Johnson Elementary in the fall of 2019. She'd seen the news reports about racist videos involving students at the high school the previous year, but that hadn't diminished her overall view of Southlake. It was just some kids being dumb, she figured. If anything, the district's forceful and unified reaction to the controversy made her feel even better about her decision to come to Carroll. "Everyone seemed to be coming together and saying, 'Racism is a problem, it exists, and we're willing to have hard conversations about it,'" Catlin said.

But a few months into the new school year, she got an email from a parent that made her start to question whether that was true.

The mother of a white student was upset about a book that her daughter had found in Catlin's classroom library, a collection of titles that students could read in their free time. The book that had drawn the mom's anger, *Blended*, by Sharon M. Draper, tells the story of an eleven-year-old biracial girl named Isabella who is struggling with her parents' divorce and her own racial identity as the daughter of a white mom and Black dad. The story includes nuanced discussions of racism and belonging, and its climactic scene depicts an encounter with a white police officer who ends up shooting Isabella as she's reaching for her cell phone. *School Library Journal* called the book "a frank, honest portrait of a modern, blended family," and recommended it for grades four and up.

The mom from Catlin's class disagreed.

In her email, she said her daughter had come home asking why a police officer would shoot someone just because of their race, Catlin recalled. That wasn't a conversation the mom said she wanted to have with her daughter, and it wasn't a message she wanted her child to learn at school. Later, at a meeting with Catlin and an assistant principal, the mom said she wanted the book removed.

That evening, Catlin vented in a social media post that was visible only to close friends: "A parent made me have a meeting with her & my principal this morning because she said this book makes all black people seem better than white people and like victims," she wrote, along with a picture of her copy of *Blended*.

Catlin refused the mom's request to pull the book. What kind of signal would that send to Black students? she thought. "That's their truth, and it's the truth of what's happening in the world," Catlin said, noting that Black parents don't have the luxury of putting off conversations about racism until their children are older. "I didn't want to take it away because it made one person feel uncomfortable."

Dissatisfied with Catlin's response, the mother filed a formal book challenge, asking to have *Blended* banned, not just from Catlin's class, but from all of Johnson Elementary's classrooms and its library. In the end, a committee that included district staff members and a parent reviewed the book and, after concluding that it was age-appropriate, voted to continue allowing it on campus, citing a district policy that said a parent's ability to control what students can read "extends only to his or her own child."

Catlin was bothered by the episode, but also emboldened. "That was a big turning point for me," she said.

She'd stood strong, and her school administration had stood with her. But major, society-altering developments were on the horizon—in Southlake and in America at large—and the next time a parent complained about what children learned at Johnson Elementary, the result would be far different.

By early 2020, the District Diversity Council was nearly finished with its work. Each subcommittee had drafted its portion of the Cultural

Competence Action Plan, or CCAP, and district administrators were beginning the process of compiling everything into a single document. All that remained was a final diversity council meeting in April to go over the details with the full committee before presenting the plan to the school board that May.

If that's how things had played out, Michelle Moore—who would be appointed school board president that May—believes the diversity plan probably would have sailed through without much debate. In that alternate reality, Moore says, the school board likely would have held a few workshops over the summer to revise and streamline the plan based on community feedback—if there even was any—and then that fall the district would have begun the work of implementing the plan.

Instead, as Moore put it, "everything imploded."

The implosion began in earnest on the evening of March 11, the day the threat posed by what most of us were calling "the novel coronavirus" became real for most Americans. That morning, the World Health Organization officially declared COVID-19 to be a global pandemic, sending financial markets tumbling. Sports fans tuning into ESPN that evening watched as an NBA arena in Oklahoma City was abruptly evacuated just minutes before tip-off after a player tested positive for the mysterious new virus. One hour later, President Trump addressed the nation: "From the beginning of time," he said from the Oval Office, "nations and people have faced unforeseen challenges, including large-scale and very dangerous health threats. This is the way it always was and always will be. It only matters how you respond, and we are responding with great speed and professionalism."

That same night, about an hour after news broke that Tom Hanks and his wife had tested positive for the coronavirus, Carroll ISD officials announced on the district's Facebook page that they, like leaders in virtually all of America's thirteen thousand public school districts, were consulting with public health experts and attempting to figure out how to keep students safe during these unprecedented times. The following week, Texas governor Greg Abbott made the decision for them. In an edict that would remain in effect for the remainder of the school year, the Republican ordered the emergency closure of all Texas schools. Practically overnight, school hallways and playgrounds went silent as most Americans—liberals and conservatives alike—heeded calls from government officials and public health experts to stay home to slow the spread of the virus and allow time to study it.

From the start, Christina Catlin said, remote schooling was a train wreck, at least at the elementary school level. She started each morning by reading aloud to her students over Zoom, learning over time, as we all did, how to master the mute button. The remainder of the children's days were filled with online assignments, largely curated from a pair of digital news and literary magazines published by the education company Scholastic. "Honestly," Christina said, "we gave them busywork. I mean, were they learning? Absolutely not. We taught nothing those last couple of months. We were just trying to get through it. Everyone was."

In the mad rush to manage the crisis, the work of the District Diversity Council was put on the back burner. The district postponed plans to present the diversity plan in May and told committee members they could resume their work the following school year. But later that month, on May 25, yet another viral video sparked a new national crisis—one that suddenly made the work of the diversity committee seem more urgent than ever.

Americans watched in horror as, for eight minutes and forty-six seconds, a forty-six-year-old Black man named George Floyd gasped for air under the knee of a white Minneapolis police officer, using his final breaths to call out for his mother. The cell phone footage of Floyd's murder hit the internet about two months after Louisville police had shot and killed twenty-six-year-old Breonna Taylor during a botched drug raid, and three months after twenty-five-year-old Ahmaud Arbery was murdered by three white men while jogging through a neighborhood in Georgia. Perhaps it was because the pandemic had everyone's emotions running high, or because the steady drumbeat of news about the killings of unarmed Black people did not slow even during a global health emergency. Or maybe it was the visceral brutality of Floyd's murder, caught on tape for all to see. Whatever the cause, the outcry that followed his death was different from that of earlier high-profile police killings.

Within hours, the video sparked a nationwide protest movement unlike anything the nation had seen in at least five decades.

Nikki Olaleye, a Black junior at Carroll Senior High School, was at home in late May, scrolling through videos of marches in big cities and small towns across the country, when a thought hit her: *Why not in Southlake?*

Nikki, the daughter of Nigerian immigrants, had moved to Southlake with her physician mother and older brother the summer before her freshman year. Coming from a predominantly white but far more progressive school district near San Francisco, Nikki described her early years at Carroll as a shock to her system. "It was lonely for a long time," she said.

Now, she saw a chance to make a difference.

She called up a few friends and fellow members of the Progressive Activism Club, a newly formed student organization at Carroll. "I was, like, 'We should do this. We should put on a protest.' And they were, like, 'You might be crazy, but OK.'" That night, Nikki designed a digital flier on her computer, inviting the community to a demonstration for racial justice the following week at Town Square: "Come support Southlake students in our fight to end racism and stand with victims of police brutality," it said, alongside a drawing of three fists raised in the air—one Black, one white, and one a shade in between.

But by the time Nikki hit publish on the Facebook post on the evening of May 31, the national conversation following Floyd's death had already begun to shift. Although most protests that spring had been peaceful, some had gotten ugly as police in riot gear clashed with Black Lives Matter activists. Images of broken-out storefronts and businesses on fire dominated cable news coverage. Amid the chaos, Trump fired off a tweet calling protesters "thugs" and said, "When the looting starts, the shooting starts." During a speech from the Rose Garden the day after Nikki published her Facebook post, the president threatened to deploy the U.S. military to quell the unrest. "I am your president of law and order, and an ally of all peaceful protesters," he said during the speech. "But in recent days, our nation has been gripped by professional anarchists, violent mobs, arsonists, looters, criminals, rioters, Antifa, and others." As he was speaking, D.C. police fired tear gas into a crowd of peaceful demonstrators outside the White House to clear a path for Trump to pose outside a church while holding a Bible.

The president's message seemed to take root in Southlake.

As Nikki's protest flier spread widely on social media, so did rumors warning that her demonstration might turn violent. Some residents were panicking over a May 30 tweet from an anonymous user that called for activists to attack homes in Southlake and other wealthy Dallas-area suburbs. Despite the post's dubious authenticity—it had come from an account named "Antifa Lockhart"—the tweet had some Southlake residents on edge. One man wrote on Facebook that business owners should be prepared to "exercise their second amendment rights" at Nikki's rally. Commenting on that same post, Leigh Wambsganss, the wife of Southlake's former mayor Andy Wambsganss, said there was no hope of changing the minds of any Black Lives Matter activists. "Sadly, they need to die," Wambsganss wrote. "But they would still vote."

Mayor Laura Hill had seen the panic building online, and she was worried. More than a year after recording the promotional video with students and promising to confront racism, Hill released a statement suggesting that Nikki's Black Lives Matter rally was not the way to do it. Holding the demonstration at Town Square near so many businesses was a mistake, Hill wrote, warning that people bent on violence might come from out of town to cause destruction. "The City always allows all groups to gather peacefully in our public parks, it is their right and I support the students' desire to be heard," she wrote. "But as Mayor and a Mother I can not in good conscience tell you to send your child. . . . Yes, we will take every precaution within our ability, but our families want guarantees that their children will be safe. There are none."

Behind the scenes, Hill worked to get the demonstration canceled or relocated. Believing that the outspoken Black mother Robin Cornish might hold some sway over the student activists, Hill texted her days ahead of the rally asking if she might be able to convince Nikki and the other students to change course. Maybe the students could do a virtual event instead, Hill suggested, or film another video at the city's expense. Cornish thought the mayor was being hysterical. "In my heart," she wrote to Hill, "I just don't see it becoming violent on Saturday."

"From your lips to God's ears," Hill wrote back. "It's over for me if anyone gets hurt."

On the morning of the protest, several Town Square shop owners boarded up their windows. As city leaders held their breath, Nikki and the other demonstrators began to gather on the lawn outside town hall. Raven Rolle, home from college for the summer, came with some friends and a stack of homemade signs, including one that read "Stop pretending your racism is patriotism." Michelle Moore came, too, nervous about the potential for violence, but wanting to show her support for students of color. In total, more than a thousand people attended. With Southlake police escorting them, they marched through the upscale shopping district, chanting "No justice, no peace!" and "Say his name! George Floyd!"

At one point, while standing under a gazebo overlooking the crowd, Nikki grabbed a bullhorn and made clear that this movement wasn't just about police violence. It was about demanding racial justice right here in Southlake—including at Carroll. "We fight so that our children won't have to feel the same way we do now: unsafe and unheard!"

Toward the end of the rally, Mayor Hill stepped forward and addressed the crowd. Shouting into the bullhorn, she challenged everyone to turn their anger into real action. "Look in the mirror and ask yourself, 'What did I do?' Was this just another year that went by? Same complaints, same disappointments, same unhappiness? Or will this be a year when you step up and say, 'I'm willing to do more?'"

A woman in the crowd shouted, "You step up!" Someone else yelled for Hill to say "Black lives matter." Instead, the mayor issued a challenge: "For real change, you must challenge yourself. You must get off the keyboard and take a seat at the table." Several people in the crowd groaned.

"Why did you discourage us from coming, then?" another woman fired back. The rest of the mayor's comments were drowned out with boos.

Nikki stood to the side, smiling. For her and her friends, the protest was a huge, affirming win. A thousand people, marching for racial justice in *Southlake, Texas*. The crowd had been passionate but peaceful. Nobody was hurt. No businesses were damaged. In that moment, it seemed to Nikki as if real, lasting change might be possible. Lots of people were feeling that way in the early days of what some had begun calling America's racial reckoning. It was a season of reflection, a time to confront injustice—both historical and present—and to find ways to make things right.

The Town Square protest caught the attention of Anya Kushwaha, a 2016 Carroll graduate who—like a lot of college students—had come home to stay with her parents in Southlake after the pandemic shuttered university campuses that spring. As the daughter of an immigrant from India, Anya had plenty of memories of Carroll classmates treating her poorly because of her ethnicity, whether it was the volleyball teammates who joked about her smelling like "stinky curry," the girl who'd made a Facebook post mocking her "excessive body hair," or the Christian kids who warned that her father was going to hell because he was a Hindu. During a lesson on the Holocaust in fifth grade, Kushwaha remembers a social studies teacher making the class line up and then pointing out the few who would have been sent to gas chambers. It wasn't until she went away to college that Kushwaha began to realize how much she'd been traumatized by those daily experiences. "So much of myself—my identity, my personality—had to be killed in order to survive there. It's suffocating, but you don't realize how suffocating it truly is until you leave that environment."

That's why she found it so inspiring to see current high school students speaking up.

After attending the rally, Kushwaha, who had just graduated from the University of Southern California with a degree in nongovernmental organizations and social change, started texting with a few other former high school classmates who were also home from college. Initially, their plan was just to write a letter calling on Carroll officials to take a firm public stance against racism. But after looping in more alumni, such as Raven Rolle, and current students, including Nikki Olaleye, the plan morphed into something much bigger.

On July 6, 2020, the Southlake Anti-Racism Coalition, or SARC, went live on Instagram, with the stated mission of "pushing for tangible, enduring anti-racist change in Southlake Carroll ISD." Over the next several days, Kushwaha and her fellow student activists published dozens of anonymous accounts of racism, xenophobia, anti-Semitism, and homophobia that had been reported to them by Carroll students and alumni, making the case that discrimination at Carroll was even worse than district administrators had realized. Soon more student testimonials were flowing into their inbox.

Within days, SARC had collected more than three hundred anonymous accounts:

"I have been called a 'dirty Jew' and have had former friends hail Hitler in front of me."

"I used to wear a hijab. I was referred to as having a 'terrorist hat.' My headscarf was pulled off my head one day. I told a female teacher and she did nothing."

"Somebody in a class of mine said, 'Why do faggots deserve rights?' and nobody said anything against it. I was too scared to say anything because I didn't want to out myself. This town needs change."

Kushwaha and the other students knew the District Diversity Council had been working on the Cultural Competence Action Plan, but they wanted to push Carroll to go further and move faster. Eleven days after their first post, SARC published a list of seventeen demands the group wanted implemented immediately at Carroll and addressed the letter to both the school district and the broader Southlake community.

Number one on their list: a demand for the school board to formally declare that Black lives matter. The students also called on the district to require all employees to pass implicit bias screenings to weed out bigoted educators, to study and overhaul the curriculum to "prevent the propagation of white supremacist and Eurocentric views" in social studies courses, and to impose a ban on racist imagery, including the Confederate flag, from all district facilities. The letter generated instant blowback on social media, but one demand—number sixteen on the list—was getting more attention than the rest. It called on Carroll to get rid of armed school resource officers and to replace them with therapists and social workers—essentially, to "defund the police," another rallying cry during that year of racial reckoning.

When Russell Maryland, the ex-Cowboy who'd volunteered to serve on the District Diversity Council, read the demand letter, especially the part about defunding police in a conservative town like Southlake, he thought, "That's going to cause some problems." Maryland would be proven right. The demands were like gasoline on the flames of fear and resentment that had begun to flicker with Nikki's protest.

Afterward, SARC was inundated with angry messages and comments accusing the group—which at the time was made up of about a dozen high school students and recent graduates—of being "radical left-wing extremists" who wanted to "destroy America." In a lengthy Facebook post calling on his fellow Southlake residents to stand strong against SARC, former mayor Andy Wambsganss called the student activist group a "little cartel of agitators and knuckleheads" and denounced their demands as "a bucket of trash." And as for the central problem that SARC was striving to address, Wambsganss wrote that "the notion of systemic racism" was a "fairytale" that had already been thoroughly "debunked." In another Facebook post about the demands, a former Republican state lawmaker shared her theory that the national Black Lives Matter organization was being funded by America's foreign adversaries and that the people behind SARC were "probably from places like North Korea, Russia, or China."

Kushwaha, twenty-two at the time, was disturbed but also bemused by the attacks. "It was either, 'Oh, these are kids who don't know what they're talking about,' or it was, 'These are adults who have been hired by George Soros and are orchestrating the decline of our government.'"

For their part, Carroll leaders responded to SARC's demands with public statements promising to complete the work of addressing racism that had begun in 2018. Behind the scenes, meanwhile, district officials, including Michelle Moore and the leaders of the District Diversity Council, agreed to meet with Kushwaha and the other student activists—a decision that would end up further inflaming outrage among conservatives. The goal was to show the students that the district was willing to listen to their perspectives, but also to convince them that the diversity plan would go a long way toward addressing their concerns. "I still felt at that point that if we could just get the CCAP before the school board, then we could get it passed and start the work of refining it and implementing it," Moore said.

But on social media, people began to conflate the work of the District Diversity Council with SARC's demand letter. They pointed to the meeting between school officials and SARC as evidence that the DDC had been infiltrated by a far-left activist group bent on defunding police and tearing down Southlake. At that point, the actual contents of the Cultural Competence Action Plan were unknown to most people in town, but now some had begun to associate it with progressive politics and Black Lives Matter activism.

That, Maryland observed, was the "beginning of the doom of the CCAP . . . the point where everything was politicized. And when things are politicized in this town or this region or this country, then all bets are off."

At last, in July 2020, nearly two years after the first viral N-word video—after hundreds of student testimonials, tear-filled meetings with parents, public forums, and promises from city and school leaders—the Cultural Competence Action Plan was unveiled to the people of Southlake and set to go before the school board for an early August vote.

The thirty-four-page draft document called for mandatory cultural sensitivity training for all Carroll students and teachers; a top-to-bottom review of district curricula to embed culturally responsive lessons at every grade level; a formal process for reporting and tracking incidents of racist bullying; an audit to ensure student clubs were welcoming and inclusive regardless of race, gender, or sexuality; the creation of a new LGBTQ focus group to foster dialogue at the high school; and changes to the code of conduct to more explicitly spell out consequences for acts of discrimination. The plan proposed an overhaul of Carroll's hiring practices to recruit more teachers of color and the creation of a new administrative position with a six-figure salary, director of equity and inclusion, to oversee the efforts across the district.

The CCAP also introduced many residents in Southlake to the increasingly prevalent term "microaggressions," the catchall way of describing racist statements and actions that might make a student of color feel disparaged, but are less obvious than, say, shouting the N-word on camera. A common example at Carroll: a white student telling an academically gifted Black classmate that she's "the whitest Black girl I know." The District Diversity Council wanted to create a system to report and track those types of incidents.

"The way we saw it, this was a fairly basic plan," Russell Maryland said. "Just a basic plan of human decency, empathy, kindness, inclusion, and understanding about other cultures."

It landed like a bomb.

Moore's phone was buzzing with notifications all week as her inbox filled up with messages from constituents and neighbors. "I'm against the diversity plan," one friend wrote to her. "This is a home issue. Parents should be the ones training their kids and not the school." That same day, an anonymous email blast started circulating, falsely claiming that Moore and the other trustees were planning to force "gender choices, LGBQ etc. on our kids as young as PRE-K." The volume of texts, calls, and emails dwarfed the blowback the district had gotten after the N-word videos nearly two years earlier.

Early on the morning of July 31, three days before the school board was slated to vote on the diversity plan, Moore's phone vibrated. "Do we have a plan to counter this crusade against the CCAP?"

The text message was from Ronell Smith, a member of the DDC who had been elected to the city council a year earlier. Smith was the Black father of biracial girls who'd brought up Carroll's motto, "Protect the Tradition," at a school board meeting after the first viral video in

2018 and had asked, rhetorically, what tradition the district was protecting. Smith, a conservative himself, didn't love every detail in the CCAP, he told Moore, but he believed it moved the district in the right direction and deserved to be defended. "I don't want these people to think they've won," Smith wrote to Moore. "If they feel emboldened, we'll never get anything done."

Some members of the school board and city leaders had begun floating the idea of delaying the vote to allow time for more community feedback. Moore agreed the plan needed to be refined. But she also agreed with Smith, who warned in a follow-up text that if school board trustees "cater to the mob," any hope of passing the CCAP "goes away forever."

"I can't let that happen," Moore responded. "I will be letting so many kids down."

On the night of August 3, more than one hundred people signed up to speak during the virtual school board meeting, every one of them wishing to comment on the diversity plan. The first speaker was Andrew Yeager, a white father of three Carroll students who called on the board to reject the CCAP. "It is a political agenda to fully change our great school. It's an attack on our tradition of excellence, which has been a unifying force for all Dragons and students of every race, religion, and ethnicity."

The next speaker complained that the CCAP added protections for LGBTQ students, which he said would unfairly punish "students who hold a biblical worldview." That opinion was echoed by a speaker who warned that "an anti-family and anti-Christian agenda has been inserted to promote homosexuality" at Carroll. Another speaker, an old friend of Moore's family, warned that tracking student microaggressions would lead to hundreds of daily false reports and "turn neighbor on neighbor, friend on friend, and provide a means to eliminate adversaries."

But most of the speakers—including Anya Kushwaha, Nikki Olaleye, and several other SARC members—supported the plan, which gave Moore the impression that, despite the outrage, she still had the backing of many, if not most, residents. After nearly two hours, it was the board president's turn to speak.

Moore opened by thanking the students and parents who had come forward with stories of discrimination beginning two years earlier. She thanked members of the DDC for collectively putting in "thousands of hours of work" to make Carroll better. And then she apologized for failing them all. If only she had done a better job communicating with the public about what the plan was about, maybe things wouldn't have gotten so heated, she said. "I would have never imagined what has happened in this community the last few days, over a plan that was really trying to create an environment that was safe and welcoming."

But failing to act would be a bigger failure, Moore said. "If we don't take action tonight, we really have to think about what message are we sending to the kids and the victims of discrimination that have come and talked to us over and over again."

With that, former board president and fellow DDC volunteer Sheri Mills motioned—while choking back tears—for the board to receive the CCAP "and authorize the superintendent to begin implementation." Another member seconded Mills's motion, but then three others unmuted their microphones and asked to pump the brakes, raising arguments like: Shouldn't we spend more time studying the plan before we vote on it? Not every board member got to serve on the diversity council. And what about all the messages from concerned parents?

"This is the most important, not just one of the important things, the most important thing that any one of us will ever work on," board member Eric Lannen said. "And I want to get it right. I don't want to have division in our community and have people upset and yelling at each other."

After nearly an hour of debate, Moore proposed a middle ground, one that she and fellow board members had begun debating in a chain of text messages prior to the meeting: Why not just vote to *receive* the CCAP, but hold off on implementing it? Then schedule board workshops to keep refining it, allowing time for the broader community to weigh in. That sounded like a good idea, a few of the other trustees said. But one member, Matt Bryant, the trustee who had asked Russell Maryland to join the diversity committee, had deep concerns.

"You stated, 'The march of progress is slow but unyielding.' So if we move at a little slower pace than what you're advising, but in the effort to understand," Bryant said, "this should be a 7–0 vote, is what this should be. This should be a unanimous vote."

Moore and Mills weren't budging. "I've spent the past twenty-two months of my life working on this plan," Mills said. "I think we owe it to the people who spent the past two years of their life to vote tonight." Moore seconded the motion and began to call the roll.

Place one, Michelle Moore: "I vote yes."

Place two, Eric Lannen: "I don't understand what we're voting on, so I vote no."

Place three: "I'm Sheri Mills. Yes."

Place four: "Matt Bryant. No."

Place five: "Danny Gilpin. I vote yes."

Place six: The board's vice president, Todd Carlton, took a deep breath before saying, "I vote yes."

Place seven, Dave Almand: "Yes."

By a vote of 5–2, the motion passed. Those five board members hoped that by simply receiving the diversity plan rather than acting right away on its recommendations, they could lower the temperature of the debate in town.

Instead, the opposite happened.

Students of color and LGBTQ teens who'd shared painful accounts felt betrayed by the board's failure to immediately adopt the plan. As for the adults in the community who saw the CCAP as a threat to their kids? They weren't about to sit back while this school board tinkered around with the fine print.

Some of those residents, as one of them would say later, had already started building an army. And now they were preparing to launch a political war.

Part II

BUILDING THE ARMY

5

Coming to a Town Near You

THE POST-IT NOTE ON which I'd scribbled a reminder in September 2020 to look into the political fight in Southlake was covered in a thin layer of dust when I finally circled back to it four months later. In that time, President Donald Trump had been hospitalized with COVID-19, Joe Biden had defeated him in the presidential election, and Trump had launched his campaign to overturn that outcome based on false conspiracy theories and outright lies about rigged voting machines, truckloads of fake ballots, and widespread election fraud. The news cycle had in a matter of weeks provided enough wild and consequential stories to keep me and my NBC News colleagues busy for years. But through it all, I hadn't been able to stop thinking about Texas GOP chairman Allen West's vague tip about conservative parents in a "very nice, well-to-do" community in North Texas "receiving threats from Black Lives Matter."

After reading a couple of *Dallas Morning News* articles about the diversity plan controversy in Southlake, I started reaching out to people in the community—which is how, on the afternoon of January 6, 2021, I ended up on the phone with Angela Jones, a Black Southlake resident and mother of three who had chaired a subcommittee of the District Diversity Council. Jones was getting me up to speed on the backlash against the Cultural Competence Action Plan, and why she believed it had been necessary to create that document in the first place. A former TV meteorologist and wife of a senior physician with the U.S. Department of Veterans Affairs, Jones and her family had moved to Southlake more than two decades earlier, like most of her neighbors, hoping to give her children a world-class education.

In many ways, Jones told me, her two oldest kids had lived what she called "the Dragon dream." Her daughter, now away at college in New York, was president of Carroll High's renowned Emerald Belles dance team her senior year and had been an all-state cross-country runner while also excelling academically. Her second child, having graduated from Carroll that spring with the ability to speak five languages, was halfway through his freshman year at one of the nation's top-ranked private universities. But those achievements, Jones now realized, had come with scars.

In a story that would soon become painfully familiar, Jones told me that, in exchange for an elite public school education, her children had dealt with near-daily insults—some subtle, some less so—which she said they'd been conditioned to accept as a normal part of life. On their own, each of these anecdotes—these microaggressions—might seem small or inconsequential, Jones told me, but they'd added up over the years. It wasn't until her daughter went away to college that she realized the "othering" that she'd experienced at Carroll wasn't normal, or OK. Jones told me one of her kids had begun seeing a psychologist to deconstruct the toxic self-image that resulted from growing up in such an environment. The hardest part, Jones told me: She and her husband had chosen this for them.

"My family worked hard to give my children the best," she told me, crying over the phone that day in January. "But at what cost? Education is wonderful. Great opportunities are wonderful. But not if your psyche has been damaged. And I believe my children have been damaged because of Southlake."

Even more upsetting, Jones said, had been watching members of her community rise up in recent months to oppose efforts that she believed would make Carroll safer and more welcoming for children like hers. It seemed to her that her neighbors had embraced a false binary, in which any critical reflection about racism in the community was treated as a total condemnation. Jones wasn't speaking up because she hated Southlake, she said. She was speaking up because she loved her home and wanted to make it better.

Being new to the story, the backlash was what I still didn't understand. The story Jones was telling didn't match West's description of a hostile Black Lives Matter takeover of the school district. I'd gone back and watched a video of the 2018 school board meeting when parents of Black children came forward with painful stories similar to the one I was hearing from Jones. Back then, people appeared to be listening to one another, and everyone seemed genuinely committed to addressing the problem. What had brought things to the point of backlash?

Jones began to offer up her theory. Over the course of two decades, she'd watched as Southlake's population had grown ever more diverse with an influx of high-achieving South Asian immigrants. Over time, she said, fewer and fewer white Carroll students were graduating at the top of their class.

"I think," Jones told me, "this has a lot to do with preservation, and I believe—"

Just then, I cut her off mid-sentence. Throughout our hour-long conversation, I'd been keeping an eye on an MSNBC live feed on a computer monitor in my home office. I was suddenly distracted by the images flashing across the screen.

"I don't know if you've noticed your TV," I told Jones, my voice shaking slightly. "The MAGA protesters just stormed the Capitol. There's shooting in the Capitol right now."

At the urging of their president, people had come by the thousands to stop Congress from certifying the results of the presidential election. Some were members of white supremacist extremist groups. Others you might have thought of as regular folks. A realtor from a wealthy Dallas suburb. A West Virginia state lawmaker. A retired New York City police officer. One man, a construction worker from Delaware, marched through the besieged U.S. Capitol with a Confederate battle flag slung over his shoulder.

I told Jones I had to get off the phone to help cover the attack. But first, she wanted to complete her thought about the demographic changes that she believed were driving the unrest in her adopted hometown.

"There's complaints now that the valedictorian and salutatorian are no longer white," she told me. "That's really what's happening. They feel their children are being displaced."

Jones was, in effect, describing a hyper-local version of what's known as the Great Replacement Theory—a once-fringe belief by some on the far right that white Americans are being demographically, culturally, and politically replaced by non-white people through mass migration. I couldn't say whether Jones's assessment was accurate; I'd only just started my reporting. But in time I would begin to realize that, at a certain level, the story I was pursuing in Southlake, and the one unfolding that day in Washington, were both part of the same long, messy American narrative.

"I'll be in touch," I told Jones before hanging up.

Then I got to work.

Allen West had told me one other thing in September, when I'd asked him to elaborate on the situation in Southlake. "Well, you can look up Southlake Families PAC and how that was established, and why it was established."

I took his advice.

Southlake Families, a long-dormant group initially formed in 2011 to oppose a municipal referendum that would have allowed retail liquor sales in Southlake, had reemerged days ahead of the August 3, 2020, school board vote on the Cultural Competence Action Plan. The group, I would eventually learn, was led by a pair of well-connected conservative activists.

Tim O'Hare, the former chair of the Tarrant County Republican Party, had previously served as mayor of the nearby town, Farmers Branch, where he'd made national headlines more than a decade earlier for passing an ordinance, later deemed unconstitutional, that banned undocumented immigrants from renting homes or apartments in town. (The goal, O'Hare had said at the time, was to prevent an influx of "less desirable people," who "don't value education" and "don't take care of their properties.") Now a Southlake resident, he'd joined forces with Leigh Wambsganss, who had been a leader of the Northeast Tarrant County Tea Party years earlier—and who more recently had written the "sadly, they need to die" Facebook comment about Black Lives Matter activists.

The PAC spelled out its priorities in a short manifesto online:

> Southlake Families is unapologetically rooted in Judeo-Christian values. We welcome all that share our concerns and conservative values. . . . Conservative principles have made Southlake an extraordinary city in which to live and raise a family, and we believe Southlake Carroll's tradition of excellence must be protected. We reject recent campaign smears calling our tradition of excellence 'racist.' . . . We must rise up and work hard to protect our traditional way of life, which is currently under attack by extremists. . . . We believe in faith, freedom and family.

Within days of the CCAP's release, as Michelle Moore and other school board members were fielding angry text messages and emails, O'Hare, Wambsganss, and the other members of Southlake Families PAC published their own interpretations of what the District Diversity Council's plan would do, painting it in radical terms.

The CCAP called for age-appropriate diversity and inclusion lessons for students at every grade level. Southlake Families said that meant the district would be forcing kids to complete "social justice training" programs to graduate.

The diversity plan proposed creating a volunteer diversity council at each school made up of students and staff to help advise the district and to plan cultural celebrations. The Southlake Families PAC website warned that those groups would essentially serve as "diversity police," creating "an environment where you are guilty until proven innocent of 'microaggressions.'"

The plan called for evaluating members of the teaching staff based on their commitment to inclusivity and rewarding students who demonstrated excellence in diversity and inclusion. Southlake Families said the plan would "require students and teachers to take a 'cultural competence test' that can be used for shaming and discipline."

Southlake's beloved school district, the PAC wrote, "is being taken over by liberal activists with a national agenda trying to force CISD to adopt a radical Cultural Competence Action Plan that parents and residents have not had the opportunity to adequately review."

To Michelle Moore, Russell Maryland, Angela Jones, and others who'd worked on the CCAP, those claims bore little resemblance to the document they'd helped produce. But Southlake Families' claims about the diversity plan—delivered in short, digestible bullet points—were far easier to understand than the actual thirty-four-page document, which was loaded with jargon and organized under convoluted numeric headings. (Action Step 3, located under Strategy 1.4.3, which fell under Objective 1.4 in the CCAP, read as follows: "Adopt recommended appraisal indicator that measures employee commitment to equity/cultural competence.")

Brandon Rottinghaus, a political scientist at the University of Houston, says when it comes to politics, "Whether it's true or not is irrelevant. If people believe that it's true, then it's politically potent." By that measure, Southlake Families PAC was winning the messaging war. And it was just getting started.

After the school board voted to accept rather than adopt the CCAP on August 3, the PAC gathered hundreds of email addresses through an online petition and blasted out instructions on how concerned residents could make their voices heard: People needed to show up at school board meetings and speak up during public comments.

Two years after Black parents had lined up to share stories of discrimination at Carroll, conservatives in town—a cohort that some had begun to refer to as Southlake's "silent majority"—were preparing for their turn at the microphone.

The Carroll school board meeting room is large and windowless, with beige walls and gray commercial-grade carpeting. Board members sit on a curved dais in high-backed leather chairs overlooking rows of wooden seats, which—at most meetings during normal times—were usually more empty than filled. To a casual observer, typical board meetings might have seemed dull or tedious. It's not that the routine work of local school boards isn't important. Balancing budgets, approving curriculum—these are among the most essential functions of local government. But those decisions rarely spark major controversy. Before Carroll's school board meetings became the front line of Southlake's political revolt, public comments—the part of the meeting where anyone can come forward to voice their opinion—usually lasted less than ten minutes. Maybe two or three people would speak.

On the evening of August 17, 2020—the first in-person school board meeting since the start of the pandemic, and the first since the board had voted to accept the CCAP two weeks earlier—nearly forty residents had signed up to comment, with dozens more waiting in the hall outside and listening over speakers in an overflow room.

Board president Michelle Moore was feeling nervous as she settled into her seat. The energy in the room was tense. As customary, the meeting opened with the Pledge of Allegiance, followed by the Texas-specific pledge that schoolchildren recite each morning across the state: "Honor the Texas flag; I pledge allegiance to thee, Texas, one state under God, one and indivisible."

After going over the ground rules—no personal attacks, no profanity, please refrain from booing—Moore opened the floor for public comments.

The second speaker of the evening, a mother named Nancy Hollis, began by introducing herself in Spanish. "Buenas noches. Cómo están?" Wearing a bright Dragon-green T-shirt, Hollis told the board she was born in Colombia. With brown hair, light skin, and a subtle Texas drawl, she might have appeared white to most people. And that was exactly the point she wanted to make.

"I am Hispanic. My kids are blond, blue-eyed, and beautiful. Can you tell? Can you tell? Neither can our staff or administration or other students. You don't know who I am based on what I look like or where I was born or what color I am. Shame on us for introducing biases based on the color of our skin and not the merit of our character."

Hollis called on the board to reject the CCAP entirely and to repudiate any policy that would require the district to consider a teacher's race before hiring them, or a student's race before disciplining them.

By the end of her three-minute remarks, she was speaking—shouting, almost—in the tone and cadence of a fire-and-brimstone preacher. "Wrong is wrong. Racism in reverse is racism. Shame!" Some in the audience had begun calling out in response—*Yes. Uh-huh. Yes!*—like members of a rapt congregation.

"Teaching teachers to watch my color. How dare y'all! No teacher should ever look at my kid when they make a mistake and see the color of their skin or their dialect. They should look at that mistake and treat that kid with the respect they deserve. Thank you."

With that, the audience erupted in applause, effectively setting the tone for the rest of the meeting. One by one afterward, parents approached the lectern facing the dais, removed their masks, and used their allotted three minutes to unload.

A white mom of three named Ashley McCurry said the CCAP did not represent the values that had drawn her family to Southlake. "People live in a constant state of being offended, and we can all agree this is not Dragon culture," she said. "Southlake prides itself on excellence, not a victim mentality and reverse discrimination or discrimination of any type. We teach our children to be excellent achievers and overcomers. We don't teach them how to live in a constant state of being a victim."

A mother named Angela Bartholomae read from prepared remarks that appeared to quote directly from the Southlake Families PAC website, claiming that the CCAP would create "diversity police" and require "students to take a cultural competence test that can be used for shaming and discipline."

"Now I have to worry about my two blond-haired, blue-eyed boys being discriminated against and having trauma and pain . . . as being labeled as a racist."

In remarks that sounded as if they could have been ripped from a forced-busing protest from the 1970s, a mother named Mary Tamargo said she moved to Southlake for its "family-oriented culture and the high regard of our schools," but now the board was "intentionally changing the fabric of our schools and this community."

"My child does not even know what the word 'minority' means, but you all are going to teach it to him. . . . How dare you teach my child about cultural competence. What makes you the authority on the definition of white privilege? Basically, you want my child to believe that because he is white, everything has been handed to him."

These parents had come to send a unified message. Schools, they argued, didn't have any business teaching their children what counted as racism. By focusing on race, the district was perpetuating the problem it claimed to be fighting. To illustrate the point, a dad named Chuck Taggart began his remarks by pulling up a photo of his son on a tablet screen and holding it up for members of the school board to see. The image appeared to show a white boy smiling in a blue baseball cap. "Is he tan enough for you?" Taggart asked. "He's got brown hair, brown eyes. He's got tanned skin. I don't know if he's too tan or too white. Would it surprise you by looking at me that this boy is—he's European. He's also African. He's also part Asian. What does that make him? Are we going to start wearing half-yellow stars or quarter-yellow stars at school?"

Taggart said that earlier that week he'd had to explain to his eight- and eleven-year-old children why their friends' parents were abruptly pulling them out of Carroll and sending them to Liberty Christian, a nearby private school where nearly 90 percent of students are white, and how this whole CCAP mess started with a video of some high school kids two years earlier. He said one of his boys responded, "What's the N-word, Daddy?"

"'Well, I can't tell you what the word is because it's a bad word.'" And that's when it hit him, Taggart told the board. "These kids have never heard the N-word, them and none of their friends. So, you know where they're going to hear the N-word from? You. You guys. You guys are gonna teach my kids what the N-word is, and any other microaggression you can come up with."

A little later, a white woman named Kathy Del Calvo stepped forward and told the board that she was worried about the message the CCAP would send to her multiracial grandchildren. "My grandchildren are all minorities. Yes, all ten of them. . . . They do not need to be treated special. They can stand on their own. We have taught them that their race or ethnicity means nothing. They need to put in the hard work to get whatever they deserve." Despite data showing that a typical Black family holds one-tenth the wealth of a typical white family in America, Del Calvo ended her remarks by disputing the notion that race plays any role whatsoever in people's ability to succeed. She said she hoped all her grandchildren learned they do, in fact, have privilege. "And that is living in the United States of America. Regardless of your color, regardless of your religion, we all have an equal chance to succeed."

Her husband, Leo Del Calvo, an immigrant from Cuba, spoke next. He approached the microphone wearing a Carroll Dragons T-shirt and a Trump face mask around his chin. "Yes, like everybody here has said, we were asleep. Our fault. We're not asleep anymore." *That's right!* a woman called from the audience. Del Calvo repeated himself: "We are not asleep anymore. You're gonna continue to hear from us."

That idea, "We're not asleep anymore," came up a lot throughout the evening. Although each of the District Diversity Council's meetings had been public, and although the city and school district had advertised the initiative through email blasts, social media posts, and online videos, several speakers accused the school board of producing the CCAP in secret, in an attempt to sneak liberal ideas past a community where two-thirds of voters had backed Donald Trump.

Most of the people who'd come to speak against the CCAP were white or Latino, but not all of them. Reginald Williams, a young Black man who'd recently graduated from Carroll, wanted the board to know he'd had a great experience at school. "Personally, I was never discriminated against. I was never made to feel like I was unwelcomed, not treated right or anything." But now Williams said he was worried about the board's plans for educating his younger, white cousins. "Why would you make them learn that, because I'm a different color than them, that means we aren't equal, they don't love me the same?"

The CCAP didn't say anything about Black and white children being unequal or not loving each other. Yet Williams's comment reflected a core belief among many of those opposing the plan. He and others argued children shouldn't be taught to see color, and that any instruction that emphasized the way racial differences are experienced would only deepen rather than heal divisions. Natan Ton, a Carroll dad who'd escaped to America as a refugee after the Vietnam War, put it this way in brief but fiery comments to the school board: "I'm not white. I don't consider myself white or Asian. We're all humans. I don't want to be labeled as Black, white, yellow, gay, lesbian. I don't want to be labeled. My kids need to assimilate."

That position, however, may have amounted to little more than wishful thinking; studies have shown that even infants are aware of racial differences, and that by the time they turn four, children have begun to internalize biases. At twelve, many children will have formed hardened perceptions about race. These findings helped form the basis for the nationwide push to speak openly with children about racism and its role in U.S. history, particularly in the years since Trump's election—an embrace of anti-racist philosophy that many in Southlake were now repudiating.

One of the final speakers of the night, after nearly two hours of public comments, was a brash marine corps veteran who was becoming an outspoken leader in Southlake's budding resistance movement. "Guy Midkiff here. Dragon parent."

Midkiff was an airline pilot. When he wasn't flying, he hosted a conservative podcast from his dining room table called *Wise Guy Talks*. Think Rush Limbaugh, but with a focus on local politics. On this night, though, Midkiff keyed his remarks to an audience beyond Southlake.

"First of all, I want to speak to America, actually. This is a cautionary tale, ladies and gentlemen. And America, you need to listen to what's going on here tonight.

"I represent many Southlake parents that are like-minded, that fear being here tonight, because they are afraid that their children will be attacked by a local neo-Marxist group that goes about attacking our children and even grown-ups that dare come in the buildings."

Midkiff was talking about the Southlake Anti-Racism Coalition. The group of students and recent Carroll graduates had been staging protests for days outside the district's main offices following the board's decision to merely accept the CCAP. The protest had led to a confrontation with Midkiff that one of the students filmed. The video shows the student activists chanting "Hey-hey, ho-ho, racist parents have got to go!" as Midkiff—wearing a "Protect the Tradition" Carroll Dragons face covering—records them on his phone. "You're hurting my feelings, guys," Midkiff says, mocking them. "I feel a microaggression."

Now, from the lectern, Midkiff told school board members that he blamed them for creating the hostility and division in the community, beginning with the formation of the District Diversity Council two years earlier. "The excuse used to divide us was video clips of teens made off-campus. . . . They parroted offensive language commonly found in popular music. And from this we have a systemic race problem that needs immediate action?"

Midkiff, like virtually all the speakers, did not acknowledge the scores of Black parents who'd come forward following the 2018 video with painful accounts of racism, the real impetus behind the diversity council.

In closing, Midkiff mentioned a post he'd seen on social media apparently showing a Southlake student or a recent graduate stomping on an American flag. Midkiff said the video made him think of a friend and fellow veteran who'd been killed in a CH-46 military transport helicopter crash in 1986. "She stands on his grave when she does that," Midkiff shouted, his voice cracking as he pounded his fist on the lectern. "You understand me? She stands on his grave!"

Midkiff's remarks stood out, and not only because of the anger in his voice. To many conservatives in Southlake, this wasn't just about local school policy. Midkiff and the people he said he was speaking for appeared to see it as part of a bigger battle, between people who loved America and those who believed the country was racist at its core.

Later, on an episode of his podcast, Midkiff set the stakes in the direst of terms, framing the fight over the CCAP as "a classical battle between good and evil, light and darkness, truth and deceit, perception and reality."

"So goes Southlake," he warned, "so goes the rest of America."

A day after the in-person school board meeting—which had ended with a renewed promise from the district to revise the CCAP based on community feedback—an article appeared on a website called the Texas Scorecard under the headline, "Is a School District Disregarding

Parents on Controversial LGBTQ Plan?" (The title was somewhat out of left field, given that the debate at that point had focused mostly on aspects of the CCAP dealing with racism, but it foreshadowed an argument that would soon become a major focus of the right in Southlake and nationally: the idea that new rules explicitly prohibiting anti-LGBTQ discrimination would violate the religious rights of Christian students.)

The Texas Scorecard story had all the trappings of a traditional news article. It carried a hard news lead: "Monday evening, Southlake parents once again confronted the elected board members of the Carroll Independent School District over their controversial Cultural Competency [sic] Action Plan." And there were quotations from some of the parents who spoke at the meeting: "America is the least racist country. Southlake is the least racist town, and I've been here three years."

But the end of the article betrayed the story's true purpose. The author, a reporter named Robert Montoya, called on parents to continue speaking out against the CCAP at future meetings. Then he listed the names and email addresses of every Carroll school board member so readers could contact them directly. Montoya was free to dabble in overt activism because the Texas Scorecard isn't a traditional news site. It's a nonprofit publication created by Empower Texans, a powerful Tea Party–aligned advocacy group funded by a pair of West Texas oil and gas billionaires who have spent tens of millions of dollars over the years pushing Texas further to the right. One of the group's top objectives, long out of reach in Texas, had been to get the state legislature to provide parents with government funding to send their children to private Christian schools. The fact that the Texas Scorecard was writing about the CCAP meant one thing: The local fight in Southlake had caught the attention of powerful forces in the far-right wing of the Texas GOP—and they'd seen an opportunity.

The folks at Empower Texans weren't the only well-connected conservatives suddenly trying to draw attention to Southlake that August. On the same day that the Texas Scorecard article was published, the CCAP quietly made it onto a nationally syndicated talk radio program hosted by former National Rifle Association spokesperson Dana Loesch.

Loesch, famous for appearing in short NRA promos that oozed with disdain for liberals and the mainstream media, happened to be a Southlake resident.

"I've been telling you that there's been a fight in my community, even in our school board," Loesch told her listeners on August 18, 2020. "The district has been flirting with the idea of implementing curriculum that teaches kids to 'decenter their whiteness,' whatever that means. And it presents as though it's all about inclusion, but it actually is teaching bigotry and teaching racism." (The words "decenter whiteness," a phrase used by anti-racism advocates to describe attempts to elevate the perspectives of marginalized racial groups, did not appear in the CCAP.)

In a profile later published in the *Washington Post,* Loesch, who'd reportedly homeschooled her two sons and later sent them to private schools, said she was infuriated when she read the diversity plan and quickly got involved in the local effort to defeat it. On her radio program, *The Dana Show*, she complained that the CCAP was using reports of harassment—"something that has always existed," she mused—as a guise to indoctrinate kids with liberal ideas. Loesch seemed to see bullying, racist or otherwise, as a natural part of growing up, and efforts to prevent it as misguided.

"It is a power jockeying thing with kids, and we've all been through it," Loesch said. "It is our species's way of determining the pecking order, so to speak. And it doesn't matter what you are. It doesn't matter if you're gay or straight, or Black or white, or smart or if you struggle. It doesn't matter. It always has happened."

After playing a clip of a Southlake dad speaking at the most recent school board meeting, Loesch explained why she was telling her national audience about a hyper-local policy debate. "I'm using what's happening in my school district as an example to you. Because this is happening in districts across the country, to the point where I've seen parents across the nation speak with each other and wonder if it is not an organized effort, honestly." At a time when a large segment of the Republican base was embracing false claims about voter fraud, she added, "These are people who are not prone to conspiracy theories, and they're not given to hyperbole."

The Dana Show—and others like it in the vast online ecosystem that makes up right-wing media—have a way of foreshadowing where the national political discourse is heading, often weeks or months before those same storylines surface on the airwaves of bigger outlets like Fox News. So it was no small thing that the former NRA spokeswoman had trained her spotlight on her own town.

Two years after scores of public school districts had started rolling out initiatives in response to the nationwide rise in racist bullying, Loesch and other conservatives had noticed the trend—and they didn't like it. The fight in Southlake, she told her listeners before signing off, might soon be coming to a town near you.

Two weeks later, the leaders of Southlake Families PAC threw themselves an unofficial coming-out party. Things had been moving fast. Leigh Wambsganss, one of the PAC's cofounders, would later refer to the time between the initial CCAP vote and the August 30 event as "twenty-seven days of building an army."

The gathering was held just outside Southlake, at First Baptist Grapevine. More than four hundred people crowded into the sanctuary. According to Wambsganss, many more were turned away because of COVID capacity rules. The event was part organizational meeting, part pep rally. The person tapped to fire up the troops that night was the same one who had turned me on to this story: Texas GOP chairman Allen West.

From the pulpit at Grapevine Baptist, West—dressed in a white suit with a white shirt and white tie—opened by talking about his own upbringing and what it says about what's possible for a Black man in America. "When you see me, what do you see? Do you see a victor, or do you see a victim?" For years, West had argued that his very existence—his career in the military and rise to power as a Republican official—represented "the antithesis of the left's messaging" on racism. He argued that Democrats had deceived Black voters into believing that they were victims, effectively stripping them of self-worth and agency. And right now, West told the audience, that's what was happening in Southlake.

"With a good-quality education, you can achieve whatever heights that you want. But if we start to listen to the soft bigotry of low expectations of the left, if we start allowing them to have that platform that says, 'You cannot achieve an American dream; all you can be is a victim,' if we continue to allow them to shame our white brothers and sisters into believing that somehow, you're racist? Give me a doggone break."

With only two months until the 2020 presidential election, West told the crowd that the fight over the CCAP was part of a bigger left-wing plot. Democrats, he said, were trying to do in Texas what they'd already done in Virginia and elsewhere: take a solidly conservative state and turn it blue. Their path for achieving that goal, West said, cut right through the fast-growing North Texas suburbs, and it started right here, at the local level.

"The most important elected position in the United States of America is school board," West said, warning that liberals had for years been quietly taking control of public schools nationwide and using their power to indoctrinate the next generation—a claim that conservatives had been making off and on for more than a century. "And the way that that continues on is if we don't get control of these school boards. The left is very strategic in what they are doing."

This dangerous liberal shift, West warned, was already well underway in deep red Texas—thanks, he said, to "the influx of people from California, Illinois, New York, and New Jersey" who did not "understand the lesson that God told Lot when he was destroying Sodom and Gomorrah."

West, it's worth pointing out, was talking to a room full of people who, for the most part, had moved to Southlake from somewhere else. Like most fast-growing Texas suburbs, it's a town of newcomers. That was one of the main reasons the city had grown more diverse. Nevertheless, West, himself a recent transplant from Florida, offered the audience some advice for what to do the next time new neighbors moved onto the block.

"Go over to their house with some pecan pie"—he pronounced it "PEE-can," like someone who had not grown up in Texas—"look at them eyeball to eyeball, and say, 'Welcome to Texas. Welcome to Southlake. Now, why are you here, huh?'"

After waiting for the crowd to stop laughing, West continued, his voice rising as he neared the climax of his speech: "'If you are here to be a part of this great state, its history, its legacy . . . welcome on in. If you are here to be a part of the state that made the United States of America energy independent, welcome on in. If you are here to be a part of a state that understands what the Second Amendment is all about—because as long as you're armed, you're a citizen, if you are disarmed, you're a subject—you can be here in Texas!'"

But, West said, if the new neighbors didn't share these conservative beliefs, his listeners should respond with seven words, delivered slowly for emphasis: "Go back . . . to where . . . you came from."

With that, the crowd of mostly white Southlake residents jumped to their feet and showered West in rapturous applause. Among those standing to cheer was John Huffman, the city councilman who'd said in a TV interview in 2018, "Racism is real . . . and sweeping it under the rug is not going to help." Huffman, having recently announced his campaign to replace outgoing mayor Laura Hill, had come out against the diversity plan, arguing in a social media post that the CCAP would impose an ideology on all children that says "the marginalized group you belong to is the most important thing about you," while promoting "a view of LGBTQ politics that is not shared by many in Southlake."

West ended his remarks by urging the crowd to continue the fight to "run the progressive socialists the hell out of Texas," and was given another standing ovation.

That night, the donations flooded into Southlake Families PAC, according to a financial disclosure filed with the state: $2,000 from Dana Loesch, $500 from Guy Midkiff, another $200 from a prominent lawyer and Dragon mother, Hannah Smith, who, perhaps inspired by West's advice about the importance of running to serve on local school boards, was about to do just that. In total that week, the PAC raised more than $125,000.

The group had momentum. It had motivated, pissed-off supporters. And now, it had money to spend.

6

Existential Threat

ON SEPTEMBER 1, 2020, two days after Allen West's speech, Tucker Carlson, then the king of cable, opened his top-rated Fox News program with a monologue about a subject that the host acknowledged had been a fixation of his for most of that year: "the riots and disorder that have paralyzed many American cities."

"Political violence is the greatest threat we face," Carlson told his four million nightly viewers, alongside footage of cars burning in Kenosha, Wisconsin, and police firing tear gas at Black Lives Matter activists in Portland, Oregon. "It is more dangerous than any virus or any foreign adversary. It could literally end this country."

This sort of hyperbole had become a staple of Carlson's prime-time program, which, according to a *New York Times* analysis, may have been "the most racist show in the history of cable news." Night after night, Carlson painted for his viewers an image of America under siege, often invoking dog whistles appealing to Americans aggrieved by what they viewed as dangerous cultural changes. The list of perceived enemies included immigrants, racial justice activists, journalists, liberal college professors, transgender people, and anyone else who threatened to undermine the status of those Carlson and his guests referred to as "legacy Americans" who held "traditional American values."

For months, Carlson admitted during his September 1 monologue, he had been obsessed with telling his viewers *who* was responsible for what he characterized as an all-out assault on America's cities that summer following George Floyd's murder. "What too few understand, though," Carlson said, "is *why* it's happening.

"Why would kids raised in the fairest country in the world support a violent revolutionary group like BLM, whose program consists mainly of destroying things?" Carlson continued, his brow scrunched into its signature squint. "Why would educated adults, the very people who should be defending our system—whom we need to defend our system—be working so hard to tear it down?"

To answer that question, Carlson wanted to introduce the nation to a man who claimed to have uncovered the shadowy roots of a toxic worldview fueling America's racial unrest. The show's producers then cut to a split-screen shot showing Carlson alongside a young white man wearing a black blazer over a plaid shirt, unbuttoned at the neck.

"Chris Rufo, thanks so much for coming on."

"Yes, thanks so much."

Rufo, a conservative political activist and journalist, had come to sound an alarm about what he saw as a hidden and emerging threat in America. Although he was speaking from a studio in Seattle, his comments that night would end up having a big impact on the diversity plan fight in Southlake—and in school districts like it all over the country.

"You know, Tucker, this is something I've been investigating for the last six months. And it's absolutely astonishing how critical race theory has pervaded every institution in the federal government."

This was one of the first—and would turn out to be the most consequential—references to critical race theory, or CRT, on Fox News. Most of Carlson's viewers had probably never heard the phrase before this moment. Rufo made no attempt to define the concept on air, but he wanted people to know that its influence was everywhere: in academia, in corporate America, in government—and in schools. "What I've discovered is that critical race theory has become, in essence, the default ideology of the federal bureaucracy," Rufo said, "and is now being weaponized against the American people."

To understand how he'd reached that conclusion, you'd have to rewind to earlier that summer. For months, Rufo had been writing articles in *City Journal*—a public policy magazine published by the conservative Manhattan Institute think tank—exposing what he described as divisive anti-racism training programs that he said were being forced on government employees, including at the federal level. The concept of mandatory anti-discrimination courses would have been immediately familiar to anyone who'd worked at major corporations or in government in the past three decades. Such programs were often viewed even by diversity proponents as bureaucratic formalities, meant to do little more than shield organizations from lawsuits. In more recent years, particularly following Trump's election, there'd been a movement to strengthen diversity programs, with the ambitious goal of teaching employees to identify and deconstruct their own biases and root out workplace discrimination at its foundation. This shift, Rufo concluded, based on a review of leaked training documents and federal contracts, had fueled explosive growth in what he'd begun calling the "diversity-industrial complex."

One of the government training programs Rufo scrutinized for *City Journal* began with the premise that "virtually all White people contribute to racism" and called on federal employees to pledge "allyship" to their Black colleagues "amid the George Floyd Tragedy." Another training given to city employees in Seattle divided workers up by race. One slide from the presentation tailored for white employees suggested that attendees would be "working through emotions that often come up for white people like sadness, shame, paralysis, confusion, denial." In his research, Rufo found that these courses frequently cited the work of National Book Award–winning historian Ibram X. Kendi, the author of *How to Be an Antiracist*, which had rocketed to the top of bestseller charts during the racial unrest of 2020.

Rufo studied Kendi's writings, he said, and traced the footnotes from his book to the decades-old academic writings of a group of Black and Latino legal scholars—most notably, Kimberlé Crenshaw, Richard Delgado, and Derrick Bell.

Crenshaw had coined the phrase critical race theory in the 1980s to describe the work of scholars who argued that the explicit racism of America's pre–civil rights era lived on in the laws and societal norms of today. CRT was, in short, an academic framework for understanding why racial disparities persist. Rather than merely viewing racism through the lens of individual biases, critical race theorists were taught to examine how the legacy of racism was baked into America's criminal justice, housing, banking, and educational systems. CRT sought to expose the ways ostensibly race-neutral policies—like the suburban zoning rules that had shaped Southlake's development—can drive racial inequality. It was the kind of thing you might learn about in a college sociology course, or a history class, or in law school.

Now on Fox News, Rufo was warning that critical race theory–inspired training programs were destroying the country. He told Carlson that "conservatives need to wake up that this is an existential threat to the United States. And the bureaucracy, even under the Trump administration, is now being weaponized against core traditional American values."

Then, in a crucial moment that would reshape American politics for years to come, Rufo telegraphed his nationally televised remarks for an audience of one: "I'd like to make it explicit," he said, reading from carefully rehearsed remarks that he'd had loaded into a studio teleprompter. "The president, the White House, it's within their authority and power to immediately issue an executive order abolishing critical race theory trainings from the federal government. And I call on the president to immediately issue this executive order and stamp out this destructive, divisive, pseudoscientific ideology at its root."

Rufo later acknowledged that it had been his goal that night to transform the phrase critical race theory into "a national brand," giving conservatives a new frame for describing what was happening around them. "All of a sudden," he told me, "when they see kindergarteners being told that they're white supremacists, or see vaccines being denied to certain racial groups, they can make the connection to critical race theory—and channel their emotional reaction into fighting a specific ideology and set of ideas." His claim about kindergartners being told they were white supremacists had appeared in an August 2020 article in the *Washington Free Beacon*, a conservative news site, but the children's book in question, *A Kids Book About Racism*, focuses on celebrating people's differences and does not mention the concept of white supremacy. And Rufo's line about white people being denied vaccines seemed to allude to a false conspiracy theory that was based on a gross misreading of health department guidelines in New York.

Even so, that night on Fox, by successfully turning a complex theoretical framework into a political catchphrase, Rufo met his goal of providing conservatives with "a central point of attack." And he found a willing audience in Trump. The morning after his Fox News appearance, Rufo got a call from a number with a 202 area code. "'Chris, this is Mark Meadows, chief of staff, reaching out on behalf of the president. He saw your segment on *Tucker* last night, and he's instructed me to take action.'"

Two days later, the White House issued a memo—followed later by an executive order—banning any federal workplace training programs based on critical race theory, which the memo falsely defined as a philosophy teaching that people of certain races are "inherently racist or evil." Later that month, in a speech focused on American history at the National Archives Museum, Trump invoked critical race theory for the first time publicly. He called the ideology "child abuse," and warned that it was on the march.

"Critical race theory is being forced into our children's schools," Trump droned. "It's being imposed into workplace trainings. And it's being deployed to rip apart friends, neighbors, and families." In a direct rebuke to the *New York Times*' 1619 Project, Trump vowed to reverse what he called an emerging narrative that "America is a wicked and racist nation," and said he would create a new "1776 Commission" to help "restore patriotic education to our schools."

After Trump's speech, references to critical race theory surged in conservative media. It was mentioned more than seventy times on Fox News that September alone, up from just a few references the whole year prior, according to a search of news transcripts. Although the average American was still likely unfamiliar with CRT throughout that fall, it was quickly becoming a popular attack line on the right.

Parents in Southlake discovered, seemingly overnight, a new way of articulating why they were so vehemently opposed to Carroll's Cultural Competence Action Plan. Critical race theory came up twice at the first

Carroll school board meeting after Trump's speech—and at every meeting for months afterward. Parents opposed to the diversity plan wielded the phrase just as Rufo had envisioned: as a blunt object to attack political enemies. "Critical race theory–based policies have been snuck into schools across the country without the approval of their communities, just like it almost happened here," a white Southlake mom told the board. Another white parent warned that the CCAP was "rooted in critical race theory," before offering Rufo's redefinition of the phrase: "It sees the world through the lens of the oppressed versus the oppressor, where the individual is reduced to the color of their skin."

The sudden fixation on a once obscure academic framework among Southlake parents underlined the growing connection between this local school board debate and national politics. It also seemed to raise the stakes. Because if you believed Trump and Fox News, then the diversity plan wasn't just a misguided local school policy or an overreaction to kids making insensitive jokes, as some conservative Carroll parents initially argued. It was part of a national plot to teach white children to be ashamed of their race, and to hate their country.

Parents aligned with Southlake Families PAC began to paint the people who'd written and supported the CCAP not as well-intentioned community volunteers with whom they disagreed, but as "Marxists" on a mission to indoctrinate their children with "leftist" ideas. Viewed through this lens, school board president Michelle Moore, a lifelong Republican, became a pariah among many conservatives in town. A mother of two Carroll high school students at the time, Moore said she could feel people's disapproving stares at Dragon football games. She started dreading going out in public. One of her best friends—someone with whom she and her family had shared Thanksgiving meals—stopped speaking to her and took a leading role in publicly attacking the board. "My health deteriorated. My self-esteem took a hit. My friendships changed," Moore told me.

Her friendship with Mayor Laura Hill was among the casualties. Hill, a mentor of Moore's for many years, had been a vocal supporter of the school board's efforts to stamp out racism at Carroll. But after the plan blew up in controversy, Hill wrote a letter addressed to Moore and the rest of the school board calling on district leaders to "reassess" their diversity efforts and "consider the damage" the plan had inflicted on "our entire city." Without directly coming out against the CCAP, Hill said the District Diversity Council process—which she previously endorsed—had "failed the citizens of Southlake."

"But most of all," Hill added, "it has failed our kids."

It didn't help that the man in charge of running the school district, superintendent David Faltys, announced in mid-August that he planned to vacate the position he'd held for more than fifteen years, having already delayed his retirement by six months to guide the district through the worst of the pandemic. Faltys's departure left Carroll without a permanent chief executive as it navigated an unprecedented political storm, adding to the pressure on Moore to somehow chart a way out of it.

Dave Almand, another Carroll trustee, said he was stunned by how quickly people turned against the board president and other members. Almand, a Republican and former squadron commander in the air force, said his support of the CCAP wasn't inspired by Marxism, but was based on a genuine desire to make Carroll more welcoming and inclusive after hearing the stories of discrimination. Yet many of his constituents were now convinced that he was trying to sneak liberal ideas into the curriculum to "convince our white students that they're bad and evil."

"Nothing could have been further from the truth," Almand said. But any time he tried to reassure conservative parents there was no political motive behind the CCAP, they would respond with three words that didn't appear anywhere in the plan: critical race theory. "They were just convinced that this whole thing was a Trojan horse to try and indoctrinate their children with CRT."

In a preview of what was to come the following spring in school districts nationwide, the debate in Southlake became an endless back-and-forth. Diversity plan opponents demanded that critical race theory be kept out of Carroll. CCAP supporters fired back, arguing that the plan had nothing to do with CRT. The sniping was made even more confusing by the fact that critical race theory had now become a stand-in for ideas that the concept didn't speak to—chiefly, that Carroll was now going to teach white kids that they were racist and teach Black kids that they were victims. In fact, critical race theory—the study of *systemic* racism—doesn't deal with whether any individual person is racist. It's an examination of systems, culture, and policies.

Yet, across the country that fall, conservatives who'd taken up Rufo's war against CRT had begun to unearth examples of what even some liberals acknowledged were cringeworthy attempts at educating children about racism. In Fairfax County, Virginia, a high school English class played a game of bingo titled "Identifying Your Privilege," with each space denoting an identity trait that carried privilege in U.S. society, including being white, male, cisgender, Christian, the child of a military veteran, and feeling safe around police. In another instance first publicized by Rufo, a teacher in Cupertino, California, had asked a class of third graders to deconstruct their racial identities, then rank themselves according to their "power and privilege." According to leaked PowerPoint slides published by Rufo, the teacher had told the class of eight- and nine-year-old students that they lived in a "dominant culture" of "white, middle-class, cisgender, educated, able-bodied, Christian, English speaker[s]," who, according to the lesson, "created and maintained" this culture to "stay in power."

As Rufo's article noted, the school district had already investigated the incident and concluded the lesson was inappropriate. Even so, conservatives pointed to anecdotes like these to discredit any attempt at addressing racism in schools. It became popular to argue that ham-fisted and overzealous diversity, equity, and inclusion lessons were a bigger threat to children than the problems of racist bullying and whitewashed curriculum that those programs were meant to address.

Progressive ideas about race might have been increasing their reach within schools nationally, but there was little evidence to support the claim that critical race theory had permeated public school curriculum. In 2020, when researchers at Stanford University studied fifteen U.S. history textbooks used in Texas, they found that the books largely focused on the accomplishments of white men, just as they always had. Latino historical figures were rarely discussed, and Black people were mentioned primarily in the context of slavery and oppression. At the same time, surveys showed that nearly half of all Americans—including more than a third of adults under the age of thirty—still believed the myth first propagated by white supremacists more than a century earlier that the Civil War was primarily fought over something other than the South's determination to continue enslaving Black people. If racial justice activists were waging an ideological war in America's public schools, as Rufo and others argued, the data suggested they hadn't made much progress.

Southlake Families PAC, meanwhile, was busy opening a new front in its attack, this time in the courts. With the PAC's financial backing, a Southlake mother named Kristin Garcia filed a lawsuit against the Carroll school district, seeking to block the CCAP based on a technicality.

Through public records requests, PAC supporters discovered that Moore had texted fellow board trustees prior to the initial diversity plan vote to go over how best to address the controversy at the start of the meeting. That, Garcia argued in her lawsuit, was a violation of the Texas Open Meetings Act.

Lawyers for the school board filed a response denying wrongdoing, and Jeremy Lyon, the man tapped to serve as Carroll's interim superintendent after Faltys's retirement, issued a statement calling the suit "an attempt to discredit and derail" the district's diversity and inclusion efforts. But school officials had clearly gotten the message. Within days of the filing, the board announced plans to add community members to the diversity council with instructions to revise the CCAP under a new, slower timeline. Behind the scenes, committee leaders had signaled a willingness to remove some of the most controversial aspects of the plan, including the provision dealing with microaggressions.

But that olive branch didn't persuade many people. Opponents learned that some aspects of the CCAP, like teacher diversity training, had already been implemented at Carroll, outside the District Diversity Council process. In one session that August, a Black assistant principal had led Carroll teachers through a presentation that included a link to an "equity rubric," which listed goals for making classrooms more inclusive, including encouraging teachers to be aware of their own "biases and privileges." In another district-wide training in September, an outside facilitator advised that "educators no longer have the luxury of being color-blind or color-mute in a society socially constructed around race." CCAP opponents also found out that the district had, without much fanfare, made changes to the student code of conduct after the 2018 N-word video, including new rules explicitly banning racist slurs at the high school and new protections for students bullied for their sexual orientation.

Convinced that the school board wasn't being transparent about its plans, angry parents kept showing up at meetings. At one, a white woman approached the lectern wearing a burgundy blazer and sunglasses resting atop her head. "Good evening," she said. "My name is Hannah Smith, and I'm the mother of four Dragons."

Smith had not come to speak only as a parent; she was there to share her perspective as a nationally recognized religious liberty lawyer. A graduate of Brigham Young University, Smith had clerked for conservative Supreme Court justices Samuel Alito and Clarence Thomas before going to work for a high-powered law firm in Washington, D.C., where her husband had been a legal advisor in the George W. Bush White House. Over the years, she participated in numerous events hosted by the Federalist Society, the conservative legal organization credited in recent decades with reshaping the federal judiciary with an originalist interpretation of the U.S. Constitution, paving the way for rulings overturning abortion rights, rolling back gun restrictions, and allowing government funding for private religious schools. Prior to moving to Southlake from Washington in 2019 in the hopes of raising her kids "in a conservative area of the country," Smith had dedicated her career to representing clients who believed their religious rights had been violated, including in cases that reached the nation's highest court. In 2014, she was part of the legal team that won a landmark Supreme Court case on behalf of the Christian conservative owners of Hobby Lobby that helped chip away at the contraceptive mandate in Obamacare.

Now, deploying her argumentative skills in comments before her children's school board, Smith said she wanted to speak about the CCAP's "callous disregard for constitutionally protected freedoms," including those that had been enshrined in law following the civil rights movement.

"How can CCAP's microaggression system be consistent with free speech rights when the vast majority are everyday unintentional snubs that are constitutionally protected speech?" Smith asked rhetorically. "How can CCAP's audits of curriculum and communications be consistent with the right of free expression of ideas, when the audits contemplate enforcing just one viewpoint: the culturally competent one? How can CCAP's audits of student religious clubs be consistent with free exercise of religion and free association rights when the audits contemplate enforcing a single viewpoint that may violate constitutionally protected religious doctrines and beliefs?"

All these issues placed the school district in legal jeopardy, Smith warned. "Get rid of CCAP," she said in closing, as a beeper signaled her time had expired, "and you'll get rid of a lot of needless litigation."

In truth, the school board's legal troubles were only just beginning. Two weeks later, a Tarrant County judge responded to the Southlake Families PAC–funded lawsuit by issuing a temporary restraining order, indefinitely blocking district leaders from taking any action to move forward on the diversity plan. Smith, who was not officially involved in the litigation, appeared to be among the first to learn about the decision. Hours after the judge signed the order, Smith emailed a copy of it to Pam Francis, one of the District Diversity Council cochairs, along with a note letting her know that any work to revise the CCAP needed to stop immediately.

The leaders of Southlake Families PAC had, in effect, bought themselves time. Now they were preparing the next phase of their assault. And Hannah Smith would be at the very center of the battle plan.

There's a long history in America of parents suing schools to control what their children learn. While researching Southlake's budding political revolt, I came across a *New York Times* article about a different coalition of suburban residents who, "armed with sophisticated lobbying techniques," were fighting to "remove books from libraries" and replace history curricula with "texts that emphasize the positive side of America's past."

"Emboldened by what they see as a conservative mood in the country," the *Times* piece said, "parents' groups across the nation are demanding that teachers and administrators cleanse their local schools of materials and teaching methods they consider anti-family, anti-American and anti-God."

The parallels to my reporting were striking, but the most remarkable aspect of the *Times* article may have been its publication date: May 17, 1981.

Long before opposition to critical race theory became a right-wing rallying cry, conservative activists had waged an all-out national assault on school lessons under the banner of a different attack line: secular humanism.

Long forgotten by many Americans, the education wars of the 1970s and '80s previewed, on a smaller scale, what was to come four decades later. Like CRT, secular humanism—the belief in human reason over religion—was redefined by conservative activists as a catch-all to describe any lesson or book that white Christian conservatives found objectionable. Members of the Pro-Family Forum in Fort Worth—an epicenter of the anti-humanist movement—distributed a leaflet titled "Is Humanism Molesting Your Child?" and issued a warning strikingly similar to the one Chris Rufo would give forty years later about critical race theory: "Humanism is everywhere. It is destructive to our nation, destructive to the family, destructive to the individual."

With the backing of far-right national organizations, such as Jerry Falwell's Moral Majority, Pat Robertson's Christian Broadcasting Network, and anti-gay, anti-feminist crusader Phyllis Schlafly's Eagle Forum, conservative parents invoked opposition to secular humanism in their calls to ban sex education, censor history lessons on racism, and infuse curricula with their version of biblical values. While arguing that secular humanism was itself a religion, and as such, should be barred from schools, activists demanded that educators present Christianity in a favorable light, that children be taught to respect America and its military, and that men and women always be depicted in traditional gender roles in classroom reading assignments.

The anti-secularism campaigns were the latest in a long tradition of reactionary movements fighting to shape what children learn in America. Christian fundamentalists waged a years-long crusade early in the twentieth century to stop the teaching of human evolution in public schools, culminating most famously with the 1925 Scopes Monkey Trial, in which a high school teacher in Tennessee was charged with violating a new state law that banned evolution lessons from public school classrooms. With America on the precipice of entering World War II in the late 1930s and early 1940s, groups like the Daughters of the American Revolution and the American Legion waged a successful nationwide campaign against popular social studies textbooks authored by progressive educator Harold Rugg, arguing that the books—which raised questions about the unequal distribution of wealth in the U.S. and made the argument for civil rights for African Americans—were "subversive" and "anti-American."

In 1974, in a direct forebearer of the anti-secularism movement, white fundamentalists launched a high-profile assault on the public school system in Kanawha County, West Virginia, which includes the state capital of Charleston, after the district introduced new multicultural textbooks as required by a recent state mandate that said "school books should portray the contributions of minorities to American culture." The protests were led by Alice Moore, a school board member and preacher's wife, who argued, for example, that the new language arts textbooks would teach students "ghetto dialect" instead of "standard American speech." Moore's supporters objected to the inclusion of writings by Black luminaries such as Langston Hughes as "anti-Christian" and James Baldwin as "anti-white." The months-long demonstrations in Kanawha County drew national attention and eventually turned violent. The Ku Klux Klan joined picketers, chanting, "Get the n——r books out!" School buildings were vandalized with Nazi insignia. Three elementary schools were attacked with firebombs and Molotov cocktails. The county board of education building was rocketed off its foundation by an explosion caused by fifteen sticks of dynamite. Amazingly, no one was killed. The unrest was finally quelled, but only after the school board made a concession: Going forward, all future textbooks would "encourage loyalty to the United States," and would "not defame our nation's founders."

Most of the grassroots organizing against secular humanism that sprang up nationwide in the decade after the Kanawha unrest emanated from predominantly white suburbs, where angry parents formed groups with names like Young Parents Alert, People Concerned with Education, and Guardians of Education. The movement's objectives were illustrated perhaps most clearly in a 1988 list of demands written by the Texas Daughters of the American Revolution and submitted to the state board of education for consideration. Jonathan Swift's eighteenth-century satire *A Modest Proposal*, the group argued, should be banned because it encouraged cannibalism. John Hersey's *Hiroshima* should be balanced with an account of the bombing of Pearl Harbor. Poems on racism by African American writers should be labeled as communist propaganda and censored. Children shouldn't be made to read Anne Frank's *The Diary of a Young Girl* because it was too sad. *Romeo and Juliet* needed to go, too, for it promoted teen suicide.

Although most of these requests were ultimately denied, Christian conservative groups scored major victories throughout the 1980s—largely through targeted lawsuits and localized pressure campaigns—before the movement's power began to wane in the 1990s. Textbook publishers edited passages, often in subtle ways, to avoid offending a conservative Christian worldview. Some school districts pulled books such as *Brave New World* (anti-religion, anti-family) and *Catcher in the Rye* (vulgar language, sexual content) from mandatory reading lists. Congress even passed a law in 1984 that included an amendment authored by GOP senator Orrin Hatch of Utah prohibiting the use of federal funds for the teaching of secular humanism. However—as would be the case decades later with a wave of Republican legislation targeting the teaching of critical race theory—Hatch failed to define the concept, leaving confused educators to guess at which ideas were and were not allowed in classrooms.

"Trying to define 'secular humanism,'" one liberal critic said at the time, "is like trying to nail Jell-O to a tree." As one of Hatch's aides would concede in 1985 when Democrats reversed the federal ban on secular humanism, the senator's amendment was meant mostly as a "symbolic thing"—a way of signaling that the federal government would not tolerate any school lessons that might be perceived as anti-American.

Thirty-five years later, a similarly vague warning was being broadcast to educators across the country—and in the fall of 2020, many of them were beginning to get the message.

When she returned to her classroom that August, fourth-grade teacher Christina Catlin's view of her "dream job" had begun to sour. Like most Texas school districts, Carroll had opted to return to in-person schooling six months into the pandemic, while also offering a virtual option for parents who worried about sending their children back before COVID vaccines had been developed. Students were supposed to wear masks in class but, to avoid drawing the ire of anti-masking parents, administrators instructed Catlin and the other teachers not to make a big deal of it when children refused to keep them on.

And yet, the parent complaints came anyway, and not just about pandemic safety measures. At Carroll, and at school districts all over the country, conservative backlash against the nation's racial reckoning was moving from school board meetings to classrooms. "The environment had completely changed that fall," Catlin observed. "It was like all the anger and resentment people were feeling was being directed at teachers. We were making their kids wear masks. We were indoctrinating them. We were training them to be social justice warriors, or whatever. And it didn't matter whether any of that was true or not."

Evidence of this shift began to surface in news headlines.

In Burlington, Wisconsin, that August, a fourth-grade teacher responded to her students' questions about protests and riots in the nearby city of Kenosha by providing them with a worksheet that posed questions like "What is the Black Lives Matter Movement trying to do?" and "How do we stop systemic racism?" Afterward, a Black student thanked the teacher, a white woman named Melissa Statz, for talking about racism. But after a picture of the worksheet turned up on a community Facebook group, Statz was bombarded with angry messages accusing her of brainwashing kids with liberal ideas. In the weeks that followed, racial slurs were graffitied on Burlington's school campuses, and parents called for Statz's firing at a heated school board meeting.

"People have just decided, if you support Black Lives Matter, you must be a liberal," Statz told NBC News in October 2020, in what would turn out to be one of the first national news reports about the growing political animus simmering in America's schools. "Somehow people have associated those words with a political party. I don't know why. I think it's a human rights issue."

The controversies were fueled in part by parents' unprecedented pandemic-era access to their children's classrooms through remote video feeds. In rural Tennessee, a white high school social studies teacher was suspended after telling his nearly all-white class that white privilege is "a fact," and later asking them to read and discuss an article by Ta-Nehisi Coates titled "The First White President," which linked the history of white supremacy with the rise of Trump. An art teacher at a publicly funded charter school in San Antonio was fired after refusing an administrator's demands that she stop wearing a cloth face mask embroidered with the words "Black Lives Matter" at school. And in a suburb outside Columbus, Ohio, a school superintendent issued a public apology after three high school staff members were photographed wearing matching T-shirts at school showing the phrases "Science is real," "Black lives matter," "No human is illegal," "Love is love," "Women's rights are human rights," and "Kindness is everything" in rainbow-colored text.

At Johnson Elementary in Southlake, Catlin said parents' complaints that fall were initially focused on what they saw as liberal bias in *Scholastic News*, the online current events magazine for children that she and her fellow fourth-grade teachers had been using to supplement their curriculum throughout the pandemic. "Things really blew up," Catlin said, when a group of fourth-grade parents found a *Scholastic News* article titled "What Does This Statue Stand For?" that examined the removal of a monument to Confederate general Robert E. Lee in Richmond, Virginia. The article framed the debate in painstakingly neutral terms: "Across the South, other Civil War statues have been taken down in recent months. Many Americans view them as symbols of racism and hate. Others believe they reflect the nation's history and should stay. The controversy has much of the country grappling with how we remember the past."

But some parents were outraged by the idea that their nine- and ten-year-old children were being exposed to contemporary debates about racism and history. There was a problem with this line of attack: The Confederate statue article wasn't included in the version of *Scholastic News* available to fourth graders at Carroll. "We were, like, 'Well, we didn't assign that, that wasn't in the magazine,'" Catlin said. "You could probably find it if you searched Scholastic's website, but it wasn't something we had assigned."

Nonetheless, parents—including some who had donated money to or volunteered with Southlake Families PAC—viewed the article's existence as evidence of liberal bias in their children's curriculum. After that, the parents seemed to be on alert for additional offenses, Catlin said, and they soon found one.

Multiple parents complained to the principal in November after Catlin and other fourth-grade teachers at Johnson Elementary asked their children to read a collection of *Scholastic News* articles that told the Thanksgiving story from the perspectives of both the Pilgrims and members of the Wampanoag tribe. One parent in particular, Catlin said, complained that the articles, which included context about subsequent atrocities committed against the Wampanoag by European settlers, "had ruined" their child's image of Thanksgiving.

This time, the complaints prompted Johnson's principal to institute new guidelines for vetting *Scholastic News* articles. Moving forward, teachers needed to review prospective reading assignments as a group, looking for potential land mines, and then get approval from administrators before asking children to read any articles that might trigger parent complaints. It was under that system, a few months later, that Catlin and the other fourth-grade teachers made a decision that she regrets. During Black History Month, the teachers decided against assigning a *Scholastic News* article titled "Setting the Record Straight," about the recent move by Major League Baseball to formally recognize the achievements of Black players who were forced to play in the Negro leagues prior to MLB's integration in 1947. The piece noted that Negro League players often faced "discrimination that was common in the U.S. at the time," which included being banned from "whites-only hotels, restaurants, and even gas stations." To make up for the past injustice, Major League Baseball had announced that the statistics and records of about 3,400 Negro leagues players would officially be included in MLB history—part of the same reordering of national memory that had led some cities to remove Confederate monuments.

There was nothing wrong with the Negro League article, Catlin argued. It was accurate and age-appropriate. But she remembers an administrator responding, "These parents will find a way to make something wrong with it."

The teachers knew censoring the piece was wrong. Children—including white children growing up in Southlake, Texas—deserved to learn the truth about the history of racism in this country. But in the end, Catlin didn't resist. Parent complaints about classroom discussions and reading assignments were only growing more heated as the school year progressed. Her principal was right, she concluded at the time; this one probably wasn't worth the fight.

7

One Election Away

"I GET THE EASY question," Leigh Wambsganss said at the start of the meeting. "Who did you vote for in the 2020 presidential election?"

The Southlake Families cofounder was seated at a conference table along with nearly two dozen other PAC volunteers, grilling a candidate who was contemplating a run for local elected office. Although Wambsganss didn't say it, the implication of her question was clear: Continued support for Donald Trump—who by then had launched his campaign to subvert American democracy—was a prerequisite for earning the PAC's endorsement.

The interviewee answered correctly: "I am a conservative Republican, so I voted for President Trump and everyone else associated with him."

The next question was even more pointed: "What is your position on the CCAP, and why?"

After winning a restraining order to halt any work on Carroll's Cultural Competence Action Plan in December 2020, the leaders of Southlake Families PAC had moved to the next phase of their strategy: winning seats on the nonpartisan school board and city council and stopping the diversity plan or anything like it from ever passing. With only two of seven seats coming open on Carroll's board of trustees that May, there would be no way for Southlake Families to win an outright majority. But Wambsganss and PAC cofounder Tim O'Hare were convinced that if they could turn the city's local elections into a referendum on the CCAP, they could kill the plan once and for all.

In the process, they would unwittingly turn Southlake into the proving ground for a new national political strategy.

To find worthy candidates, Wambsganss and O'Hare staged a series of private interviews in late 2020 and early 2021 at the law office of Wambsganss's husband. Before being considered for an endorsement, prospective candidates had to promise not to run if the PAC didn't choose them. The goal, Wambsganss would later explain, was to consolidate all the conservative votes in town behind a single slate of candidates. "Nothing matters if we don't get a majority on the school board," she later told the *National Review*. "None of this matters if we do not win seats."

In total, the PAC interviewed six candidates for the two school board positions and screened a few considering runs for city council. After the questions about fealty to Trump and opposition to the CCAP, PAC members would continue to read from their interview script.

The questions themselves, even more than the candidate's answers, painted a picture of the PAC's objectives for Southlake and its public school system:

Do you support Black Lives Matter?
Have you ever participated in a BLM rally?
Do you support full-time, armed officers on the school campus?
Do you support the pro-life movement, from conception to natural death?
Are you willing to take a public stance in support of the Second Amendment?
Are you a Christian?
How active are you in your church?

Nobody stopped to explain how a candidate's views on any of these items might factor in their work on a school board or city council, but that didn't appear to be the point. Southlake Families, it seemed, was looking to curate the same ideological purity that Republican primary voters had come to demand from national political figures. To be truly conservative, at least according to the PAC's definition, seemed to mean never associating or compromising with people of different political beliefs.

At one point during one of the interview sessions, O'Hare made it explicit. Reading from the list of questions, he asked point-blank if the candidate sitting at the conference table would commit to checking the voting histories of every citizen who volunteered to serve on future advisory boards or committees and would pledge never to appoint any Democrats. That would mean, for example, barring anyone who'd ever voted in a Democratic primary from serving on the standing committee tasked with evaluating Carroll's budget priorities, or the one tasked with reviewing curriculum. O'Hare ended the interview by asking if the candidate would support rebranding the city's annual "Home for the Holidays Tree Lighting Celebration" to explicitly make it a Christian event.

With that, after about an hour of questioning for that candidate, the Southlake Families PAC was done.

By early 2021, just as I'd begun my reporting in Southlake, the PAC had selected its slate of five candidates for mayor, city council, and school board. To replace Mayor Laura Hill, who'd served the maximum two terms and would soon be eyeing a run for the Texas statehouse, the PAC announced it was backing John Huffman. This was the councilman who'd spoken out against racism in 2018, but who'd since come out against the diversity plan, saying, among other things, that the CCAP reflected "a view of LGBTQ politics that is not shared by many in Southlake." For the two city council seats, the PAC was supporting an anesthesiologist and a business owner who'd also protested the CCAP. For the two all-important school board seats, the PAC had bestowed its blessing upon Cam Bryan, a civil engineer and dad of four who'd spent years volunteering in town as a youth football and basketball coach, and his highly accomplished running mate: the religious liberty lawyer Hannah Smith.

To aid its efforts, Southlake Families would amass a campaign war chest of nearly a quarter-million dollars—an eye-popping figure for elections that typically featured spending of no more than a few thousand dollars per candidate. School board candidates Smith and Bryan would combine to raise an additional $137,000 to spend on green yard signs, hats, T-shirts, and social media advertisements. In the process, their joint campaign to rid their city of "critical race theory" would help transform this small-town election into something bigger—and nastier.

It would be as if all the nation's most bitter political divides had been superimposed onto a local, nonpartisan school board contest. The way some residents began to see it, the outcome would be about far more than a school diversity plan. It would be a statement about what Southlake stood for, and, ultimately, whose ideas were welcome there.

The knives were most of the way out by the time the Carroll school board, with four months to go until the election, called in Lane Ledbetter to help quell the unrest in Southlake. Ledbetter, the son of legendary Dragons football coach and former athletic director Bob Ledbetter, had graduated from Carroll in 1989 and gone on to become a respected public school administrator. Before the board hired him to replace David Faltys as Carroll's new superintendent in December of 2020, Ledbetter, who's white, had been the top official at the Midlothian Independent School District, a majority-white but fast-diversifying school system in the suburbs south of Dallas, where he'd overseen efforts to make the school culture more welcoming for students of color. That included, just a few months prior to taking the job in Southlake, hiring a Black woman to serve as Midlothian's first director of diversity, equity, and inclusion: "We are confident she will accomplish many great things in this role and help us create an environment where each child's uniqueness is celebrated," Ledbetter said then.

Now members of the Carroll school board were hoping that, given his family's revered status in Southlake, Ledbetter would be uniquely positioned to heal the divisions in town. He would need to move quickly, though, because by the time of Ledbetter's first Carroll school board meeting in January 2021, those divisions were nearing a boiling point. This was thanks, in part, to yet another social media video.

The Southlake Anti-Racism Coalition, the group of Carroll high school students and recent graduates, had recently cut together and published footage of parent comments at school board meetings—*"My child does not even know what the word 'minority' means, but you all are gonna teach it to him"*—and scored the montage with a mocking circus theme song. Conservative parents were outraged, but things really turned heated after the pop star Demi Lovato, who grew up in nearby Grapevine, blasted the SARC video out to her more than 100 million worldwide followers on Instagram on January 8, along with the caption: "It is horrifying to see how some of the parents at Carroll ISD in Southlake, Texas, are literally *fighting* to uphold white supremacy." Afterward, a lawyer representing one of the Southlake dads featured in the video sent the student anti-racism coalition a cease-and-desist letter, arguing that the group had deceptively edited his client's comments to portray him as a racist, and threatening legal action.

Separately, residents aligned with Southlake Families PAC dug up a lawsuit accusing a Black volunteer leader of the District Diversity Council of defrauding an elderly investor and published the documents online. In retaliation, parents who supported the diversity plan began to circulate a twenty-seven-year-old news article about one of the white residents now leading the fight against the CCAP, revealing that she'd been sentenced to six months in prison and ordered to pay more than $1 million in restitution after pleading guilty in 1994 to federal bank fraud. Parents filmed each other while arguing and cussing at one another over dueling campaign signs. The uglier the fighting got, the more it seemed to drown out the voices of students who'd come forward with painful stories of discrimination.

From behind the dais in Carroll's meeting room that evening, Ledbetter said coming home to lead Carroll, even amid such strife, was a dream. He talked about how excited he was to send his own kids to such an "amazing" district. He used that word—"amazing"—four times in his opening monologue.

Then he pleaded for unity.

"We're not going to solve the problem in this district on social media," he said, referring to the diversity plan fight. "We're not going to solve the problem in this district through public comment. We're not going to solve it in the courtroom. It's going to be solved by bringing people together in this community and sitting down with a willingness to work together."

Seeming to channel his retired football coach father, Ledbetter gave what amounted to a rousing pep talk. Parents, he said, needed to stop attacking each other. Social media insults and legal threats weren't how Southlake had earned a reputation across Texas as an excellent place to raise a family. This wasn't how smart, caring adults solved problems.

"The more we come and we speak against each other, the more we post on social media, the more division we are creating in this community. . . . My number-one priority in this district right now coming forward is to get through this situation."

His message seemed to resonate. The public speakers that followed his remakes that night were far more magnanimous than at any recent school board meetings. Some residents who'd previously accused the district of orchestrating a secret plot to brainwash their children and grandchildren thanked Ledbetter for striking a positive tone, and they promised to work with him to find a solution.

For the first time in months, Moore, the embattled school board president, thought that things might finally settle down. But the ceasefire was short-lived. Within days, residents went back to sniping on social media. And less than three months later, Moore discovered just how far some of them were willing to go to block the types of changes she believed were needed at Carroll.

She remembers being in a state of shock after she got the call from her lawyer: A grand jury had indicted her and the board's vice president, Todd Carlton, for allegedly violating Texas's Open Meetings Act. Now she needed to turn herself in at the county jail. "You've got to be kidding me," Moore told her lawyer, fighting back tears.

The criminal charges stemmed directly from allegations first made in the Southlake Families PAC–funded civil lawsuit, which accused Moore of illegally texting fellow board members about district business ahead of the CCAP vote. In Texas, legal experts say it's exceedingly rare for prosecutors to pursue criminal charges for Open Meetings Act violations, leading some in Southlake, including Moore and her lawyer, to suspect a political motive by Tarrant County's Republican district attorney, Sharon Wilson. Wilson denied the allegation.

Moore felt as if she was drifting through a haze later that day as she checked herself in at the jail and posed for her mug shot. She'd never had anything more than a speeding ticket. Now, because of her work to make her school district more welcoming for students of color, she was facing up to six months behind bars.

After signing some paperwork and walking out of the jail on a $500 bond, Moore got in her car. There was a school board meeting that evening, and she didn't want to be late.

One afternoon that March, Southlake resident Jennifer Hough found what looked like a new local newspaper stuffed inside her mailbox. The words "Southlake Families News" and "Volume one" were plastered across the masthead. And underneath it, in huge boldface type, the lead headline screamed a question: "Is CISD in crisis?"

Hough, a white mother of two Carroll ISD students and an outspoken supporter of the diversity plan, scanned the page until her eyes landed on the fine print at the bottom: *Pol. Adv. Paid for by Southlake Families PAC.*

Oh my God, Hough thought, is this really where we're at?

The PAC had spent a few thousand dollars producing an eight-page political mailer, designed to look like a broadsheet newspaper. Every household in Southlake got at least one copy. The paper was filled with headlines and articles written by Wambsganss and other PAC volunteers about the school district's diversity plan, describing the CCAP as an attempt to "indoctrinate children according to extremely liberal beliefs." One headline warned that the plan would discriminate against Christian student clubs by forcing them to comply with diversity audits. On page two, another article claimed that scrapped plans for a diversity and inclusion week at Carroll would have amounted to a school-sponsored celebration of Black Lives Matter activism. And on page three, near an article about the dangers of tracking and disciplining students for microaggressions, there was what looked like a stock photo of a white child in handcuffs under the headline "Student Criminalization."

Hough was having an emotional reaction to the newspaper, but probably not the one the PAC was going for. She believed the mailer was aimed at people like her: white, Christian Southlake moms who would do anything to protect their kids. But her views on race and politics no longer aligned with many of her neighbors', a shift that really took off in 2016 after her daughter came home talking about kids in her fifth-grade class chanting "Build the wall." After the viral N-word video in 2018, and after hearing accounts of Black and LGBTQ students who said they'd been bullied at school, Hough got even more involved, eventually cofounding a nonprofit, Dignity for All Texas Students, to support the diversity plan.

That spring she and her friends were backing a slate of candidates who'd promised to press forward with Carroll's diversity and inclusion efforts. Against Hannah Smith, Dignity for All Texas Students was supporting Ed Hernandez, an immigrant from Mexico and a business consultant who had three children in the district. For the other school board seat, the organization was backing Lynda Warner, a white mother of biracial children who'd volunteered on school board committees and was among the parents who came forward with accounts of racism after the 2018 N-word video.

In public, if not behind the scenes, the campaign was fairly polite. Smith and Bryan stayed above the fray, allowing Southlake Families to do all the mudslinging on their behalf. The candidates met only a few times in person, not for debates but at forums, where they struck a neighborly tone. At one in late March, the moderators opened by asking a series of banal questions about what inspired the candidates to run for school board, their top priorities if elected, and which academic programs they wanted to see added at Carroll. Thirty minutes in, they finally broached the elephant in the room, ever so gently. Without naming *what* had been dividing the city and school system, one of the moderators asked, "What is your specific plan of action to unify our community?"

Hannah Smith got to take the first crack at it.

"We have been through a very difficult time in our community over the last year and a half to two years," Smith said. "I love Southlake.

I don't think that we are a racist community. I don't think that we have racist schools."

To illustrate the point, Smith relayed a story that she said one of her kids had shared recently. Sitting in her sixth-grade classroom, Smith's daughter noticed a few classmates teasing a boy next to her. "He was of Southeast Asian descent, and these boys behind him started calling him names. Started teasing him about his different name and were really ugly about it. And this poor kid started to cry."

Smith said her daughter saw what was happening and spoke up.

"She said, 'You need to stop treating him that way.' You know, 'He can't choose what his name is. His parents named him that. Please stop doing that to him. You're making him cry and you're being a bully.'"

The lesson Smith took away from that story was not that Carroll needed to do a better job of educating children on how to show kindness to people from different cultures, but that students like her daughter were the ones who had the power to unify Southlake. "I think we need to look at our children and their wonderful examples. They love each other. They want our schools and our communities to heal. Thank you."

Later in the forum, one of the moderators finally asked a direct question about the plan that had torn the community apart and inspired each of the candidates to run in the first place: "Name one thing you support in the CCAP, and one thing in the plan that you disagree with."

Warner and Hernandez both said they disagreed with tracking and punishing kids for microaggressions, an idea that had become toxic in Southlake. But each said they supported other aspects of the CCAP—the ones focused on providing staff and students with diversity training rather than punishment. "I really think this is an opportunity to take on every incident and make it a teaching moment for our kids," Hernandez said.

When it was her turn, Smith reiterated her belief that the CCAP violated students' constitutionally protected rights, including freedom of speech and freedom of association. And while she and Bryan both argued that the narrative about racism in Southlake had been vastly exaggerated, they did see one area where Carroll could improve, and it wouldn't require any special new rules or a new director of diversity with a six-figure salary to oversee it. As Bryan put it: "I actually do believe that if we train our teachers to be able to enact and enforce the student code of conduct, we can eliminate bullying and discrimination from all of our schools."

The student code of conduct. Most school districts have one. It's the set of rules that says what students can and can't do, and how they can be punished. It's the document that says you can't cheat on an exam or bring a knife to school. After the 2018 N-word video, Carroll's code of conduct was updated to include more explicit protections for students who were bullied based on their race or sexuality. Prior to the update, racist bullying and taunts could be treated by teachers as a lowest-level offense, on par with chewing gum in class or spitting.

All four candidates seemed to agree that the district's current approach to enforcing the rules, even with those updates, was not getting the job done. Too many students had come forward with stories about school staff brushing aside bullying complaints. But what to do about it? That's where the candidates differed. To Smith and Bryan, the solution was simple: The school district just needed to do a better job of enforcing the rules already on the books. Warner and Hernandez, on the other hand, believed nothing would change without new educational programs to teach educators and students about bigotry and kindness, programs that would attack what they viewed as the root of the problem.

A viewpoint conspicuously absent from the debate was that of Carroll students, who—even as the adults in town went on bickering—were learning to live with the consequences of what everyone seemed to agree was a broken system.

The same month of the school board candidate forum, Mia Mariani, now a sixteen-year-old junior at Carroll, was at home, logged on to her virtual physics class, when suddenly her phone started blowing up with Instagram alerts. Four boys in her grade had created a private chat and named it "Debate Channel." Then one of the boys added Mia to the thread, and two of them started blasting messages at her:

lol who the fuck has pronouns in their bio nobody takes that serious
you can't be a they, they is plural
Hahah

Mia, who listed both female and gender-neutral pronouns ("she/they") in her Instagram bio, felt her hands shake as she started scrolling through the messages. Even before the derision at homecoming her freshman year, she'd gotten used to anti-LGBTQ insults from Carroll classmates. She'd come out as queer in eighth grade. But most of the taunts in middle school weren't aimed directly at her, just kids using the word "gay" as a way of saying something was dumb, or general commentary from classmates about homosexuality being a sin. Things got worse after Mia entered high school and joined Carroll's Gay-Straight Alliance, or GSA. The club itself was wonderful, she said. The only problem was when other students figured out who was in it. Kids would say, "Oh, let's go to the GSA so we can figure out who all the queers are." To Mia, that sounded like a threat, which is why she always made sure the hallway was empty before ducking into the classroom where the club met.

In some ways, the pandemic had been a relief. In virtual classes, at least Mia was able to focus on her work and not what the kid two rows back was saying about her.

That was, until now.

The same boy who'd sent the initial message making fun of Mia's pronouns sent another—"It's a mental illness, not a sexuality"—followed by a rolling-on-the-floor-laughing emoji. Mia never responded, but the boys kept typing, mocking her gender identity and attacking her over old social media posts she'd written in support of Joe Biden's 2020 presidential campaign:

dumb cunt. i truly loath the people who voted for biden
fuck you cunt
yuh i fucken wanna punch liberals
your all great president is really fucking us over

dumb cunts don't even know who he is
he's run for president like 4 times
He a dumb retard
And he secretly gay
and the ONLY reason camala is vp is because her legs are
open wider than a $5 meth whore
fuck you

Mia felt sick and, even though she was at home, afraid for her safety. Did those boys know where she lived? She set her phone aside and started drafting an urgent email to Carroll Senior High's principal, Shawn Duhon—the same administrator who'd told Raven Rolle two years earlier, after she'd heard a classmate saying the N-word, that she was "too pretty" to let racist comments get under her skin. Mia shared pictures of the messages and the names of the boys who'd sent them. After nearly a week, Duhon finally scheduled a Zoom meeting to discuss her complaint. Just like Raven, Mia recorded the conversation.

"Hi, how are you?" the principal said as Mia turned on her camera.

"I'm alright. How are you?"

Duhon opened by explaining why it had taken him so long to get back to her: He'd been busy interviewing the boys who'd harassed her, along with their parents. That set off alarm bells in Mia's head. Why hadn't her parents been invited to this meeting? Duhon then shared his conclusions about what happened, based on his conversations with the boys.

"In visiting with them, they were inviting people into the Debate Channel," Duhon said, as Mia nervously fiddled with a hair clip. "Talking with one of them specifically, he said that he wanted to hear opposing views and opinions. And I said, 'OK, that makes sense.' He goes, 'I like politics, and I wanted to debate.' I said, 'OK. Very reasonable, very understanding.'"

Now Mia's hands were shaking. What was he talking about? Hadn't he read their vulgar messages? But before she could say anything, Duhon pivoted to an issue that he believed needed to be sorted out: Had Mia accepted an invite to join the Debate Channel? No, she told him. She didn't have to click anything to join the Instagram chat. And so what if she had?

"It wasn't exactly a debate as they were calling me slurs and saying—"

"Yeah, I want to get to that," Duhon said, cutting her off.

He then returned to his line of inquiry about whether Mia had clicked anything to join the chat, trying to figure out whether she'd consented to be part of the "debate." He spent nearly ten minutes on this subject before pivoting to his next question: Why, exactly, did Mia think that the messages targeted her?

"I never saw your part of the debate," Duhon said, continuing to frame the torrent of four-letter insults as routine political discourse. "And in general, I never saw anything specific that they said to you."

She was the only one they added to the chat, Mia said, feeling her grip tighten on the hair clip she was holding. "It was all being directed at me. They just started being mean to me."

But that's not how the boys intended it, Duhon told her. One of them explained it all to him in an email. "He was basically saying that they were directing things more at the Democratic party," Duhon said. "Because they were trying to create dialogue. They were trying to create a debate."

But don't worry, Duhon continued. He did tell the boys they needed to be more "professional" and "respectful" when they debated politics in the future. And, he said, he gave the boys a warning—about how this kind of behavior, if ever made public, might harm their chances of getting into a good college.

"I told them this could very well come back to haunt them in years to come if in fact the one admissions officer that's reading their application is a particular side of a party. They took that a little bit to heart because they didn't know that colleges are doing that these days." Duhon assured Mia he'd also counseled the boys on how their words might hurt someone's feelings—someone, he said, like Joe Biden. "'If President Biden was to know that you're saying this about him, you know, there might be some consequences to that.'" Duhon said the boys took his warning seriously.

Finally, after nearly twenty minutes, Mia started to cry.

"They didn't clarify they were talking to a group," she said, angry at Duhon for failing to see what was obvious to her, and angry at herself for letting him see her get emotional. "They were talking to *me*. It was all directed at *me*. They called *me* a cunt. They called *me* slurs. They called *me* all this stuff. They started slandering *me* because of the pronouns that I use. It was all at *me*. There was no debate."

At one point, Duhon, sounding flummoxed, turned to an assistant principal seated next to him: "They were just wanting to debate."

On the call, Mia asked Duhon to take another look at the boys' messages. After he'd read them aloud, censoring the curse words, Mia grilled him as tears streamed down her cheeks.

"You understand how they're being mean to me, right? Because I use 'she/they' pronouns. They're calling it a mental illness. And they're misgendering me."

Whether or not Duhon understood those things was unclear. As an educator, he seemed less than up to speed on the realities of his LGBTQ students. Mia and her friends were growing up in an era of broadening acceptance and confronting backlash from conservatives and even some progressive parents who'd begun warning that young people were changing genders on a whim because of indoctrination and peer pressure. To Mia, this wasn't political, and whether she should be allowed to live as her authentic self wasn't up for debate.

Duhon did promise to take a closer look at everything. But he explained there wasn't much he could do even if he ultimately sided with Mia since she wasn't physically at school when the alleged harassment took place—a statement directly contradicted by Carroll's student code of conduct. District policy gave administrators authority to discipline students for off-campus behavior when it disrupted activities at school, just as they'd done in response to the 2018 N-word video.

"Well, sweetie," Duhon said before ending the meeting, "you have a good evening."

After saying goodbye, Mia closed her computer, then cried alone in her room.

Later that month, her parents filed a formal complaint against Duhon and demanded that Carroll train administrators on how to sensitively handle reports of anti-LGBTQ bullying. In a written response, senior district administrators denied that request, citing the restraining order issued in response to the lawsuit backed by Southlake Families PAC, which they said prohibited Carroll from implementing any type of diversity training. An assistant principal tasked with investigating Duhon's handling of Mia's harassment complaint concluded that his boss acted appropriately, writing that the boys' messages did not "satisfy the criteria necessary to constitute bullying."

Mia's father, Elio Mariani, was furious.

"It's shocking because these are employees that are working with our children every day," he said. "If they can't have a basic understanding of some of these things, just a basic proficiency, that is maybe endangering our kids."

Like Raven Rolle two years earlier, the whole encounter left Mia feeling like the adults in Southlake weren't looking out for kids like her.

"I just wanted something to happen. I wanted the boys to get in trouble. I wanted to have, I don't know, comfort in the fact that I'm not going through this for no reason. Instead, I felt even more unsafe, because the people who are supposed to keep me safe were hurting me."

Mia was just a high school junior, not old enough to vote. But that spring, she was paying close attention to Southlake's school board elections—watching, she said, for a sign of hope.

With days to go until the election, outgoing mayor Laura Hill appeared at a campaign event alongside all five Southlake Families PAC–endorsed candidates for school board, city council, and mayor. Wearing a Dragon-green dress and standing in front of U.S. and Texas flags, Hill told the crowd that the choice on May 1 could not be clearer.

"The [city's] wealth, the good planning, the great schools, have in large part to do with conservative mayors and primarily majority conservative councils that have served your city." But now, Hill warned, the people of Southlake were "one election away" from losing it all.

More than two years had passed since Hill started talking with Black parents like Robin Cornish and Black students like Zaneta Ogunmola and promising to take action to address racism. She'd put together the

Mayor's Alliance for Unity and Culture and hosted bridge-building community events. But since then, Hill had turned against the Carroll school board and the volunteer diversity council she once endorsed.

Now she painted those campaigning in support of the CCAP as disgruntled liberals. "Oh, they loved [Southlake] when they made the decision to come here and educate their children here. But now it's not good enough for them."

With Hannah Smith and Cam Bryan smiling behind her, Hill explained that it had been conservatives who'd made Southlake great. And now, they were its last line of defense.

"So right now that's up to us. It is absolutely up to us. There is a fork in the road. We're standing at it. I hope you'll join me in voting for all of these folks."

A fork in the road. Two paths to choose from. The stakes had been set. Now it was up to the people to decide which way to turn.

8

Blowout

SATURDAY, MAY 1, 2021: Election Day in Southlake, Texas. Two feuding factions were set up on sidewalks across the street from the city's picturesque redbrick town hall. On one side, a small group of volunteers held signs in support of the candidates for school board, city council, and mayor who'd campaigned on a promise to support new diversity and inclusion programs at the Carroll Independent School District. On the other side, a much larger and louder crowd had gathered to cheer on the slate of conservative candidates backed by Southlake Families PAC. In a scene that had the look and feel of a football pep rally, they were blasting music through portable speakers, waving huge green campaign signs, banging on cowbells, and yelling for passing drivers to honk their horns in support.

Between the two groups, my colleague Antonia Hylton and I were standing on a sidewalk, calling out to strangers as they headed inside to cast ballots. "Excuse me sir, we're reporters with NBC News. Would you mind telling us what brought you out to vote today?"

The passerby didn't glance up at us: "No, thank you."

We were doing what's known in the journalism business as man-on-the-street reporting, holding out a microphone to random residents in the hopes of gaining some insight about what was motivating so many of them to vote. By the end of the evening, more than nine thousand Southlake residents would cast ballots—three times the normal turnout for local elections here. But so far, our attempt at taking the pulse of the electorate wasn't going well.

"Hi, sir," I called to a middle-aged white man, "would you be open to sharing how you feel about this race?"

He delivered his one-word reply without slowing his stride: "Nope."

It's not unusual for people to decline spontaneous interview requests from reporters, but there may have been another reason so many were breezing past us that morning. In the months leading up to the election, some folks in Southlake had begun to view me and Antonia as villains in the diversity plan saga. That January, I'd published a written article about the CCAP fight, shining a national spotlight on the local controversy, while centering the piece on the experiences of Robin Cornish, the Black mother who'd sent five children through the Carroll school district before becoming a leading voice calling for change. A few weeks later, Antonia brought that story to the more than six million regular viewers of *NBC Nightly News*.

Afterward, our email inboxes were flooded with messages from parents, students, and educators from across the country who'd seen our reports and wanted us to know that similar fights over racism and diversity were simmering in their suburbs. Those messages were our first clue that the story we'd begun documenting in one North Texas town was the story of America in 2021.

In Southlake, the reaction to our reporting had been polarized. Some conservatives cast us as out-of-town agitators, bent on tearing down a good city. Juan Saldivar, a Mexican American parent and army veteran who'd spoken against the CCAP, wrote a post on social media calling my reporting "fake journalism" and saying, "All you deserve from Americans of all stripes is the double-barreled middle finger. Come see me and I will give it to you myself." Someone in town even coined a clever nickname for me: "Mike Fiction-baugh." The attacks on Antonia, a young Black woman, were sometimes uglier. A few residents suggested her professional success—she'd graduated from Harvard University and won an Emmy by the age of twenty-five—could be attributed largely to affirmative action policies like those they claimed were embedded in the CCAP.

Distrust among conservatives had long been a defining obstacle to doing journalism in America, before Trump inflamed anti-media animosity to new heights with his signature "enemy of the American people" attack line. In this environment, Antonia and I weren't just struggling to get random voters to stop and talk to us. Of the more than fifty diversity plan opponents we contacted, including those running for school board, almost none were willing to talk on the record.

Undeterred, we called out to an older white couple as they headed in to vote.

"Ma'am, care to share any of your thoughts about why you're voting?"

"No," the wife said without stopping, then shouted back at us over her shoulder: "It's a great town. I want to keep it that way."

Ours wasn't the only national spotlight shining on Southlake that week. In the final days before the election, there had been a sudden rush of coverage about the CCAP fight in conservative news outlets. The *Federalist*, a far-right online magazine, published a series of articles, including one under the headline "Parents Revolt After Texas's No. 1 School District Tries to Institutionalize Racism."

Nearly identical language appeared on a Fox News chyron the following day as one of the network's daytime hosts introduced a segment about the Southlake controversy: "Texas Curriculum Institutionalizes Racism." The anchor interviewed Juan Saldivar, the Carroll parent who'd offered me a "double-barreled middle finger." Saldivar said he was troubled by some of the lessons his fourth grader was learning from *Scholastic News* articles assigned by her teachers, but his biggest concern was with what the district had planned for her as she got older. "If these diversity, equity, inclusion programs are forced down our throats, I will pull her out."

The local race also drew attention from the cable news host who'd helped introduce the nation to the dangers of critical race theory eight months earlier. "Until recently," Tucker Carlson said, introducing a segment on his primetime broadcast, "the Carroll Independent School District of Southlake, Texas, was one of the highest-performing school districts in the state of Texas. But beginning in 2018, the school district implemented something called a cultural competence plan."

These types of policies were being forced on children all over the country, Carlson warned. But unlike in other towns, the Fox News host said, parents in Southlake were revolting. He then introduced his guest, Southlake resident and former NRA spokeswoman Dana Loesch. "I mean, we're seeing this everywhere," Carlson said. "It's come to your town. Tell us what parents are doing about it."

"Yes, Tucker, thank you so much."

Carlson listened with his mouth agape as Loesch explained how this whole mess began a couple of years ago because, she said, "some teenagers said something bad" on social media. "And the school and a lot of very far-left Marxist activists decided to exploit this as a way to implement critical race theory education in this school district." But parents weren't powerless, Loesch said, and then urged Carlson's viewers to visit the website of Southlake Families PAC to learn how to fight back in their own communities.

"Amen," Carlson said. "This is happening everywhere. They'll come in and they'll wreck your school, they'll hurt your children, they'll take your money, they'll bully you, and no one does anything. And I'm just so grateful to hear of parents who are doing something. Dana, thanks so much for coming on today and telling us that story."

Carlson's hyperbolic warning about woke Marxists coming to "hurt your children" must have hit a nerve with some of his viewers. That night, a retiree in Hilton Head, South Carolina, sent Southlake Families PAC $500. A real estate developer in Skillman, New Jersey, gave $25. A stay-at-home dad in central Ohio chipped in another ten bucks.

With just a few days left until the election, donations like these, large and small, poured in from across the country.

As polls closed on the night of the election, workers at Southlake's Cambria Hotel were scurrying to set up a buffet at an election party for the slate of pro–diversity plan candidates. Just then, the first batch of results were posted on the county's website. Members of the hospitality staff were still setting out appetizers, but already the party was over.

Elisha Rurka, who'd been running for a seat on the Southlake City Council, got the news from a campaign volunteer. With her ear still pressed to her cell phone, Rurka turned to school board candidate Ed Hernandez, who'd just walked in, and mouthed the word "blowout."

"This is the town we live in," she told him. "Do you want to move?"

Hernandez didn't respond. He just frowned, then headed for the bar.

He and the other CCAP-defending candidates knew they were underdogs, especially since the nonpartisan race was framed by Southlake Families PAC as conservatives versus liberals in a diversifying suburb that was still solidly Republican. It didn't help that the CCAP opponents had raised nearly twenty times more than they had. Even still, the margin of their defeat was stunning. Each of the Southlake Families PAC candidates for school board, city council, and mayor won their race with about 70 percent of the vote—an even bigger share than the 63 percent of Southlake residents who'd backed Trump in 2020.

Rurka said she was only joking about wanting to move, but she hadn't completely ruled out the possibility. "We all love our town," she said. "It's just, this whole last year has been crazy. It doesn't feel like the same place in some ways."

Across the room, Jennifer Hough, one of the white moms who'd organized in support of the diversity plan, was just learning the outcome. With one arm wrapped in a sling, she struggled to scroll through the results on her phone. She'd slipped and fallen that week while running to get out of a lightning storm—an apt metaphor, perhaps, for what had just happened to her town.

"It feels like hate wins," said Hough, who didn't bother sticking around for the concession speeches.

As word of the results spread through the hotel lobby, Hernandez headed out to the patio with a beer. He said he was feeling great, ready to celebrate a hard-fought campaign, but his forced smile and slumped posture were telling a different story. "I think that they did a great job of making these into partisan races. They did a great job of fearmongering, of labeling me as, you know, this guy from the radical left and Marxist, which I'm not. But at least I learned that that works."

When asked what message he thought the election results would send to students at Carroll, Hernandez shook his head. "I want to save that answer for Monday. Today is a celebration. I don't want to think about all these kids that shared their stories, their testimonies. I don't want to think about that right now, because it's really, really hard."

Hernandez paused and stared down at his drink, tears wetting the corners of his eyes, before adding: "I don't want to talk about it."

Across town, one of the students Hernandez was trying to avoid thinking about studied the results in disbelief. Two months had passed since Mia Mariani filed a complaint against the boys who sent her vulgar messages mocking her gender identity. Since then, the district had rejected her parents' demands for accountability. Now, alone in her room, she was losing hope that anything would ever change.

"It just hurts," she said. "I think what's happened to me and what I've learned here—whether educational or just bad things that have happened—I think I'm going to carry that with me."

About twenty-five miles away in downtown Dallas that evening, fourth-grade teacher Christina Catlin had just recited her marriage vows and was celebrating at a reception hall with friends, family, and several of her Johnson Elementary colleagues. Ms. Catlin—now Mrs. McGuirk—was mingling with guests when a fellow teacher came up to share the news. The parents who'd been hounding her and her colleagues over assignments from *Scholastic News* had just won two seats on the school board.

McGuirk, in her sparkling white wedding dress, turned to her maid of honor, fellow fourth-grade teacher Rickie Farah, and said, "Welp, we're screwed."

Back in Southlake, the city's new mayor-elect John Huffman grabbed a microphone and addressed a packed room of supporters at Delucca Gaucho Pizza & Wine.

"Hey, listen, y'all, if anybody doubted that Southlake still believes in the goodness of its people . . . if anybody doubted that the men and women of Southlake are going to rise up and defend their reputations, and their city, and their schools, and their kids . . . if anybody doubted where we stood on CCAP and that we will not tolerate our kids being taught that what's most important is the color of their skin . . . if anybody doubted those things, tonight was your answer!"

The victory party was packed with Southlake Families PAC leaders and donors, including Leigh Wambsganss, Tim O'Hare, and outgoing mayor Laura Hill, who wasn't the only city leader in attendance who'd once supported the work of the District Diversity Council.

Ronell Smith, Southlake's lone Black city councilman, had spoken out against racism after the first N-word video in 2018 and, on the eve of the August 2020 CCAP vote, had urged school board president Michelle Moore to approve the diversity plan. "I don't want these people to think they've won," Smith had texted Moore at the time. "If they feel emboldened, we'll never get anything done." Now, with a year until his own reelection campaign, and having changed his position on the righteousness of the CCAP based, he said, on conversations with constituents, Smith posed for photos with PAC-endorsed candidates and congratulated them on their victories.

During her speech that night, Hannah Smith told the crowd that their fight to take control of the Carroll Independent School District was just beginning. "We need you behind us, because this is when the real work begins."

At a school board meeting two days later, Smith's supporters answered her call. They put on matching green T-shirts and crammed into Carroll's public meeting room to declare victory.

In a scene that would soon be repeated in school board meeting halls across the country that spring and summer, parents waved homemade signs from the audience and cheered after every speaker. One white woman held a poster showing a masked little white girl with pigtails next to the words "I can't breathe," appropriating George Floyd's dying words in protest of the district's policy of requiring students to wear masks at school to slow the spread of COVID. At one point, the proceeding was stopped for several minutes as two men got into a physical altercation over a sign. Amid the chaos, a woman stood up, jabbed her finger at board president Michelle Moore, and yelled, "Be a leader!"

Later, a mom walked up to the microphone carrying a poster with a blown-up picture of Moore's face: "That's your mug shot on there," she said, "just in case you were wondering." Another woman, a mom named Tara Eddins, told Moore she needed to resign. Otherwise, she warned, "we will continue to breathe fire upon this corrupt school board."

Despite her best efforts, Moore wasn't having much luck keeping order. She banged her gavel and repeatedly called for the audience to follow the board's policy against cheering during meetings. When another mom shouted back at her, Moore's level demeanor started to crack. "You know what?" Moore fired back, raising her voice for the first time in the nine months since the school board room had been transformed into a political battleground. "I'm going to speak. I'm speaking. And I'm asking you to please stop."

Finally, after nearly two hours, a few people from the losing side got a chance at the microphone, including Robin Cornish.

This was the same room where, more than two years earlier, she and other Black parents first called for changes at Carroll. Now she'd come to let the board know that she still believed in her late husband Frank Cornish's vision for Southlake. She opened by reading the words etched onto the Town Square plaque that the city had put up in Frank's memory: "May his vision of a diverse, inclusive community continue to inspire future generations."

"The seventy percent who have an issue with those words might want to go back to where *they* came from," Cornish said, parroting Allen West. "And to us in the struggle for diversity and inclusion, I say, don't give up. Stand up, dust yourself off, stay in the fight."

"This is just one battle," Cornish said, as two white women in the audience turned to each other and rolled their eyes.

"The war is not over."

9

The Southlake Playbook

IN THE DAYS AFTER Hannah Smith's and Cam Bryan's blowout election wins, Southlake's political revolt was continuing to make national headlines, and quickly becoming the stuff of legend on the American right.

The *Federalist* compared the conservative uprising in Southlake to the early days of the Tea Party movement in 2010, when anti-Obama blowback propelled a new generation of far-right Republicans into power. "Only this time," the magazine wrote, "the stakes are far higher, with conditions ripe for a new takeover."

The *Wall Street Journal* editorial board praised the outcome in an op-ed titled "Southlake Says No to Woke Education," writing, "Perhaps parents in other parts of the country will take the lesson that they can resist indoctrination that tells students they must divide and define themselves by race and gender rather than focus on learning and achievement."

Laura Ingraham opened her nightly Fox News broadcast with big news out of a small town in Texas. The clear message from Southlake, she told viewers of the *Ingraham Angle*, was: "We're winning." Like Carlson, Ingraham had spent months calling on her audience to fight the rise of Black Lives Matter and critical race theory in American society. "More of you are smartly heeding that call, because in Saturday's election in Southlake, Texas, candidates opposed to the far-left BLM curriculum won the two open seats on the Carroll Independent School District board with nearly seventy percent of the vote."

It may have been the first time that a Fox News prime-time program led with the results of a local school board election. Six months after Trump's election defeat, conservative pundits appeared hungry for something to celebrate—some indication that the political winds were shifting ahead of the 2022 midterms. After years of selling their viewers a dark vision of America besieged by sinister forces from the left, the Southlake story presented the bosses at Fox News with an opportunity to feed their audience something markedly different: hope that their side would prevail.

Activist Chris Rufo, the man most responsible for turning critical race theory into a conservative battle cry, was so excited by the outcome in Southlake that he failed to fact-check his celebratory tweet: "In 2020, Joe Biden narrowly won this district. Today, anti-woke candidates won by 40 points," Rufo wrote, seeming to conflate Southlake's 2020 presidential results—which skewed heavily for Trump—with those of the broader, more liberal Tarrant County, whose electorate had swung narrowly for Biden.

Nevertheless, Rufo's point was fast becoming conventional wisdom on the right: Southlake, the argument went, held the answer for how Republicans could regain the ground they'd lost over the years in fast-growing and rapidly diversifying suburbs nationally. Days later, former Trump advisor Steve Bannon declared on his *War Room* podcast: "The path to save the nation is very simple—it's going to go through the school boards." Before long, right-wing outlets like the *National Review* were pumping out admiring profiles of Southlake Families, holding the group up as a model to be replicated.

The sense that Southlake's uprising was a winner for conservatives nationwide was the headline message when, a few weeks later, the leaders of Southlake Families threw themselves a victory party. The event was held at the home of Leigh Wambsganss; PAC cofounder Tim O'Hare introduced the day's special guest speaker.

"He is a true patriot, and he is the man that has made pecan pie the most famous dessert in Southlake, Texas. Please welcome Allen West!"

Texas GOP Chairman Allen West was himself looking to ride the Southlake wave to electoral glory. Not long after this event, West would announce that he was stepping down from the state GOP to launch a campaign to challenge Texas governor Greg Abbott in the Republican primary. Standing on a podium set up in Wambsganss's living room, West opened by calling on Kristin Garcia, the mom who'd filed the lawsuit that effectively derailed Carroll's diversity plan, to come forward and stand next to him.

"Throughout history," West said, "whenever there's been a struggle for liberty, there was always one person that stood up. . . . When I think about Thomas More, when he stood up against King Henry VIII and refused to bow down to him because he would only bow down to his sovereign Lord. When I think about thirteen little colonies that came together against the greatest power the world knew at the time. And when I think about a simple woman by the name of Rosa Parks, who said, 'I'm not going to go to the back of the bus. I'm going to sit right here.'"

West then gestured toward the woman standing next to him: "Kristin," he said, "is the Rosa Parks of Southlake, Texas." Garcia smiled bashfully with her hands folded in front of her, and mouthed the words "Thank you," as the room erupted in applause.

Like Rosa Parks, West said as Garcia returned to her seat, the movement that she'd helped ignite in Southlake was never meant to be only a local fight. "This is a best practice. This is a lesson learned. You have to put this in a white paper. You have to make a video. You've got to make sure that you export this to every single major suburban area in the United States of America."

He paused between those words for emphasis: *Every. Single. Major. Suburban. Area. In the United States.*

That August, eighteen months after the initial shutdowns to prevent the spread of COVID, a disturbing scene unfolded in a darkened parking lot outside a school board meeting in Williamson County, Tennessee, a wealthy and predominantly white community in the suburbs south of Nashville. As the Delta variant of the coronavirus burned through the population that summer, once again filling hospital beds across the nation, the school board in Williamson County had made the politically divisive decision to follow the advice of public health experts and reinstate the district's mandatory mask policy for the upcoming school year.

After the vote, an angry crowd swarmed mask proponents as they headed to their cars. "Take that mask off," a woman shouted, getting into the face of another resident. Later, two men followed a mask-wearing official to his car, shouting, "We know who you are!"

"You can leave freely," one of the men yelled, "but we will find you!" The other man made the threat more explicit: "You will never be allowed in public again!"

Video of the altercation went viral on social media, becoming the latest in a long line of chaotic school board meetings to make headlines that summer, as conservative parents nationwide revolted against pandemic safety measures and lessons on racism that they attacked under the umbrella of "critical race theory." Similar scenes had played out in Loudoun County, Virginia, where parents opposed to a district diversity plan shut down a meeting chanting "Shame on you!" and in Rockwood, Missouri, where a school superintendent felt compelled to hire private security to stand guard outside the homes of Black senior administrators responsible for overseeing the district's diversity and inclusion programs.

School board meetings grew so volatile that summer and into early fall that the National School Boards Association wrote a letter to President Joe Biden requesting help assuring the safety of school employees and board members. Attorney General Merrick Garland followed up by sending a memo to the FBI and federal prosecutors noting a "disturbing spike in harassment, intimidation, and threats of violence" against school officials, and directing agency leaders to come up with strategies to address those concerns. "While spirited debate about policy matters is protected under our Constitution," Garland wrote, "that protection does not extend to threats of violence or efforts to intimidate individuals based on their views." Conservative activists seized on the missive to spread a conspiracy theory that the Justice Department planned to target parents opposed to critical race theory and to prosecute angry suburban moms as "domestic terrorists."

Many suburban moms embraced that title as a badge of honor that summer, as conservative parents rallied around groups like No Left Turn in Education and Moms for Liberty that had formed to take the fight directly to school boards. Robin Steenman had launched a local Moms for Liberty chapter to fight the mask mandate and lessons on racism in Williamson County, the site of the ugly parking lot showdown. An air force veteran and white mother of three, Steenman's own children did not attend public schools in the Nashville suburb, but as a taxpayer she was determined to rid the district of any lessons or curriculum that she believed focused too heavily on the history of racism in America. Steenman, her critics liked to point out, had opened this campaign in a wealthy Tennessee community where tourists could still book guided tours of plantations where enslaved Black Americans once toiled in cotton fields.

On June 30, soon after Republican Tennessee lawmakers passed one of the first state bans on the teaching of critical race theory, Steenman and her supporters sent Williamson County Schools an eleven-page letter listing dozens of books and lessons that they believed violated the new law. Like Tennessee's anti-CRT law, Steenman's attack on books would soon be replicated in states across the country.

She and the other parents argued that reading an illustrated children's book about the life of Ruby Bridges—a Black six-year-old who integrated a Louisiana public school in 1960—might expose students to "psychological distress," because the book's depiction of an angry white mob gave the impression that all white people were "bad." Although Steenman said she admired Martin Luther King Jr.'s call to judge others based only on the "content of their character," she and her supporters wanted the district to ban the children's book *Martin Luther King, Jr. and the March on Washington*, because it contained historical images—including depictions of white firefighters blasting Black people with hoses—that might make white children feel bad about themselves.

"There's so much positive that has happened in the sixty years since," Steenman told a Reuters reporter, "but it's all as if it never happened."

The district refused to remove the books, arguing that they presented important historical facts in a clear, age-appropriate format. Later, the school board agreed to minor adjustments in the way teachers presented some of the material, but that did not appease Steenman, who'd come to believe that speaking at board meetings and writing stern letters wouldn't be enough to affect real, lasting change. If she and her supporters were going to take control of their public schools, they would need to win seats on the school board.

To achieve that goal, Steenman looked to the example set in a Texas town some seven hundred miles away. Six months after Southlake Families PAC's landslide election victory, Steenman filed paperwork to form a new political action committee of her own. She and her allies named it Williamson Families PAC and quickly launched a website, which featured a mission statement taken nearly word for word from SouthlakeFamilies.org, with only a few creative edits: "Williamson County is built upon the rock of Judeo-Christian values that are the foundation of our country. We welcome all that share our concerns and conservative values."

In case there was any doubt about where she'd drawn her inspiration, Steenman made it explicit in an interview with the *Tennessee Star*, a conservative online newspaper. "Williamson Families is a recipe that's been done before. It was done in Southlake, Texas," she said, before repeating the now famous story of how an affluent suburban community much like her own had rallied to defeat the "specter" of CRT. "So I said, 'Wow, that really works. That could really work here.'"

Like Southlake Families, Steenman's political action committee held a kick-off celebration. Instead of Allen West, theirs featured John Rich, a famous country singer known for supporting Republican politicians. And like the Texas-based PAC that inspired it, Williamson Families quickly raked in nearly $200,000 and set its sights on recruiting candidates for the following year's school board elections. As in Southlake, Steenman and others on the PAC privately interviewed prospective candidates, looking to weed out those who were insufficiently conservative. The Williamson County–based PAC also hired a heavy-hitter GOP consulting firm called Axiom Strategies—the same firm that had recently begun advising Southlake Families. Axiom, known for its work on Senator Ted Cruz's presidential campaign and Glenn Youngkin's campaign for governor that fall in Virginia, was now in the business of bringing sophisticated, national-level political strategies to local school board races.

Steenman wasn't the only white suburbanite inspired by Southlake. Leigh Wambsganss reported receiving more than a thousand emails after the Southlake Families PAC election triumph from conservatives looking for tips on launching their own hyper-local political action committees. "Parents in Southlake taught parents across the country that you can be called a racist and you can be called a homophobe, knowing that none of that is true, and you can keep standing," Wambsganss said. "People across the country are looking for leadership, they're looking for a blueprint."

Newly sworn in Carroll school board member Hannah Smith was also in hot demand. That July she'd been invited to speak at the Conservative Political Action Conference, the twice-annual gathering of far-right activists and politicians known as CPAC. Since its founding in the aftermath of the Watergate scandal in 1974, CPAC had long been a barometer of the American conservative movement and an incubator for Republican policy ideas. Two days after Trump gave a CPAC keynote address filled with grievances and lies about the outcome of the 2020 election, Smith spoke from the same stage during a panel focused on defeating critical race theory. "Can you imagine the psychological trauma that we're inflicting on our school-aged kids by telling them they're inherently bad if they're born white, or if they're born a person of color, they're inherently a victim?" Smith asked those gathered in the 3,300-seat Dallas ballroom.

Smith then rattled off a litany of steps that conservative activists could take to fight back: Bombard school districts with open records requests to learn what they're teaching; be on the lookout for CRT code words, like "equity," "diversity" and "social emotional learning"; set up a community Facebook group where residents could educate each other; write out talking points for fellow parents before they speak at school board meetings so that they'd be able to "articulate the reason why CRT is so bad."

"Also," Smith continued, "we set up a political action committee in our town, and the PAC was really very influential in helping get people organized into different committees. A legal committee, a communications committee, a grassroots neighborhood committee, a prayer team. There's a lot of ways that you can get your community organized, but you have to have a strategic focus so that you can fight back."

In closing, Smith shared a link to her campaign website, where she said conservative organizers could find her contact information. A moment later, a fellow panelist ended the CPAC session with a warning: "I just want to say that we are at war. It's a war between tyranny and liberty. It is the life and death of this country as we know it."

Just as in Williamson County, new Southlake Families–inspired PACs were sprouting up all over the country. A group seeking to block diversity lessons in Spalding County, Georgia, formed a political action committee with a mission statement including the same copied-and-pasted phrase "unapologetically rooted in Judeo-Christian values," and noting that the group would "welcome all that share our concerns and conservative values." McKinney First, a political action committee formed to root out critical race theory in another North Texas school system, included identical language on its website. In the affluent majority-white suburbs west of St. Louis, parents said they consulted with Southlake Families leaders before creating Francis Howell Families PAC with the mission of supporting school board candidates who would ensure that schoolchildren learned "respect for our nation's founding principles." To stop the spread of CRT in the Houston suburbs, there was Spring Branch Families PAC. Outside Austin, politically connected parents formed Lake Travis Families PAC.

Nearly a dozen local PACs formed that year in the Dallas–Fort Worth suburbs alone—so many that a liberal Fort Worth newspaper coined the phrase "the Southlake Playbook" to describe the surge of conservative organizing around local nonpartisan school boards. That fall, when a school district in the North Texas city of Grapevine was contemplating whether to discipline a Black high school principal named James Whitfield after he'd come under fire for allegedly embracing critical race theory, a parent defending Whitfield coined a slogan of his own while pleading for the school board to reverse course: "Please," he said, "do not Southlake my Grapevine." In the end, the board voted to cut ties with Whitfield, the first Black man to serve as principal at Colleyville Heritage High School.

For conservatives, however, there may have been a hidden downside of rushing to copy Southlake's nascent political movement. Southlake Families had no doubt produced an easy-to-replicate strategy for turning school board contests into partisan affairs, leveraging conservative anger to win seats. But the informal field guide known as the Southlake Playbook was, at that point, silent about what conservatives should do once they'd gained power.

In politics, there's an adage, summarized perhaps most artfully in the musical *Hamilton*, when President George Washington counsels his headstrong and idealistic secretary of the treasury: "Winning was easy, young man. Governing's harder."

10

The Parents Are Our Clients

LATE ON THE EVENING of October 4, 2021, the board of trustees of the Carroll Independent School District reconvened after more than three hours in closed session. Although Southlake Families PAC had officially won just two of seven seats on the school board by that point, the resignation of one diversity plan–supporting trustee that summer, and the frequent absence of another, had, in effect, given PAC-aligned conservatives control of the district. Now trustee Hannah Smith was about to fulfill one of her campaign promises—by disciplining fourth-grade teacher Rickie Farah, Christina McGuirk's maid of honor.

"I move to grant the appeal and to request the administration issue a formal letter of reprimand," Smith said from her seat behind the dais.

The complaints from parents at Johnson Elementary the previous school year hadn't let up after the initial blowup over *Scholastic News*. In the lead-up to Smith and Bryan's election victories, Farah had become a primary target of Southlake Families and several of its donors after one of Farah's students found a copy of a best-selling children's book titled *This Book Is Anti-Racist* in her classroom library. The fourth grader's mother, a white woman named Sarah Muns, whose family had donated a combined $2,000 to the Smith-Bryan ticket, was outraged that her daughter was allowed access to an anti-racism field guide that she said violated her family's "morals and faith." Confronted with the complaint, Farah initially agreed to remove the book after discovering that it was intended for grades five and up. But Muns was upset that Farah followed that concession by telling her daughter that she would have to get the teacher's permission before taking any more books home from class.

Muns called that bullying and retaliation and elevated the matter to senior district officials, who'd investigated and ultimately found no cause to punish the teacher. When Muns wrote about the situation on Facebook in the spring, then candidate Smith had chimed in with a public note of encouragement: "Sarah, we have your back. Cam and I will not tolerate this. Thank you for your support."

Now, having listened to her campaign donor's case in closed session that evening in October, Smith motioned to overturn the ruling by superintendent Lane Ledbetter's staff clearing Farah of wrongdoing.

The action was somewhat unusual; typically, school boards focus on setting district policy while leaving day-to-day operations, including teacher discipline, to administrators. Before voting against Smith's motion, board member Sheri Mills, who'd served on the District Diversity Council and fought to pass the CCAP, issued a warning to any Carroll educators who might have been up late watching the meeting on the district's live feed. "I would like to let the teachers know, if you are worried about teaching in this school district, that you should watch this vote," Mills said. "I want you to know that you are right to be worried."

A moment later, the board voted 3–2 to reprimand Farah, with Michelle Moore joining Mills's no vote. The disciplinary action, approved along party lines, was largely symbolic. The document would go into Farah's employee file, and although it might have made it harder for her to find work at another school in the future, it wasn't expected to directly affect her job at Carroll.

The bigger and more immediate impact was the message that the board had just sent to the district's 1,100 employees. With the vote, cast at 10:35 P.M. on a Monday, the Southlake Families–controlled school board had set in motion a chain of events that would spark a different sort of backlash, and—in ten days' time—draw a harsh global spotlight onto the city of Southlake and its beloved school system.

A couple of days later, I started getting messages from teachers in Southlake. One of them was Christina McGuirk, by then in her fourth year at Carroll and now fully disillusioned with the community that had embraced her as Ms. Catlin. McGuirk and the other teachers had been following my reporting with Antonia Hylton in Southlake—including a six-part podcast series we'd released covering the CCAP fight. The teachers didn't want to be named publicly, but they wanted us to know that they were deeply concerned about some of the policies the district had begun implementing.

The vote to reprimand Farah that week had sent a jolt of panic through Carroll's teaching ranks. Two days later, administrators followed up by notifying staff members across the district that they would be receiving training during a staff development day that Friday on new guidelines governing which books would be allowed in classrooms, and instructions for getting rid of any that didn't meet new content standards.

One educator sent me a copy of a rubric that Carroll administrators had distributed ahead of the training. It asked teachers to grade books in their class based on whether they provided multiple perspectives, and to discard any that presented singular, dominant narratives "in such a way that it . . . may be considered offensive." It appeared that the guidelines were based in part on the so-called anti–critical race theory law passed in Texas that summer, which prohibited schools from teaching children that they should feel "discomfort, guilt, anguish, or any other form of psychological distress" because of their race. The law also required teachers to present multiple perspectives when discussing "widely debated and currently controversial" issues in class.

After the new guidelines went out, Carroll teachers started revolting.

The rubric was too vague, they argued, and after what happened to Farah, they were afraid of being punished by the school board because of a complaint from a politically connected parent. The books in question, the teachers emphasized, weren't even part of the assigned reading curriculum; their classroom libraries were filled with a wide range of titles that students were allowed to browse in their free time, with the goal of encouraging a love for reading. To protest the changes, an English teacher at a Carroll campus wrapped her classroom library with yellow caution tape. Photos from another classroom showed bookshelves covered with black sheets of paper and a sign that read, "You can't read any of the books on my shelves."

"How am I supposed to know what forty-four sets of parents find offensive?" one of the teachers quipped. "We've been told: 'The parents are our clients. We have to do what they want.' And this is what they want."

Ahead of the mandatory training, teachers began taking stock of which books might have to go under the new rules. One elementary school teacher said she would need to get rid of *Separate Is Never Equal*, a picture book about a Mexican American family's fight to end segregation in California in the 1940s. Another said she was setting aside *A Good Kind of Trouble*, which drew its name from a famous quotation by the late civil rights activist and congressman John Lewis, because the girl at the center of the story gets involved in the Black Lives Matter movement. A high school English teacher said it would take her months to review the hundreds of books in her classroom and that, based on the guidelines, she would likely need to get rid of many of them. She no longer felt safe keeping a copy of the young adult novel *The Hate U Give* by Angie Thomas, in part because it depicted racialized reactions to a police shooting, or any books by Nobel Prize–winning author Toni Morrison.

"One of the questions we're supposed to ask is 'Does the writer have a neutral stance on the topic?'" the teacher said. "Well, if you are Toni Morrison, how can you have a neutral stance toward racism? Now history is being depicted through this rose-colored lens, and all of this is creating a chilling effect that's going to hurt our students."

Hoping to quell the outrage, Carroll administrators sent out a flurry of mixed messages on the day of the training. One said that teachers would indeed be required to pull books from their shelves for review based on the content rubric. Another, from Superintendent Lane Ledbetter, claimed that no teachers had been instructed to remove books—a statement that was plainly contradicted by yet another email to teachers a few hours later advising them to close their classroom libraries until they'd had a chance to review all the books in them.

As the training session for elementary school educators got underway that Friday afternoon, teachers demanded clarity. What did administrators mean when they said they needed to "vet" all the books in their classroom? Did that mean reading them cover to cover? Or could they rely on *School Library Journal* reviews? What if they had a children's book that focused on a key figure in the civil rights movement? Were they supposed to set it aside?

"I think we're all just really scared," one teacher said during the training.

"Terrified," added another.

"I think you are terrified," Gina Peddy responded. "And I wish I could take that away. I do. I can't do that."

Peddy, a longtime Carroll employee, had been the district's executive director of curriculum and instruction for more than a decade. She'd earned a reputation as a thoughtful and compassionate educator. On this day, she'd been given the unenviable task of helping teachers understand their new marching orders. On the one hand, Peddy wanted to reassure them that everything was going to be OK.

"We hired you as professionals," she told the teachers. "We trust you with our children. So if you think the book is OK, then let's go with it. And whatever happens, we will fight it together."

But she'd also come to level with them.

"We are in the middle of a political mess," Peddy said. "And you are in the middle of a political mess." Switching back to reassurance mode, Peddy added, "And so, you're going to do what you do best, and that's to teach kids."

The teachers, however, weren't buying it. They kept bringing up the school board's vote that week to override the administration and reprimand Farah, who only a few months earlier had been named Johnson Elementary's teacher of the year. What made leadership think they could do a better job protecting any of them? After thirty minutes, Peddy seemed to acknowledge the conflicting messages. She stepped away and called one of Ledbetter's deputy superintendents to ask for clarity on what teachers should be doing. A few minutes later, she returned with some answers—and a suggestion.

"As you go through, just try to remember the concepts of thirty-nine seventy-nine," Peddy said, referring to Texas House Bill 3979, the state's anti-CRT law, "and make sure that . . ." Peddy paused briefly, then threw out a hypothetical. "If you have a book on the Holocaust," she continued, "that you have one that has an opposing—that has other perspectives."

"What?!" one teacher said, incredulous.

"How do you give opposing views on the Holocaust?" said another.

"Believe me," Peddy responded through the shocked commotion. "That's come up."

"So all of our historical fiction will have to go?"

Another teacher wondered aloud if she would have to pull down the children's classic *Number the Stars* by Lois Lowry, or other historical novels that tell the story of the Holocaust from the perspective of its victims. Was she supposed to find a story told from the perspective of Nazis? Or one from the point of view of Holocaust deniers? Should they also balance accounts about the horrors of slavery by adding books written from the perspective of white supremacists?

The teachers walked away from that meeting more confused than ever. Several of them huddled in a hallway afterward and tried to make sense of what they'd just heard. "I am offended as hell," one of them said in a hushed, emotional voice, "by somebody who says I should have an opposing view to the Holocaust in my library."

Enough was enough, a few of the teachers decided right then. They weren't going to go along with this. This wasn't what they'd signed up for when they'd come to work at one of the top public school districts in Texas.

It was time to take a stand.

That same evening, secretly recorded audio from the teacher training popped up on my phone in a message from a source who wished to remain anonymous. I was warming up frozen pizzas for my kids as I listened—and then relistened—to Peddy's advice to teachers, and was so distracted by what I was hearing, I ended up burning the pepperoni.

At that point, I'd spent a year covering the political fight over the ways schools addressed racism and history, trying along the way to understand where this movement was heading. Now here was a senior school administrator who, to comply with a vaguely worded state law—and under pressure from a new hyper-conservative school board—was directing teachers to provide opposing perspectives . . . on genocide?

For the next several days, Antonia and I worked to report out the story. We spoke to educators who were in the room to verify the authenticity of the secret recording, and to understand its full context. I contacted education experts, who said they were outraged to learn about Carroll's new book guidelines, and I called the Republican author of the state's anti–critical race theory law, who denied that his legislation required teachers to present both sides of any historical atrocity, be it slavery or the Holocaust. To bring the story to a national television audience, Antonia found two Carroll teachers who were willing to be interviewed on camera, with their faces silhouetted and voices altered to prevent them from being identifiable.

One of them was McGuirk.

The teacher had gone back and forth all week on whether she'd wanted to sit for the interview. Even with her identity obscured, she worried about the blowback if anyone found out. Her mother, a career educator, helped her decide. "Everyone needs to know what's happening to teachers," she'd told her daughter. "If you don't speak up, then who will?"

McGuirk felt as if she might throw up as she pulled up to the Dallas-area hotel where the interview was to be filmed. That might have been nerves, or because McGuirk was newly pregnant (she didn't know it yet). An NBC News producer let her in through a side door and led her to a private conference room where Antonia was waiting for her and the other Carroll teacher who'd agreed to talk. McGuirk's hands were shaking, but once in the interview chair, she felt a rush of confidence that she'd made the right choice.

"The district says that they have not told teachers to ban books," Antonia said in an exchange that made it into the piece that aired that week on *NBC Nightly News*. "What are you seeing?"

"That's a lie," McGuirk responded sharply. "It is a flat-out lie."

Later, in a moment that didn't make it into the final cut, McGuirk explained why she and other teachers were willing to put their jobs on the line to bring this situation to light. "We felt like no one was going to listen until a teacher spoke up."

People certainly listened.

On the afternoon of October 14, five months after Southlake Families PAC won control of Carroll's school board, an article by Antonia and me headlined "Southlake school leader tells teachers to balance Holocaust books with 'opposing' views" appeared online. That evening, the McGuirk interview aired on *Nightly News.* Very quickly, the story went international.

The words "Holocaust" and "Southlake" became the number-one trending topic on Twitter, and to some the story became a symbol of the overreach of the conservative movement against critical race theory. The story got picked up by nearly every major news outlet in the country, including the *New York Times*, *Washington Post,* and *USA Today,* and inspired condemnation from across the globe. The Auschwitz Memorial responded by posting tips for teaching about the Holocaust on social media and tagged Carroll's Twitter account. *The Daily Show with Trevor Noah* mocked the Holocaust comment on Comedy Central, along with the idea that teachers should have to present two sides to any issue. "I just wish that they had this policy when I was in school," Noah deadpanned. "Yeah, you say I have homework, Mr. Davenport, but I say that's some bullshit. Who's to say who's right?"

Jewish authors and descendants of Holocaust survivors went on cable news and wrote scathing editorials. Lois Lowry, the *Number the Stars* author, appeared on CNN the next morning, telling Jewish anchor John Berman that she'd initially chuckled when she heard the audio from the teacher training on NBC News. "It seemed silly," Lowry said. "But the more I thought about it, it wasn't laughable. It was ignorant. And ignorance so easily morphs into evil."

To the chagrin of teachers who'd spoken with us, including McGuirk, Gina Peddy was being bombarded with threatening emails and phone calls from strangers accusing her of anti-Semitism. A number of people in Southlake came forward to defend her, however, arguing that the administrator had misspoken while under pressure, and blaming the Southlake Families–controlled school board for putting her in an impossible situation. Ledbetter, Peddy's boss, issued a statement apologizing for the comments and acknowledging that "there are not two sides of the Holocaust." Southlake mayor John Huffman issued a statement of his own, saying that the city stood with its Jewish neighbors, and accusing Antonia and me of being on a mission to "tear down the hard-working, generous, wonderful families of our incredible city."

At a tense school board meeting four days after the story broke, residents came forward to express their outrage. Teachers teared up as they described feeling unsupported and under attack. For some, the episode had ripped open old wounds. A Jewish former student named Jake Berman gave testimony about anti-Semitic bullying that he'd endured at Carroll in the early 2000s.

"I received everything from jokes about my nose to gas chambers, all while studying for my bar mitzvah," Berman said. The bullying was so severe that, Berman said, he contemplated suicide, and his parents eventually pulled him out of the school system. He'd long ago moved on from Southlake, but he'd come back to speak that night because he believed Peddy's comment exposed the problem with the wave of new laws nationally limiting how teachers talked about racism and other controversial subjects.

"The facts are that there are not two sides of the Holocaust. The Nazis systematically killed millions of people. There are not two sides of slavery. White Europeans enslaved Black Africans in this country until June 19, 1865, a moment we're barely 150 years removed from. There are not two sides to Jim Crow, there are not two sides to racism. These are facts."

More than fifty people addressed the board, many of them demanding that the district take steps to repair its reputation. Others echoed Mayor Huffman's statement blaming the media: "NBC's obsessive reporter Mike Fiction-baugh is on a teacher witch hunt," Southlake Families PAC supporter Leo Del Calvo said. "He's trying to divide this community."

One of the final speakers of the night approached the microphone and drew in a deep breath. In a shaky voice, she opened by explaining that she'd known ever since she was a little girl that she wanted to be a teacher.

"Teaching is what I know I have been called to do," Christina McGuirk said as tears formed in her eyes. "I love your kids. They are my 'why?' My goal as their teacher is to make sure I provide an environment that allows them to learn, grow, and have fun daily—to provide a space where all students feel safe. And I wish some of you made me feel safe in return."

Days earlier, a group of a few dozen Carroll teachers had made plans to speak at the meeting and show the board that they stood in solidarity with Farah. McGuirk was one of only five who followed through. She told the board she "felt betrayed, unsupported, and quite scared" because of their vote to reprimand her friend and colleague.

"I love your children, and I want to continue being the best teacher I can for them. Please help rebuild my trust in Southlake. Thank you."

When McGuirk returned to her seat, she glanced at her phone. While she was speaking, she'd received a text from a parent and Southlake Families PAC donor who'd once had a child in her class. The woman also had spoken during public comments that night and was seated nearby.

Her message sent a rush of panic through McGuirk: "I am so disappointed you went to NBC."

The fourth-grade teacher took another deep breath, then closed the text without responding. That mom was probably just guessing. There's no way, McGuirk reassured herself, that she had evidence to back up her accusation.

It wasn't long before Southlake's Holocaust controversy faded from the national spotlight, but the issue at the center of it—a debate over library books—was just heating up. In the latest evolution of America's raging school board wars, parents across the country started bombarding districts with complaints about books that they claimed indoctrinated children with anti-American views on racism. Increasingly, too, the focus was on books some parents felt exposed children to inappropriate content dealing with gender identity and sexuality.

Soon suburban parents were repeating a new set of talking points at board meetings. Librarians who stocked shelves with children's books depicting LGBTQ characters—especially titles marketed to teenagers that included descriptions of sex—were accused of pushing "pornography" on children and of sexually "grooming" them. Many of the books under fire were newer titles, purchased by school librarians in recent years as part of a nationwide movement to diversify the content available to public school children—a shift inspired in part by research showing that children are more likely to become avid readers when they have access to books that reflect their identities and experiences.

The fight had gotten particularly heated in Texas, where Republican state officials, including Governor Greg Abbott, went so far as to call for criminal charges against any school staff member who provided children with access to young adult novels that contained explicit descriptions of sex. Separately, state representative Matt Krause, a Republican from Tarrant County, made a list of 850 titles dealing with racism or sexuality that he said might "make students feel discomfort," therefore violating the state's anti-CRT law, and demanded that Texas school districts investigate whether the books were in their libraries.

After parent activists learned that they could formally challenge school library content, they flooded districts with written requests to ban certain books. A mom in Katy, Texas, asked her child's school to remove a children's biography of Michelle Obama, arguing that it promoted "reverse racism" against white people. A parent in the Dallas suburb of Prosper wanted the school district to ban a children's picture book about the life of Black Olympian Wilma Rudolph, because it mentioned racism that Rudolph faced growing up in Tennessee in the 1940s. In the affluent Eanes Independent School District in Austin, a parent proposed replacing four books about racism, including Ibram X. Kendi's *How to Be an Antiracist*, with copies of the Bible.

Censorship movements tend to come in waves. In the early 2000s, a conservative backlash to the Harry Potter book series, which some Christian leaders condemned as a satanic depiction of witchcraft, fueled a surge of book ban attempts nationally. But the scale of the latest protest was likely without precedent. The free speech advocacy group PEN America documented more than 2,532 instances of individual books being banned from schools nationally between July 2021 and June 2022.

Nearly half of the removed titles featured LGBTQ characters or themes; one in five directly addressed issues of race or racism. Unsurprisingly, Texas topped PEN America's list, accounting for nearly a third of the bans.

Mary Ellen Cuzela, a mother in Katy, a sprawling and booming suburb outside Houston, had never thought much about what library books her kids might have access to at school before that fall. But in September, she'd heard then candidate Glenn Youngkin mention a Virginia school district's fight over "sexually explicit material in the library" during his campaign for governor. Curious, Cuzela searched the Katy Independent School District's catalog and was surprised to find that one of the books at the center of the Virginia fight, *Lawn Boy* by Jonathan Evison, was available at her children's high school.

Cuzela picked up a copy from the public library and "was absolutely amazed" by what she read. The book, which traces the story of a Mexican American character's journey to understanding his own sexuality and ethnic identity, was "filled with vulgarity," Cuzela said, including dozens of four-letter words and explicit sexual references, such as a mention of oral sex between fourth-grade boys during a church youth group meeting.

"I don't care whether you're straight, gay, transgender, gender fluid, any race," she said. "That book had it all and was degrading for all kinds of people."

Cuzela soon discovered that several other young adult books that had been targeted in Virginia and other Texas districts were available at Katy. She shared her findings with some "like-minded parents," and together they set out to get administrators to do something about it. The school system, a diverse district of nearly 85,000 students—ten times the size of Carroll—had already made national headlines that fall when administrators temporarily removed copies of *New Kid* and *Class Act* by Jerry Craft from school libraries after a white mother complained that the graphic novels, about Black seventh graders at a mostly white school, would indoctrinate students of color with a "victim mentality" and make some kids feel guilty for being white.

But Cuzela said she and her friends were having a hard time getting

Katy administrators to take their concerns about sexually explicit books seriously. Although the district was putting in place new controls to allow parents to track which books their children checked out of school libraries, Cuzela and her supporters believed the change was insufficient. So, they hatched a plan—one that drew inspiration from a strategy being deployed at school board meetings all over the country that fall. Cuzela and five other moms showed up at a Katy board meeting with a stack of books, and one by one, they took turns reading passages during public comments.

Cuzela read an excerpt that included the word "pussy" from *Me and Earl and the Dying Girl* by Jesse Andrews, a novel later adapted as a film that chronicles the relationship between a teen boy and a girl with leukemia as they navigate her illness amid all the usual awkwardness that comes with being high schoolers. Another mother read a sexually explicit passage from *All Boys Aren't Blue,* a coming-of-age memoir in the form of essays by queer Black author George M. Johnson covering topics like family, toxic masculinity, gender identity, and consent. The book includes brief passages describing Johnson's first sexual relationships, as well as sexual abuse he suffered—all presented with the aim of educating queer teens and their allies. "I didn't want to spend my money on this filth," the Katy mom told the school board, after stumbling over the phrase "oral sex."

"Why are we sexualizing our precious children?" another mother asked the board, after reading a passage about two teens kissing from *The Breakaways* by Cathy G. Johnson, a graphic novel featuring a transgender middle schooler that includes no sexually explicit language. "Why are our libraries filled with pornography?"

The audience, packed with parents and community members who shared the mother's concerns, applauded as she returned to her seat. Within days, Katy administrators pulled most of these books off shelves and later launched reviews of dozens of others. Cuzela hoped administrators would go further. Although she didn't believe most librarians were knowingly stocking shelves with "pornographic material," she said she agreed with Abbott's call for criminal charges against any who did. It did not appear to matter that none of the books in question met the legal definition of pornography, which draws a distinction between literary descriptions of sex and content created for the explicit purpose of sexual stimulation. For truly pornographic content, book ban opponents noted, teens likely would have been searching the internet, not their high school libraries.

Without fail, parents leading this new phase of school board activism reported that they were merely fighting to shield their children from graphic sexual content that violated their family's values. But many parents and activists were conflating references to gender identity and sexual orientation with sex and pornography. To some it seemed any depictions of LGBTQ people—an illustration showing a child with two moms, for example, or a children's book about a pair of male penguins raising a chick—were viewed as inherently sexual. The phrase "OK, groomer" was fast becoming a popular right-wing insult on social media, used as a weapon against anyone who defended classroom discussions and books dealing with gender identity or sexual orientation. Teachers and librarians who argued that it was important to allow children access to a wide range of age-appropriate books, including those depicting LGBTQ characters, were not regarded as well-intentioned educators with whom some parents happened to disagree; they were accused of being child predators.

I later learned firsthand the power of such a loaded accusation. I'd written a story about the growing campaign to ban certain library books in Katy, which included an interview with a seventeen-year-old student whose parents were not accepting of her LGBTQ identity. "As I've struggled with my own identity as a queer person, it's been really, really important to me that I have access to these books," the student told me. "You should be able to see yourself reflected on the page." The girl's school library had been one of the few places where she felt free to be herself. Now that space was under attack.

A day after the article was published, my phone started blowing up with calls and text messages. A few Katy moms, it turned out, had read the piece and were deeply troubled that I'd spoken to a student about her sexual orientation. In emails, text messages, and voicemails, the mothers accused me of being a sexual predator.

"Speaking to a child this way is one of the initial steps taken when adults groom minors," one of the moms texted me. "We feel this is grounds to file a police report."

I don't know if the moms ever followed through with their threat, and it didn't really matter. The baseless allegation had done its damage. I felt sick all day afterward and began to question whether it was worth continuing to report on these stories.

If the teachers who'd blown the whistle on Carroll's new book guidelines were hoping that coverage of the administrator's Holocaust comment would inspire conservatives in town to change course, they were likely disappointed. Two weeks after the controversy, in a special election to replace the CCAP-supporting school board member Dave Almand, another Southlake Families PAC–backed candidate, a white father of three named Andrew Yeager, won by another landslide margin, cementing the new majority.

Among the board's first actions afterward was to settle Kristin Garcia's PAC-funded civil lawsuit. Under the terms of the agreement, the district would formally disband the long-dormant District Diversity Council, officially reject the Cultural Competence Action Plan, and repay Garcia's six-figure legal fees—with money from a risk management fund that ultimately would go back into the coffers of Southlake Families PAC. The board also agreed to embed language from the state's anti–critical race theory law in the district's employee code of conduct, including a line prohibiting teaching students that "slavery and racism are anything other than deviations" from America's true founding ideals. (This was one area, it seemed, where conservatives did not want educators to present students with multiple perspectives.)

The fear of being on the wrong end of a parent's complaint had several educators rethinking their futures at the district. Sarah Chase, a longtime librarian at Carroll Senior High School, decided to retire early, in the middle of the school year, after being pressured to remove the book *Beyond Magenta: Transgender Teens Speak Out* from her library. A Southlake Families donor had copied school board member Hannah Smith on a message complaining about the book: "There is extreme sexual content in that book that isn't even appropriate for me to put in an email." Under a school board policy meant to prevent censorship, the parent should have been asked to file a formal challenge. A committee of school employees and community volunteers should have reviewed the book in its entirety and determined whether it was appropriate, keeping in mind that, according to district policy, a parent's ability to control what students can read "extends only to his or her own child." But none of that happened. Instead, fearing blowback, Chase agreed to pull the book. She immediately regretted her decision to give in rather than fight. It made her realize she no longer loved the job that had been her life's passion.

"I'm no saint," the fifty-five-year-old Chase said of her decision to quit. "I got out because I was afraid to stand up to the attacks. I didn't want to get caught in somebody's snare. Who wants to be called a pornographer? Who wants to be accused of being a pedophile or reported to the police for putting a book in a kid's hand?"

That winter, Carroll's board of trustees embarked on a top-to-bottom reexamination of district policy. They put together volunteer committees to study changes to the curriculum and the student code of conduct and packed the groups with parents who'd donated to Southlake Families PAC. Superintendent Lane Ledbetter, who'd been brought on with a mission to heal the town's political divide, now dutifully carried out the new board majority's directives. When asked after Southlake Families PAC's initial election triumph whether he believed racism was even a problem in need of addressing in Southlake, Ledbetter declined to answer.

The new school board did briefly consider hiring a consultant to train teachers on diversity and inclusion. Hannah Smith, who would soon be appointed board vice president alongside Cam Bryan as president, had helped find a possible presenter. She was a Black woman and former stand-up comedian named Karith Foster who'd gone on Fox News that year to denounce critical race theory, and whose "INversity" program promised to "take the 'division' out of diversity training" by focusing on what people "have IN common" and using "INtentional language" to make conversations more "INclusive." Smith told a reporter that she'd pushed for the program "because I thought, 'Well, if we're going to say no to [the CCAP], we have to have an alternative.' Because there has to be some training, I think, to help our teachers and our students understand what's involved with our student code of conduct, what it prohibits, and how they can be more educated on what they can and cannot do." The idea was later discarded, however, after the district fielded complaints from liberal parents who were turned off by Foster's comments about critical race theory, and from conservative parents who argued that INversity sounded too much like any other diversity program.

In the end, the controversy over library books and Peddy's Holocaust remarks inspired just one concrete policy change at Carroll. It was not one the whistleblower teachers had hoped for: The school board voted that winter to prohibit employees from secretly recording district business. Peddy's instruction wasn't the problem in need of solving, it seemed; the publication of it was.

To parents like Angela Jones, who'd spent more than three years fighting to implement policies that they believed would make Carroll more inclusive and welcoming for students of color and LGBTQ kids, there now appeared to be no chance of that happening.

But Jones insisted she wasn't giving up.

"Unfortunately, it's going to take outside forces to make change," she told me on the night of Yeager's election to the board. "Southlake had opportunities to do it on its own, but the community decided not to do that."

Ten days later, Jones's hope came into focus. On November 12, 2021, three letters arrived at Carroll's administrative offices. The U.S. Department of Education had gotten some complaints about discrimination against Black and LGBTQ students in the schools. And now—more than three years after a viral video triggered Southlake's failed reckoning over race, identity and belonging—the federal government was investigating alleged civil rights violations at the Carroll Independent School District.

Part III

SO GOES AMERICA

11

Christianity Will Have Power

BY EARLY 2022, MANY fighters on the front line of America's school board wars had moved beyond the battle against critical race theory, having identified a new foe that some on the right were pitching as an even bigger danger to schoolchildren: the growing embrace of LGBTQ identities.

Chris Rufo, the activist who'd helped make CRT a household phrase a year earlier, saw big potential to motivate voters, telling the *New York Times* that spring that "the reservoir of sentiment on the sexuality issue is deeper and more explosive than the sentiment on the race issues."

Later, he took that message onto *Tucker Carlson Tonight,* warning millions of Fox News viewers that a California school district was "training kids as young as kindergarten to experiment with sexual identities, such as transgender, queer, pansexual, gender fluid," and that this trend was sweeping the country. The school training documents that served as the basis for Rufo's claims, in fact, said nothing about training children to experiment with different genders or sexualities, but instead advised teachers to ask students which pronouns they wanted to use in class and listed a glossary of LGBTQ terms to help educators understand and support all children.

Nevertheless, Carlson expressed shocked outrage and said it seemed public schools were working to "destroy human civilization." Carlson then suggested that teachers who talked to children about gender or sexual orientation should face prison time, or vigilante violence. "I mean, up until recently the rule was you troll my minor children about their sex life and you're going to get hurt," Carlson said. "I think that should be the rule still."

Whether he realized it or not, Rufo's hunch about the motivational power of anti-LGBTQ animus—particularly when focused on perceived threats to children—was supported by decades of historical precedent. And much of the pent-up sentiment he now hoped to tap into was inextricably entangled with a half-century-old campaign to exalt God in America's public schools.

The seeds of the movement were planted on June 25, 1962, when the U.S. Supreme Court issued a landmark decision banning the encouragement of prayer in public schools. Prior to the court's 6–1 ruling in *Engel v. Vitale*, and a related ruling banning compulsory scripture reading the following year, children across the country often began each school day by reciting a Christian prayer and reading aloud from the Bible. To some conservative Christians, the court's decision to, as they put it, "take God out of schools" was the original sin that triggered what they viewed as this country's moral decline in the years that followed—a period that coincided with the legalization of abortion, anti-war demonstrations, forced racial integration, and the women's empowerment movement.

This was the unofficial start of what we now refer to as America's religious right. But that fledgling alliance of white evangelical pastors and segregationist politicians did not blossom into a full-fledged national coalition until after 1977, when Anita Bryant—a famed singer, beauty queen, and spokeswoman for Florida orange juice—connected outrage over the court's prayer decision with her vitriolic campaign to block gay people from working inside schools.

More than four decades before parents nationwide started packing school board meetings to protest library books depicting LGBTQ characters, Bryant had waged a crusade against an ordinance that would have prohibited employers in Miami from denying jobs to people based on their sexual orientation. Above all else, Bryant and her supporters were outraged at the prospect that private Christian schools like the one Bryant's children attended could be forced to hire gay and lesbian teachers, who they uniformly mis-portrayed as child predators. "As a mother," Bryant said, "I know that homosexuals cannot biologically reproduce; therefore, they must recruit our children."

Playing to those fears, Bryant, an evangelical Christian, formed an organization called Save Our Children, always framing her anti-gay bigotry as an act of love: "I know that there is hope for the homosexuals," Bryant told a reporter. "If they're willing to turn from sin they can be ex-homosexuals, the same as there can be an ex-murderer, an ex-thief or an ex-anybody."

After a monthslong media blitz, which included newspaper advertisements and television commercials falsely linking homosexuality with pedophilia, Save Our Children succeeded in defeating the Miami ordinance in a special referendum, with local voters rejecting it by a 2–1 margin. "All America and all the world will hear what the people have said," Bryant told reporters afterward, laying out plans to take her organization national. Her activism made her into an overnight star on the right, helped give rise to Jerry Falwell's Moral Majority, and stoked anti-gay resentment across the country. When a gay man was viciously stabbed to death in San Francisco two weeks after the Miami vote, witnesses told police that one of the attackers had been yelling, "Here's one for Anita!"

For her follow-up act, Bryant pledged to take on a cause that she believed would address the root of America's turn toward depravity: "putting prayer back in school."

But in the decades that followed, Bryant and her allies repeatedly failed to achieve that goal. In case after case, courts affirmed that school-sponsored prayer was prohibited under the establishment clause of the First Amendment, which Thomas Jefferson had famously called "a wall of separation" between church and state.

In one case from 1992, William Pritchard, then a seventeen-year-old senior at Carroll High School in Southlake, filed a lawsuit against his school district over its thirty-year tradition of hosting a Christian prayer at the start of Dragon football pep rallies. The case stirred a hornet's nest of resentment in Southlake, which at the time was still 97 percent white and overwhelmingly Christian. A Southlake mother named

Linda Ahlers spearheaded a counterprotest, quickly collecting 1,500 signatures in a town of eight thousand. "This country is out of control," Ahlers told a reporter. "We hand out condoms to teach our children how to have sex, but we can't let our children pray."

In the end, the Carroll school board settled the case by agreeing to adopt policies to ensure that no students would feel pressured to participate in religious activities at school. The case was part of a string of similar court battles limiting the role of religion in public schools. Not all believers were dismayed by these restrictions: Many Christians, Muslims, and Jews embraced the precedent, which they believed prevented the government from usurping parents' authority to instill religious values in children. Students were still free to worship or pray as they saw fit; they just couldn't be compelled or pressured to do so at school.

The anti-LGBTQ movement Bryant helped birth also appeared to sputter out in the ensuing decades, as state after state passed laws prohibiting discrimination based on sexual orientation. Then, in June 2015, the Supreme Court appeared to deliver the movement's death knell, with another ruling that shocked the conscience of evangelical Christians. With the stroke of a pen, the 5–4 ruling in *Obergefell v. Hodges* legalized same-sex marriage in all fifty states.

It seemed to many that the debates over school prayer and LGBTQ rights had been settled, once and for all.

Seven months after *Obergefell*, in January 2016, Donald Trump gave a speech that most people remember for the wrong reason.

Speaking at a small Christian college in Iowa, Trump—still seen by some at the time as a long shot for the Republican nomination—famously bragged that he could "stand in the middle of Fifth Avenue and shoot somebody" and not lose any supporters. But there was another, more significant message embedded in his speech that day. One that didn't make as many splashy headlines.

Standing in front of the crowd of evangelical supporters, Trump warned that Christianity was "under tremendous siege" in America, and that he alone would put a stop to the persecution. Once he was elected, he promised, people would be saying "Merry Christmas" again.

And, he added, "Christianity will have power."

Most people might not have been paying close attention when Trump uttered that line in early 2016, but many prominent evangelicals were. And they believed him. In the years that followed, Trump's rise to the White House—and his fight to stay in office after losing his reelection—breathed fresh life into the flickering flames of the movement that began in 1962.

Now, with a new enemy in their crosshairs—what Chris Rufo and others had begun calling "woke gender ideology"—conservative activists were about to pour gasoline on the fire and watch it spread.

From the stage of a conference center in Dallas in late 2021, the evangelical author and self-styled historian David Barton invoked the recent school board elections in Southlake as reason for renewed hope in America. Barton, the founder of the conservative Christian advocacy group WallBuilders, was speaking at the ProFamily Legislators Conference, a national gathering and strategy session of state lawmakers aligned with the newly empowered religious right.

Southlake's example and the groundswell of interest in school board politics, Barton believed, signaled a new opportunity for evangelicals. "I think really good things are happening in the nation," he told lawmakers at the conference.

For more than three decades, Barton—who considered Trump one of the five greatest presidents in U.S. history—had traveled the country, speaking at churches and in front of legislatures and on Christian television programs, spreading a revisionist version of United States history. In Barton's rendering, America was founded, not as the world's first secular republic, but as an explicitly Christian nation. The separation of church and state was a lie cooked up by progressives based on a misreading of Thomas Jefferson. Any laws and court rulings limiting the influence of religion in schools and government were an affront to America and an affront to God.

Barton also viewed LGBTQ people with extreme contempt. After touring the site of Nazi atrocities in Poland, he'd remarked that the same evil spirit that was responsible for the Holocaust was now at work advancing the "homosexual lifestyle."

Along the way, he'd become "the most celebrated and broadly influential Christian nationalist historian in America," journalist Katherine Stewart wrote in her book, *The Power Worshipers*, which documented an expansive network of activists, political action committees, and far-right megadonors working behind the scenes to impose biblical values in government. According to Stewart, Barton's writings were composed mostly of "mash-up quotes wrenched out of context and dragooned into service of the Christian Nation myth." The History News Network named Barton's book, *The Jefferson Lies*, "the least credible history book in print." Christian scholars and historians roundly panned his writings.

Despite the errors and omissions, Barton's pseudo-history provided the philosophical underpinnings for the Christian right's relentless, decades-long campaign to place Jesus at the center of public life. On that front, Barton and his allies had been quietly gaining ground. By 2021, a majority of Republican voters reported embracing core tenants of Christian nationalism—the belief that America is a Christian nation and should by governed by biblical law. Now the fights over critical race theory and LGBTQ inclusion had opened a path for Barton to push his message further into the mainstream.

From the stage in Dallas that November, he rattled off statistics showing that nearly 40 percent of young people identified as LGBTQ, a trend that he blamed on the godlessness of public education. "This is the stuff we've been teaching in the culture and in the schools for a long time," Barton said. "And parents are just now waking up."

He then laid out his vision for what public schools should look like in America, as inspired by the writings of the founding father Benjamin Rush. "The first purpose of public schools is to teach students to love and serve God," Barton told the audience. "The second purpose of public schools is to teach students to love and serve their country. And the third purpose of public schools is to teach students to love and serve their family."

That's the way the Framers intended it, Barton declared. Now it was up to Christians to make it a reality.

A few months later, a white homeschooling mother of nine named Monica Brown signed up to speak at a school board meeting in Granbury, Texas, about seventy miles southwest of Southlake. Brown, who for years had kept copies of David Barton's books on her shelves at home, wore a pink button-up blouse with her hair pulled back in a bun.

"'Repentance' is the word that's on my heart," Brown told the board. She then called on the school district to reform its ways.

Two weeks earlier, Brown and another Granbury mother had filed a police report alleging that the school district was making pornography available to minors. Although the women provided no evidence to back up that explosive claim—none of the literature available to teens at Granbury met the legal definition of pornography—the case was quickly picked up by Scott London, a Hood County deputy constable who had ties to the far-right Oath Keepers militia. Four days later, London visited Granbury High School to investigate the allegation—the start of a monthslong criminal probe that seemed to go nowhere but terrified librarians all the same.

Moving forward, Brown now told the school board, a local Christian pastor, rather than the librarians she'd sought to prosecute, should decide which books were allowed on public school shelves. "He would never steer you wrong, and he will put you in a safety zone with your books," Brown said.

The idea of inviting a religious leader to decide what students can read at school represented a radical departure from the long-held philosophy of nonsectarian public education in America. But Brown clearly wasn't the only Granbury resident who endorsed the proposal. As she walked away from the lectern that evening, the audience showered her with rapturous applause.

In public, Brown denied specifically targeting LGBTQ books. At one school board meeting, she said her only objective was to protect children from sexually explicit content—gay, straight, or otherwise. "There's nothing about LGBTQ involved in this," she said. "There are

LGBTQ books that are sexually explicit, yes. They are wrong, too. If they are between men and men, women and women, cats and women, dogs and women, whatever, that is not appropriate educational content."

That claim, however, didn't square with many of the books that she flagged for removal at Granbury. Several of the titles on her list featured LGBTQ storylines but contained no sexually explicit content. Of the nearly eighty library books Brown and her supporters wanted removed, three out of five featured LGBTQ characters or themes. In one instance, Brown criticized a biography of notable women in part because it included the story of Christine Jorgensen, a trans woman who made national headlines in the 1950s for speaking openly about her gender-confirmation surgery. Brown suggested replacing that book with a Christian biography series about girls and women who used their talents to serve God—"biographies of truly great Americans," she wrote.

Brown's social media posts also betrayed her anti-LGBTQ beliefs. In the years after the U.S. Supreme Court legalized same-sex marriage in 2015, Brown posted frequently about the "dangerous" gay agenda that she believed was on the march across mainstream American society. She warned in posts that Disney was secretly pushing LGBTQ lifestyles on children in movies such as *Toy Story 4*, and shared a link to a video alleging that pop star Katy Perry was conspiring with satanic forces to convince teens to embrace homosexuality.

Until now, she'd mostly vented these views in private. The nationwide backlash against CRT and LGBTQ inclusion had given fundamentalist moms like her new confidence—and a platform.

(Later, amid her fiery public campaign, Brown's adult son, Weston, came forward to reveal that his mother had cut him out of her life after he'd come out as gay five years earlier, leading Brown's opponents to believe that her school board activism on behalf of district students might have been motivated in part by her opposition to her own child's path.)

As other evangelical parents rallied to Brown's side, Granbury school board meetings began to take on a distinctly religious tone.

Quoting Jesus, one woman issued a warning to any school officials who refused to remove sinful content from district libraries: "If anyone causes one of these little ones who believe in me to sin, it would be better for him to have a large millstone hung around your neck, and dropped to the bottom of the sea."

Just like Southlake a year earlier, Brown's campaign in Granbury was becoming a national symbol of the far-right political movement overtaking school board politics in 2022. That spring, a secret recording surfaced of the district's superintendent, Jeremy Glenn. Under pressure from parents like Brown and conservative members of the school board, Glenn had directed librarians to remove books on LGBTQ identities, seeming to undercut any claim that the removals were focused only on sexually explicit content.

"And I'm going to take it a step further with you, and you can disagree if you want," Glenn told the librarians. "There are two genders. There's male and there's female. And I acknowledge that there are men that think they are women and there are women who think they are men. Again, I don't have any issues with what people want to believe, but there's no place for it in our libraries."

In essence, Glenn appeared to adopt the same position as the boys who'd told Mia Mariani that her gender identity was a mental illness, but without the profane speech. He didn't believe in the legitimacy of transgender identities, and therefore, no books on that subject should be available to the 7,500 students who attended Granbury. Glenn had previously and very publicly signaled his views on LGBTQ inclusion in a book of Christian devotionals he coauthored, which included a warning that those pushing for broader acceptance of homosexuality were doing so through the indoctrination of children in schools, as "was done by Hitler when he took over Germany."

"I'm cutting to the chase," Glenn further instructed the librarians. "It's the transgender, LGBTQ, and the sex—sexuality—in books. That's what the governor has said that he will prosecute people for, and that's what we're pulling out." (On the contrary, Greg Abbott's letter calling for criminal investigations referred only to "pornography or obscene content" and made no mention of LGBTQ people.)

After Glenn's comments were leaked, the Texas chapter of the American Civil Liberties Union filed a complaint against the Granbury school district with the U.S. Department of Education's Office for Civil Rights, which was responsible for enforcing federal anti-discrimination laws in public schools. Glenn's remarks and the district's subsequent decision to remove dozens of library books had fostered a "pervasively hostile" environment for LGBTQ students, the ACLU wrote in its complaint. "These comments, combined with the book removals, really send a message to LGBTQ students in the districts that, 'You don't belong here. Your existence is shameful. It should be censored,'" one of the ACLU lawyers said.

This wasn't just about demanding acceptance for the sake of it. The nationwide backlash against queer representation in schools coincided with a surge in mental health struggles among LGBTQ students. According to one national survey released that spring, nearly half of all LGBTQ youth reported seriously considering suicide in the previous year, and nearly one in five transgender and nonbinary young people reported that they had attempted to kill themselves.

The ACLU's legal argument was emblematic of a new strategy that was being embraced by civil rights activist groups nationwide that year as they sought to counter conservative gains on school boards. If local leaders refused to take concrete steps to protect students from discrimination, groups like the ACLU hoped they could get the federal government to step in.

Southlake had by then already become the poster child for this new strategy.

After the Office for Civil Rights opened three civil rights investigations at Carroll in November 2021, the NAACP Legal Defense and Educational Fund, a national civil rights law firm based in New York, got involved, filing an amended complaint with the education department on behalf of the Southlake Anti-Racism Coalition and four students who said they'd experienced harassment at Carroll. Afterward, the Department of Education opened two additional civil rights investigations concerning the Carroll school district, bringing the total to five.

NAACP lawyers detailed the allegations at Carroll in a summary of its complaint. One Black high school student, the youngest child of Angela Jones, reported being called the N-word and a "porch monkey" nearly every year at Carroll. Reporting the abuse, he said, had led to retaliation from peers. Another student described suffering such severe racial and anti-LGBTQ harassment that their parents eventually pulled them out of the district. A third student said he was bullied relentlessly over his sexual orientation, including physical violence that left welts on his legs, the NAACP said. The student expressed a desire to kill himself before withdrawing from the district. The fourth student in the NAACP's complaint was Mia Mariani, the queer, nonbinary student who'd reported vulgar harassment from classmates, only to be told by her principal that the boys were merely trying to have a debate.

Unsatisfied with the school's response, Mia's parents had now gotten the federal government involved. They realized the investigations likely wouldn't be resolved until months or even years after Mia had graduated from Carroll. "At this point, it was about making sure that no other students would have to go through the abuse that my daughter endured," Elio Mariani said.

News of the civil rights investigations raised alarm among conservatives in Southlake. With the federal agency refusing to comment beyond confirming that the investigations existed, some local officials rushed to fill in the gaps with conspiracy theories.

Southlake mayor John Huffman issued a statement suggesting that the federal investigations might have been launched to retaliate against the city for electing school board members who opposed the diversity plan. Southlake Families PAC sent an email to supporters floating the possibility that the civil rights investigation was being steered by the Department of Justice—a federal agency separate from the Department of Education—as part of a broader plot to treat conservative parents as domestic terrorists. And U.S. representative Beth Van Duyne, a Republican whose district included Southlake, responded by writing a letter to Secretary of Education Miguel Cardona, cosigned by several GOP lawmakers including senators Ted Cruz and John Cornyn of Texas, expressing fears that the Biden administration was "weaponizing federal resources to intimidate parents."

There was no evidence that the investigations at Carroll had been opened in response to Southlake's local elections or as part of a liberal plot against parents. But, as with many conspiracy theories, there was a nugget of truth buried under the hyperbole. In fact, if the federal probes uncovered systemic problems at Carroll, the agency would have the power to require the school district to implement some of the same types of diversity and inclusion training programs that Southlake voters had rejected in a pair of landslide elections. And if the district refused? The Department of Education could pull federal funding—which accounts for about 2 percent of the district's budget—and refer the matter to the DOJ.

Some parents were counting on it.

"The only way we're going to get any change in here is if the Department of Education comes in and does something," said Jennifer Hough, one of the moms who'd lobbied for the diversity plan. "Our kids are going to keep suffering unless they come in and say, 'Y'all have to do something to protect these kids.'"

The investigations had, in effect, put Southlake and its conservative school board on a collision course with the federal government, and with history. The civil rights laws the agency was enforcing—Title VI of the Civil Rights Act of 1964 and Title IX of the Education Amendments of 1972—had been adopted in the 1960s and '70s as a result of that era's struggle for racial justice and women's rights, around the same time that the religious right was beginning its campaign to reverse these societal changes.

A half century later, the investigations at Carroll would test the department's power and willingness to enforce those landmark civil rights protections, even if it meant overturning the wishes of local voters in Southlake and elsewhere who demanded that conversations about racism, gender, and sexuality be kept out of schools.

In total, the Office for Civil Rights fielded a record nineteen thousand discrimination complaints during the fiscal year that ran from October 2021 to September 2022—more than double the total from the previous year. The surge likely reflected a buildup of grievances resulting from the worst public health crisis in a century and the most divisive political climate in decades, Catherine Lhamon, the education department's assistant secretary for civil rights, told the *New York Times*. "The scope and volume of harm that we're asking our babies to navigate is astronomical," Lhamon said.

That fall, yet another North Texas school district landed in the agency's crosshairs. Responding to the ACLU's complaint, the Office for Civil Rights opened an investigation into the Granbury Independent School District—one of the first cases explicitly tied to the nationwide movement to ban library books about gender and sexuality.

Lou Whiting, a nonbinary senior at Granbury High School who'd helped organize student protests in response to the book removals, cried when they learned that the federal government was investigating.

"It's just really good," Whiting said, "to hear that there are people who are listening to us and actually doing something about it."

12

Seven Mountains

INSIDE THE CROWDED HOTEL convention hall, a mustachioed man onstage was in the middle of giving a speech that sounded as if it might have been ripped from the script of a dystopian Hollywood blockbuster. "Over fifty-four countries have now been taken by the machines," he said, causing some in the audience to gasp. "Venezuela, Australia—they're gone."

It was August 5, 2022. Die-hard supporters of America's far right had converged on Dallas for the latest gathering of the Conservative Political Action Conference, or CPAC. At the moment, attendees at the Hilton Anatole conference center were listening with rapt attention to Mike Lindell, the CEO of My Pillow and an ascendant figure in far-right Republican politics best known for spreading bizarre and easily debunked claims about rigged voting machines. "You don't get to vote out the machines once they're there," Lindell said, as a woman seated near me in the audience scribbled down notes. "Once they're there, you don't get your country back."

As Lindell was warning the CPAC faithful about what would happen should patriots like them fail to reinstall Trump as president—"If the lights go out here, they go out everywhere"—other attendees browsed rows of promotional booths in the adjacent convention space. One table was selling hats emblazoned with the words "Trump Won," "Take America Back: 2024," and "Let's Go Brandon"—a coded phrase that meant "Fuck Joe Biden." At another table, women lined up to purchase sparkling silver heels with "Trump" spelled out in gold sequins on the back. A few booths down, attendees were invited to write notes of encouragement to imprisoned January 6 rioters.

A stroll through the convention space revealed the extent to which the classroom wars over race and identity had become a core pillar of the conservative movement—right up there with Trump, God, and guns. One booth was lined with illustrated children's books, but not the sort you'd find in most public libraries. There was a book called *More Than Spots & Stripes*, about a dispute between striped and spotted cheetahs, which was meant to teach children as young as four about the "harmfulness of critical race theory." Another, titled *Elephants Are Not Birds*, told the story of a young elephant who was tricked by a vulture named Culture into believing that he could fly simply by identifying as a bird—an allegory about gender identity. The publisher of these titles, Brave Books, had been founded just a year earlier with the goal of countering the spread of "harmful progressive influences" in schools.

The official theme of that year's CPAC was "Awake, Not Woke." In addition to panels about rigged elections and the persecution of Christians and Capitol rioters alike, speaker after speaker focused their comments on liberal indoctrination. Senator Ted Cruz drew a standing ovation when he declared, just in case anyone was wondering, "My pronouns are 'Kiss my ass!'" After a panel featuring a speaker who suggested that the U.S. government may have planned the COVID pandemic for the purpose of thinning the world's population with phony vaccines, the CPAC announcer introduced the start of a session titled "Faith Over Fascism," which was focused on defeating the spread of "wokeism" in schools.

"They're banning Dr. Seuss. They're banning *Little House on the Prairie*. And they're giving kids books that would make the citizens of Sodom and Gomorrah blush," the moderator said, painting liberal parents as censorious at a time when conservatives nationally were challenging library books by the hundreds.

"Well, that's really true," replied Carroll school board vice president Hannah Smith, now a regular on the CPAC stage. Smith encouraged those gathered in the audience—many of whom had applauded moments earlier in response to a false claim about COVID vaccines killing hundreds of thousands of people—to volunteer in their children's schools and to serve on committees charged with shaping curriculum. That way, Smith said, they could "be the eyes and ears of what's going on on the ground" and "raise the red flag" if they observe a lesson or book that they found troubling.

"The main concern that I have with critical race theory is that it really turns on the head the American fundamental premise of color blindness before the law," Smith said. "Critical race theory really attempts to look at color to make people equal, but the American dream and the American promise is that we don't look at color, and everyone is already equal."

Another Carroll trustee, Andrew Yeager, one of several Dallas-area school board members in attendance that weekend, applauded from the audience.

The clearest symbol, however, of the right's aggressive foray into local school politics—and the ways in which that fight had now become entwined with a resurgence of Christian nationalism—could be found, not on the CPAC stage, but at one of the promotional booths.

A huge banner screamed in bold letters "Patriot Mobile: America's ONLY Christian Conservative Wireless Provider." And standing beneath it, greeting convention-goers, was the person who'd helped make that company into a leader in the fight to install conservatives on school boards: Southlake Families PAC cofounder Leigh Wambsganss.

More than six years earlier, in 2016, the owners of a fledgling wireless provider called Eos Mobile filed paperwork to rebrand the company under a new name: Patriot Mobile. The company's CEO at the time, a Southlake resident named Brandon Moore, announced the change in a press release that January. "We are excited to adopt a name that will resonate with our customer base. Patriotism is part of our American DNA, and it only makes sense to use a name that our conservative customers can relate to and embrace."

The business plan was straightforward: Patriot Mobile—which rented space on T-Mobile's cellular network at a wholesale rate and resold it to customers—would market itself as a cell phone company for Christian conservatives, with a pledge to donate a portion of users' monthly bills to traditional conservative causes. The goal was to win loyal customers by supporting groups and politicians who promised to oppose abortion, defend religious freedom, protect gun rights, and back the military.

At least, that was the idea back then.

Brandon Moore, who'd since left Patriot Mobile for reasons unknown to me, could not have predicted—in a twist that's almost too strange for fiction—that the company he created would one day embark on a crusade to disparage school board members like his wife, the embattled Carroll trustee Michelle Moore. Brandon Moore didn't want to discuss his former company, but Michelle told me that the Patriot Mobile of 2022 bore little resemblance to her husband's original vision.

The company's transformation mirrored that of the GOP over the same period. After the 2016 presidential election, the company's branding shifted to embrace the style of politics popularized by Trump. One of Patriot Mobile's most famous advertisements included the slogan "Making Wireless Great Again," alongside an image of Trump's face photoshopped onto a tanned, muscled Rambo body holding a machine gun. The irreverent approach helped turn the company into a darling among some big names on the far right. "You can give your money to AT&T, the parent company of CNN, and you can pay the salary of Don Lemon, or you can support someone like a Patriot Mobile and give back to causes that they believe in," Donald Trump Jr. told a gathering of conservatives in February 2022. "That's not cancel culture, folks. That's using your damn brain."

As the company grew, Patriot Mobile also began to align itself with politicians and religious leaders who promoted a once obscure strand of political theology known as Christian dominionism—a fringe offshoot of the evangelical movement of the 1970s and '80s.

Sometimes referred to as the Seven Mountains Mandate, dominionism is the belief that Christians are called on to dominate the seven key "mountains," or spheres, of public life: family, religion, media, entertainment, business, government, and perhaps most important, education. Some followers believe that by fulfilling the Seven Mountains Mandate they can bring about the return of Jesus. The vision, first articulated a half century ago by Pentecostal leaders of the religious right and popularized in the early 2000s, ties back to a passage in the apocalyptic Book of Revelation:

> And they that dwell on the earth shall wonder, whose names were not written in the book of life from the foundation of the world, when they behold the beast that was, and is not, and yet is. And here is the mind which hath wisdom. The seven heads are seven mountains.

Lauren Boebert, the far-right Republican congresswoman from Colorado known for denying the legitimacy of the 2020 presidential election and for her love of assault rifles, began endorsing Patriot Mobile in 2022, around the same time she gave a speech rife with dominionist talking points. Speaking at a Sunday church service, she called on evangelicals to "rise up and take our place in Christ" to "influence this nation as we were called to do" and usher in "the second coming of Jesus." The comments alarmed some political and religious scholars who warned that it signaled a growing embrace of Christian nationalism within the GOP.

John Fea, a professor of American history at Messiah University in Pennsylvania, spent years studying Seven Mountains theology. Fea says that the idea that evangelicals have been called on to assert biblical values across all aspects of American society moved from the fringes of conservative thought to the center of GOP politics after Trump's election. "This was kind of a sleeping giant," Fea says. Trump—a twice-divorced billionaire who bragged about the ease with which he sexually assaulted women and who famously misnamed a book of the Bible as "Two Corinthians" while campaigning—may have seemed an unlikely figure to shepherd a revival of America's religious right.

But many evangelicals were emboldened by his blunt commentary about America's moral decline and inspired by his willingness to wage cultural wars against their perceived enemies. Trump ended up winning a larger share of white evangelical voters—about 80 percent—than Mitt

Romney, a candidate firmly tied to his Mormon faith, or even the devout George W. Bush.

Fea explains that "'Make America Great Again'" to some conservatives meant "'Make America Christian Again.' Restore America to its Christian roots." And whereas past Republican presidents sought to keep fringe Christian leaders at arm's length, Trump—having pledged that Christians would have power in his administration—invited them directly into the fold, naming the Pentecostal televangelist and Seven Mountains adherent Paula White as his chief spiritual advisor. Charlie Kirk, the far-right Christian commentator, celebrated the GOP's religious reawakening during remarks at CPAC in 2020. "Finally," Kirk said, "we have a president that understands the Seven Mountains of cultural influence."

The following year, one of the leading proponents of the Seven Mountains worldview, pastor Rafael Cruz, began leading weekly Bible studies for employees at Patriot Mobile's corporate office in Grapevine, which the company live-streamed for its customers. In one Patriot Mobile sermon, Cruz, an immigrant from Cuba and the father of the firebrand senator Ted Cruz, dismissed the concept of separation of church and state as a myth, arguing that America's founders meant that ideal as a "one-way wall" preventing the government from interfering with the church, not preventing the church from having dominion over the government—a widely disputed claim popularized by David Barton. Cruz then called on people who "are rooted in the righteousness of the word of God" to run for public office. "If those people are not running for office, if they are not even voting, then what's left?" he said. "The wicked electing the wicked."

It was around that same time, as opposition to critical race theory and LGBTQ inclusion was emerging as a political attack on the right, that Fea began to observe another shift in the Christian dominionism movement. Rather than focusing only on winning federal elections, far-right Christian groups and leaders around the country started talking about the need to take control of local schools—"the ideal battleground," Fea said, "if you're looking to fight this battle.

"This is a spiritual war, they believe, against demonic forces that undermine a godly nation by teaching kids in school that America is not great, America is not a city on the hill, or that America has flaws," Fea said. "If you can get in and teach the right side of history, and social studies and civics lessons about what America is, you can win the next generation and save America for Christ."

In one of his Bible study sessions at the Patriot Mobile break room in early 2022, Rafael Cruz called on the company and its employees to look to an example set a year earlier in the town next door. "I am so thankful also for what happened in Southlake," Cruz said, "where Christians got involved and transformed a school board from having seven evil, liberal people promoting all this garbage. . . . Some committed Christian people said, 'Enough is enough.'" Left unsaid was the fact that most of the supposedly evil liberals on Carroll's school board were in fact churchgoing Republicans, and that one of them was the spouse of one of Patriot Mobile's founders.

Cruz then quoted a line that's often misattributed to the founding father Samuel Adams: "'It does not take a majority to prevail, but only an irate, tireless minority, keen on setting brush fires of liberty in the hearts and minds of men.'"

With that, the pastor looked around the room and issued a challenge: It was time, Cruz said, to go light some fires.

One month earlier, Patriot Mobile had filed paperwork to establish a new political action committee—Patriot Mobile Action—and brought on Wambsganss, on the heels of her triumph with Southlake Families PAC, to lead it. With nearly $600,000 to spend, Wambsganss got to work achieving the mission that Allen West had laid out in her living room a year earlier, when he called on Southlake conservatives to spread their movement to other suburbs—starting first with some school systems close to home.

Wambsganss and her team quickly zeroed in on four North Texas districts—Keller, Grapevine-Colleyville, Mansfield, and, once again, Carroll. After interviewing prospective candidates, Patriot Mobile Action settled on a slate of eleven for the May 2022 elections in the four school districts.

Following her own playbook from Southlake, Wambsganss hired a pair of heavy-hitter GOP consulting firms, paying nearly $150,000 to Vanguard Field Strategies to run get-out-the-vote canvassing operations and shelling out another $240,000 to Axiom Strategies to produce and send tens of thousands of political mailers to homes across the four districts.

In Mansfield—the town where white demonstrators had strung up Black effigies to protest integration sixty-five years earlier—Patriot Mobile blasted out fliers baselessly blaming a recent classroom shooting at a local high school on critical race theory–inspired disciplinary policies. The mailer, which appeared to imply that the district had stopped disciplining Black children because of "woke" politics, included an image of a white child cowering in a school hallway under the words "Restore safety. Restore sanity. It's time for a new school board."

"I believe those fliers were designed to play to parents' fears and to divide this community," a Black Mansfield mother said. Another parent said the mailers miscast educators and progressive parents of color as evil—turning neighbors into enemies.

Patriot Mobile used the same image of a despondent white child in mailers sent to residents in the Grapevine-Colleyville school district: "Vote for a new school board that will support students, not shame them." In Keller, the school district west of Southlake, Patriot Mobile sent fliers endorsing three candidates under the slogan "Saving America starts with saving our public schools." The PAC sent mailers with the same message to support a pair of Southlake Families–endorsed candidates for Carroll's school board, hoping to expand the board's conservative majority.

The Patriot Mobile slate got an extra boost from the pulpit on the Sunday before the election. "Please hear me," said Robert Morris, the senior pastor at Gateway, a Southlake-based megachurch with a reported congregation of more than 100,000 people nationwide. "If you haven't looked at the material that is in schoolbooks that are in our school libraries, I want you to look. . . . It is as pornographic as anything you've ever read." Morris, who'd served as a member of the Trump campaign's evangelical advisory board and spoken at a conference focused on advancing the Seven Mountains Mandate, then directed his parishioners to look up at the big screens behind him as a series of slides flashed the names of most of the Patriot Mobile–backed school board candidates. Emphasizing that he was not explicitly endorsing anyone—which would violate federal law and put the church's tax-exempt status at risk—Morris asked his congregation to remember the candidates' names and to pray for their fellow Christians. And, he added, "we need to vote."

Unlike in Southlake, the elections that spring in Mansfield and Grapevine-Colleyville were anything but foregone conclusions. Each of those districts were more diverse than Southlake, and their electorates were more evenly divided between conservative and liberal. But never had an outside group spent so much money in those places to drum up partisan enthusiasm in traditionally low-turnout local elections. After all the votes had been counted on the evening of May 7, 2022, Patriot Mobile's candidates had gone a perfect 10–0, having won several of the races by just a few percentage points. (The eleventh Patriot Mobile candidate failed to win more than 50 percent of the vote in a three-way race; he later won in a runoff.)

The clean sweep once again caught the attention of conservatives nationwide. In a series of interviews afterward, Wambsganss said it was just the beginning. Patriot Mobile, she said, planned to continue spending on school board elections, with the goal of spreading the movement to local districts across Texas and, eventually, the country.

A little more than a year after former Trump advisor Steve Bannon called on conservatives to "save the nation" by winning seats on local school boards, Wambsganss and Glenn Story, Patriot Mobile's president, appeared on his conspiracy theory–fueled *War Room* TV program to spotlight the work Patriot Mobile was doing to fulfill that vision.

"The school boards are the key that picks the lock," Bannon said during his interview with Wambsganss and Story. "Tell us about what you did."

Story turned to the camera and said, "We went out and found eleven candidates last cycle and we supported them, and we won every seat. We took over four school boards."

"Eleven seats on school boards, took over four!" Bannon shouted as a crowd of CPAC attendees erupted in applause.

Bannon, who at the time was awaiting trial on two counts of contempt of Congress for his failure to comply with a subpoena issued by the House select committee investigating the January 6 insurrection, asked Wambsganss whether she'd started to see changes in those school districts. "Oh, tremendous," Wambsganss said. "Those eleven seats in four ISDs means that now North Texas has over 100,000 students who, before May, had leftist leadership. Now they have conservative leadership."

Bannon replied: "Amen."

The Patriot Mobile–endorsed leaders of Southlake's school board, meanwhile, continued to exert their growing electoral mandate. Seven months after Carroll teachers spoke out about new restrictions on classroom library books, sparking an international controversy, district employees discovered that a new clause had been tacked onto their annual employment contracts, listed under the heading "Non-Disparagement."

"You agree to not disparage, criticize, or defame the District, and its employees or officials, to the media," it read. The language, which mirrored the types of NDAs often included in legal settlements, seemed intended to shield the district from future scandals. It ended up sparking one instead.

National teachers groups condemned the contract language as an unprecedented attempt to muzzle educators. As one Carroll teacher wrote, "Only a district that is knowingly doing something wrong would choose to silence its entire staff." Alice O'Brien, general counsel at the National Education Association, a teacher's union, drew a parallel between Carroll's non-disparagement clause and the broader campaign to limit the ways teachers talk about racism and sexuality. "Instead of censoring the truth," she said, "let's focus on addressing the real issues facing Texas students, starting with paying educators more and making sure students have the resources they need to succeed."

The blanket NDA likely wasn't enforceable. Michael Leroy, a labor law expert, says that prohibiting public employees from criticizing a government-funded school district is "absolutely indefensible" under the First Amendment: "I mean, that's not even a close call."

But if the goal had been to send a message to teachers, school district leaders may have succeeded on that measure. And they were just getting started.

That same week, fourth-grade teacher Christina McGuirk (the former Ms. Catlin) got an email addressed to her and a few colleagues, including her best friend Rickie Farah, from a parent and Southlake Families PAC supporter named Tara Eddins. A white mother, Eddins had been among the most outspoken opponents of the district's diversity efforts, winning praise among local conservatives for her confrontational and often colorful commentary at school board meetings. She'd once told Michelle Moore that she planned to attend her criminal trial "with bells on." At another meeting, Eddins demanded to know why Carroll—this was amid a national mental health crisis among teenagers—was paying counselors to give students lessons on suicide prevention. "At Carroll ISD, you are actually advertising suicide," Eddins claimed, arguing that many parents in the affluent suburban school system had been forced to hire tutors because the district's counselors were too focused on mental health and woke indoctrination instead of helping students prepare for college. Eddins frequently emailed senior district administrators with criticisms and suggestions, once writing in a message to Superintendent Lane Ledbetter and school board members Hannah Smith and Cam Bryan that more attention should be focused on discussing "the failure and breakdown of the black family unit." The PAC-endorsed school board had rewarded Eddins's activism by appointing her to serve on a volunteer committee tasked with reviewing and overhauling the district's curriculum.

McGuirk's heart was racing as she opened the email from Eddins, who'd copied district administrators and school board members. "Did you know April is contract negotiation month?!?" Eddins wrote to the teachers, and then shared a link to an audio file. "Take a look at this link, gals, and get those resumes ready!!!"

When McGuirk clicked play, she immediately recognized it as a recording of her interview with *NBC Nightly News* from the previous fall. Someone had managed to undo the complex digital distortion that audio engineers had applied to mask her voice and the voice of the other Carroll teacher who'd spoken to us. Oh my God, McGuirk thought as she played the clip again, recognizing her own voice with near-complete clarity.

The audio still sounded slightly distorted, making clear this wasn't a leak of NBC's raw footage, but instead a feat of digital wizardry. Exactly *how* this was possible, and who did it, remains a mystery. Audio experts said it likely would have required sophisticated software and someone with advanced technical knowledge to reverse the distortion techniques used by major broadcast outlets to mask the voices of confidential sources. The audio file linked in Eddins's email also included the unscrambled voice of a third Carroll educator who'd spoken anonymously to CNN in a separate interview about the Holocaust controversy.

Based on the other names copied on Eddins's email, however, it did not appear that conservative activists had successfully identified the two other teachers who'd also given television interviews. In McGuirk's case, Southlake Families supporters had compared the unscrambled audio of her October interview with a recording of her speaking publicly in defense of Farah at a school board meeting that same month.

"I never in a million years would have imagined people would go to such extreme lengths to punish a teacher," McGuirk said. "I think they were trying to make an example out of me. Basically, here's what happens if you don't fall in line with Southlake Families."

Her initial plan was to ignore the email and hope that school officials would do the same. She hadn't done anything wrong, she reminded herself. There was no rule in her current contract that said teachers couldn't talk to reporters. But at school the next morning, McGuirk received another email that made her start to panic. This one was from Ledbetter's assistant; the superintendent wanted McGuirk to meet him at his office after school that afternoon.

McGuirk's principal was stunned; normally staffing issues were handled at the campus level. "You have to be strong," the administrator encouraged her. But McGuirk, nearly seven months pregnant, wasn't feeling very strong as she arrived at Carroll's central administrative offices that afternoon, accompanied by a lawyer from a state teachers union. "How's your pregnancy going?" one of Ledbetter's deputies asked, making small talk as McGuirk sat down across from them.

"Not good," McGuirk replied. "I'm stressed out."

Ledbetter cut to the chase. He told McGuirk that the school board had voted the night before to approve annual contracts for all the district's teachers, but the members had set hers aside for special consideration. Before the board voted on whether to bring McGuirk back for the following school year, there was one question that needed to be answered, he said. Ledbetter then set his phone on the table and hit play on the same audio file that Eddins had emailed. McGuirk's lawyer had advised her not to show emotion during the meeting, but as she sat across from her superintendent and listened to the recording of herself criticizing his administration on national television, she began to cry.

After the audio file finished playing, Ledbetter asked McGuirk, "Are you telling me this isn't your voice?" Before she could answer, the union lawyer interjected.

"I have advised her not to answer that question."

"This is your chance," Ledbetter said to McGuirk. "Is this your voice?"

She took her lawyer's advice and declined to answer, although the tears streaming down her cheeks must have signaled the truth. "OK," Ledbetter responded. "That's all we needed to know." He said he would pass this information along to the school board and that they would decide what to do with her contract at the next meeting.

But as she walked out of the superintendent's office that afternoon, feeling depressed and defeated, McGuirk's future at Carroll had already been decided—by her.

The majority in town no longer wanted her teaching their children, she told herself, polluting their minds with what she considered irrefutable truths. Yes, racism exists. No, there is nothing to debate about the horrors of the Holocaust. Yes, some kids have two dads. It's OK to be different. She still believed that every child deserved to learn those lessons. But with her own baby on the way, she was too tired to keep fighting.

Four years after accepting what she thought was her dream job, hoping at the time to live out her Christian faith by showing love to the children of Southlake, Christina McGuirk resigned. The only question now was whether the twenty-eight-year-old would ever teach again.

13

The Florida Blueprint

IN JULY 2022, A mother stood onstage at a conference center in Tampa and listed the ways that Florida governor Ron DeSantis, now running for a second term, had defended parents like her. He'd been among the first in the country to order public schools to reopen during the pandemic, and he'd enacted more policies than perhaps any governor in the country to purge what he called "woke ideology" from public schools, universities, and even private businesses.

"American parents watched as elected officials abdicated their responsibility—but not Governor DeSantis," said Tiffany Justice, the cofounder of the anti-CRT activist group Moms for Liberty, which had blossomed into a powerful force in conservative politics since its founding one year earlier. "I talk to moms all over the country who wish that Ron DeSantis was their governor," Justice said, with a reverent quiver in her voice. "And I am often told that they cannot wait to vote for him for president."

A moment later, "Sweet Florida"—a country song written as a tribute to DeSantis—began to blare from speakers as the governor walked onstage. *Down in sweet Florida, our governor is red, white and blue . . . he's shooting us straight, tellin' us the truth.*

As the music faded, the founders of Moms for Liberty pulled out a wooden sword and presented it to DeSantis. This was not just any sword, one of the women told him. "This is called a Rudis. It is what the gladiators were awarded with after they had fought a long hard battle for freedom." The ballroom, packed with conservative activists from all over the country, cheered like they were at a concert.

The crowd liked the governor's combative style. They liked that he never backed down from a fight. And most of all, they seemed to like his policies—what his campaign would soon begin calling the "Florida Blueprint."

"For those of you not from here," DeSantis said at the start of his keynote address, "welcome to the freest state in the United States."

It seemed like a winning message. In the midterms that November, as Republicans loyal to Donald Trump underperformed nationally, DeSantis went on to defeat Democratic nominee Charlie Crist by nearly twenty percentage points, the largest margin in nearly four decades of Florida gubernatorial politics. He even won reliably blue Miami–Dade County, the first Republican to do so in a generation. To those watching closely, DeSantis's reelection campaign appeared to be less about who would reside in the governor's mansion and more like an audition for the White House.

In the years after the 2020 presidential election, DeSantis, a forty-four-year-old attorney and military officer, had emerged in the minds of Republican Party insiders as the most—and perhaps only—viable candidate to supplant Donald Trump as the face of the GOP. His willingness to defy public health experts during the pandemic by opposing mask and vaccine mandates earned him fawning coverage on Fox News. But it had been his early and relentless embrace of school board controversies that truly separated him from other GOP politicians jockeying to emerge from Trump's shadow.

After the state board of education banned critical race theory from Florida classrooms at his urging in 2021, DeSantis followed up in 2022 with a bill titled "Stop Wrong to our Kids and Employees"—aka, the Stop W.O.K.E. Act—which prohibited schools and private businesses from giving any instruction that might lead students or employees to believe they bear "personal responsibility" for historic wrongs because of their race, sex, or national origin. The irony of restricting the speech of private companies in "the freest state in the United States" was not lost on civil rights groups, including the ACLU, which quickly filed a lawsuit seeking to overturn the law. A judge issued an order blocking its enforcement for private businesses while the case was pending, but not for schools. As a result, some districts and colleges scrapped diversity and inclusion training programs to avoid running afoul of the new rules.

Later, the state cited the law to justify its decision to ban a new Advanced Placement course in African American studies from being taught in Florida high schools. DeSantis's education department claimed that the curriculum—developed by the College Board, the nonprofit group that runs the SAT test and AP college-prep programs nationwide—was "inexplicably contrary to Florida law and significantly lacks educational value." To further punish the College Board, the DeSantis administration explored replacing the SAT in Florida with an alternative college aptitude test favored by Christian homeschooling families and private schools.

Next, DeSantis set his sights on the emergent battles over sexual orientation and gender identity. He threw his total support behind the controversial Parental Rights in Education Act, better known by the name opponents had chosen for it: Florida's "Don't Say Gay" law. The legislation prohibited classroom discussions about sexual orientation or gender in kindergarten through third grade and placed age-appropriateness restrictions on such lessons for older students. Critics said the law's authors had intentionally conflated sexual orientation and sex—just as Anita Bryant had done in Florida decades earlier—and argued that the legislation would force LGBTQ teachers into the closet by making it illegal for them to display a photo of their spouse on their desk or keep picture books depicting queer characters in their classes.

DeSantis seemed to relish the controversy. "I'm like, OK, they want to die on the hill of forcing sexuality and gender ideology in elementary school?" he told the Moms for Liberty conference. "You've got to be kidding me." The governor then invoked a hypothetical that he frequently used to defend the Parental Rights in Education Act: "We're not gonna have some first grader be told that, 'Yeah, your parents named you Johnny. You were born a boy, but maybe you're really a girl.' That is inappropriate to be doing in school, and we're not going to allow that to happen in Florida."

The fact that DeSantis never produced evidence of any Florida teachers directing children to change their gender was inconsequential to this crowd. Many of his supporters seemed to view any effort by schools to accommodate nonbinary and transgender students as an attempt by educators to force LGBTQ identities on impressionable children. In one high-profile case, parents initially gave school officials in Florida's Leon County written permission to honor their child's request to be called by gender-neutral pronouns at school, even though the parents did not personally support the idea. Later, the parents filed a federal lawsuit accusing the district of taking additional steps to affirm their child's gender identity without their knowledge. Yet, when DeSantis cited the Leon County case to defend the need for his legislation, he presented a far less nuanced account, making it sound as if school officials had forced the teenager to switch genders without the parents' knowledge. "Some people in the school had decided that the daughter was really a boy and not a girl," DeSantis claimed. "So they changed the girl's name to a boy's name, had her dress like a boy and all this stuff without telling the mother or getting consent from the mother."

In effect, DeSantis had taken a genuine and complicated debate vexing educators nationally—how should schools accommodate the choices of transgender and nonbinary students when those children's parents are unsupportive?—and turned it into a caricature, painting teachers as far-left ideologues on a mission to turn children queer. The lack of evidence for DeSantis's version of events in the Leon County case did not slow the spread of the story in right-wing media, which routinely cast the governor as a rare politician with the courage to stand up to dark cultural forces on behalf of parents.

DeSantis's work to solidify that reputation was not limited to signing legislation. He also aligned himself with far-right figures and Christian conservatives leading those fights nationally. And like Trump before him, he found a way to make their enemies his enemies.

When DeSantis signed the Stop W.O.K.E Act, he was joined onstage by anti-CRT activist and Washington state resident Chris Rufo, whom he later appointed to serve on the board of a Florida state college, with the goal of purging the school of progressive pedagogy. After the Walt

Disney Company, one of Florida's largest employers, came out against the "Don't Say Gay" bill, DeSantis moved to terminate the company's special tax status and accused it of pushing sexuality in its children's films. To bolster his image as an opponent of pandemic restrictions, DeSantis elevated fringe medical experts who spread false claims about the deadliness of COVID vaccines, including a dermatologist who said that Biden's chief medical advisor, Dr. Anthony Fauci, "should face a firing squad." And when Chaya Raichik was outed as the anonymous woman behind Libs of TikTok—an incendiary social media account that trafficked in anti-trans rhetoric—DeSantis directed someone in his office to reach out and offer the far-right influencer refuge in the guesthouse of the Florida governor's mansion.

"It was incredible, I don't even have the words for it," Raichik told Fox News host Tucker Carlson, describing DeSantis's gesture in her first interview after being named publicly. In that same interview, Raichik expanded on the philosophy behind Libs of TikTok, the viral social media account that had won DeSantis's admiration.

"The LGBTQ community has become this cult," Raichik said. "They brainwash people to join. They convince them of all of these things, and it's really hard to get out of it." The woman DeSantis praised then called LGBTQ-affirming educators "evil" and uttered a line that could have been lifted from the anti-gay campaigns of the 1970s: "They want to groom kids. They're recruiting."

For his part, DeSantis never explicitly mentioned the LGBTQ community during his address to Moms for Liberty. He instead framed his efforts as he always did: a fight against those who seek to indoctrinate children with "woke gender ideology."

DeSantis ended the speech by encouraging everyone to vote conservatives onto their local school boards and to support his reelection campaign. "We have a great opportunity," the governor said, "to really solidify the state of Florida as this country's citadel of freedom."

That summer, a group of social studies teachers arrived at an administrative building in Broward County for a new voluntary training program that, according to DeSantis, would provide guidance to educators statewide on how to teach "accurate American history without an ideological agenda." How, exactly, the DeSantis administration defined "accurate American history" became clear over the next three days, as trainers guided the teachers through a PowerPoint presentation infused with Christian conservative interpretations of the nation's founding.

According to one slide seeming to echo the view promoted by David Barton, it wasn't true that America's constitutional framers endorsed a strict separation of church and state. "The Founders," the slide read, "only wanted to protect freedom of worship" from government intrusion, not the other way around. Another slide argued that although two-thirds of the founding fathers were slave owners, it was important for educators to emphasize to their students that "even those that held slaves did not defend the institution"—a sweeping claim unsupported by the historical record. Another slide argued for the merits of originalism, a judicial theory favored by conservatives that calls for a strict reading of the Constitution as the founders intended it at the time of its writing. Under that framework, one of the trainers advised teachers, the Supreme Court had erred when it ruled in 1962 that school-sponsored prayer violated the establishment clause of the First Amendment. (Originalism was also the foundation for the Supreme Court's bombshell decision that summer to overturn *Roe v. Wade*, eliminating the right to abortion in America.)

"It was very skewed," Barbara Segal, a government teacher at Fort Lauderdale High School, told the *Tampa Bay Times* and *Miami Herald* after completing the training. "There was a very strong Christian fundamentalist way toward analyzing different quotes and different documents." Another social studies teacher told the newspapers, the first to report on the content of the trainings, that it seemed as if a "Christian nationalism philosophy" had been baked into the program.

That may have been because the course was developed with the help of Hillsdale College, a small but influential private Christian liberal arts school based in Michigan with ties to Donald Trump. When Trump's White House created the 1776 Commission in 2020 to counter the *New York Times'* 1619 Project, the administration appointed Larry Arnn, president of Hillsdale, to lead the group, which counted among its members several conservative educators but no professional historians. The commission's final report, released on Martin Luther King Jr. Day in 2021, minimized the role of slavery in American history and compared the modern progressive movement to the fascism of leaders like Benito Mussolini, who "sought to centralize power under the management of so-called experts." Arnn and his team at Hillsdale later adapted the report into a school social studies curriculum and began marketing it to charter and private schools across America, including in Florida.

The man whose college DeSantis tapped to reeducate Florida teachers seemed to have a low view of them generally. In secretly recorded remarks obtained by a television journalist in Nashville, Arnn told Tennessee's Republican governor that America's teachers were "trained in the dumbest parts of the dumbest colleges in the country," and warned that the nation would soon see "how education destroys generations of people. It's devastating. It's like the plague." The Hillsdale president later walked back the comments, writing in an op-ed that he had "deep and abiding affection for teachers" and that he did not mean to say they were unintelligent. "Dumb also means 'ill-conceived' or 'misdirected,'" Arnn wrote, "which is, sadly, a fitting description for many education schools today."

DeSantis echoed those remarks a month later when he announced a plan to allow military veterans to teach in Florida schools without a bachelor's degree. In defending the policy, the governor slammed college education programs as "a magnet for a lot of ideology." Later, he said he wanted to expand the law to offer teacher's licenses to police, firefighters, and EMTs. "We would prefer people with real world experience and academic proficiency in the core subjects when they're teaching English, math, science, not saying, 'Oh, I went to the school of education somewhere and they taught me kind of how to teach,'" DeSantis said. "Because I've seen that, and I've been very underwhelmed by it."

But the policies advanced by conservative activists like Chris Rufo and adopted by DeSantis and other Republican governors did not reflect an attempt to remove political ideology from education. Rather, they elevated ideologies favored by conservatives while minimizing or banning those they opposed. Books and lessons that applied a critical lens to the lasting influence of racism in U.S. society were prohibited; those minimizing the effects of racism were made mandatory. When DeSantis appointed Rufo and other hardline conservatives to run New College of Florida, a liberal arts college, the goal was not only to eliminate progressive influences from campus, but to replace them with conservative worldviews. As DeSantis's chief of staff told the *National Review,* the governor hoped to transform the public school into a "classical college, more along the lines of a Hillsdale of the South." Likewise, when several Republican-controlled state legislatures voted to ban the *New York Times'* 1619 Project from schools, they followed up by imposing rosier perspectives. Texas, for example, created the 1836 Project, an educational program named for the year the state won independence from Mexico, with the goal of promoting a patriotic view of Texas history. (Another noteworthy development from 1836: The Constitution of the Republic of Texas was ratified, legalizing slavery and excluding indigenous groups from gaining independence.)

From 2021 to 2023, PEN America tracked three hundred state bills that sought to censor or restrict classroom speech—policies that the free-speech nonprofit dubbed "educational gag orders." Following Florida's lead, red state lawmakers introduced a wave of bills banning discussion of gender and sexual orientation, including some that included criminal penalties for teachers and librarians. In a throwback to the education wars of the 1970s and '80s, an Oklahoma lawmaker introduced a pair of bills banning "secular humanism," which the Republican defined as a religion that is "inseparably linked" to critical race theory, sexual orientation, and gender identity. Under the bill, any public schools that "promote the plausibility" of these concepts would "excessively entangle the government with the religion of secular humanism" and violate the Establishment Clause of the U.S. Constitution.

Writing for the *Guardian,* Jason Stanley, the author of *How Fascism Works*, argues against the framing of these policies as part of a "culture war." It's no longer merely a battle of values when officials begin wielding the power of the state to ban certain ideas, he asserts. "The passing of these laws signals the dawn of a new authoritarian age in the United

States, where the state uses laws restricting speech to intimidate, bully and punish educators, forcing them to submit to the ideology of the dominant majority or lose their livelihoods, and even their freedom." Timothy Snyder, a Yale University history professor, likened the policies favored by DeSantis to "memory laws" adopted by Russian President Vladimir Putin, which criminalized criticism of Soviet actions during World War II: "Such measures work by asserting a mandatory view of historical events, by forbidding the discussion of historical facts or interpretations or by providing vague guidelines that lead to self-censorship. . . . The point is not to protect historical facts but to cultivate national feeling."

This explicit tipping of the educational scales in the U.S. was in some instances making it difficult for high school teachers—and even some college professors—to speak openly with their students about the nativist political forces that may have helped inspire those policies in the first place. This reality was put on harsh display in May 2022, in the days after a white gunman opened fire and killed ten Black shoppers at a Buffalo, New York, grocery store. In a screed posted online prior to the massacre, the eighteen-year-old gunman had detailed his plans to target Black people and repeatedly cited as motivation his belief in the Great Replacement—the conspiracy theory that said white Americans were being "replaced" by people of color through immigration, interracial marriage, and integration.

Replacement theory, once relegated to fringe online forums, had in recent years become popular among some mainstream conservatives, espoused by leading figures in the GOP. That included, most prominently, Fox News host Tucker Carlson, who, according to an analysis by the *New York Times*, had "amplified the idea that Democratic politicians and others want to force demographic change through immigration" in more than four hundred episodes of his show, totaling more than fifty hours devoted to the theme. Marjorie Taylor Greene, the far-right congresswoman from Georgia who famously embraced the QAnon conspiracy that said Trump was waging a secret war against a cabal of Satan-worshiping pedophiles, later warned followers that "Joe Biden's five million illegal aliens are on the verge of replacing you—replacing your jobs and replacing your kids in school. . . . They're also replacing your culture, and that's not great for America."

After Buffalo, educators nationwide were once again grappling with how to discuss a mass shooting that appeared to have been motivated by bigotry, just as they had in 2019 after a shooting rampage targeting Mexican immigrants at a Walmart in El Paso; in 2018 after a massacre of Jewish parishioners at a synagogue in Pittsburgh; and in 2015 after a white gunman killed Black Christians at a church in Charleston, South Carolina. This time, however, these already difficult classroom conversations were being complicated or suppressed under restrictive classroom speech laws. Fearing for their jobs, teachers in some majority-white suburban communities reported avoiding the conversation altogether; others took a more provocative approach.

Two days after the Buffalo shooting, a white teacher named Elizabeth Close walked into her high school ethnic studies class in Austin, Texas, and began by reminding her students about the new state law that required her to provide balanced perspectives on "widely debated and currently controversial issues."

Close then told her students that under the law, she was obligated to inform them that there was more than one way to view the Buffalo massacre. On one hand, she explained that authorities were investigating the killings as a racially motivated hate crime carried out by a teenager, not much older than them, who'd written of his belief in a racist conspiracy theory. "But I'm also supposed to tell you that that's just one perspective," Close told her students. "Another perspective is that this young man was out defending the world—or his kind—from being taken over."

Close waited for her comment to fully register with her students, then added: "If you guys want to know why I'm thinking about quitting at the end of the year, it's because of these types of policies—the fact that I have to have this conversation with you."

The teacher said she couldn't fathom a way of responsibly discussing the subject, in a classroom that included students of color and immigrants, without violating Texas law. So, already thinking about quitting, she didn't bother holding back.

Close explained the history of replacement theory and noted that some leaders in Texas had embraced aspects of the belief, including the state's Republican lieutenant governor Dan Patrick, who'd claimed on Fox News a year earlier that Democrats were allowing millions of immigrants to enter the country as part of a liberal plot "to take over our country without firing a shot."

The teacher knew the lesson might land her in hot water with parents or politicians, but she didn't care anymore. "If we're not able to have these discussions," she said, "how else are students going to envision a better future?"

There may have been another reason Ron DeSantis wanted to make it easier for military veterans, police, and other non-educators to become teachers: Florida did not have enough of them. Public schools statewide reported more than five thousand vacancies as classes resumed in the fall of 2022, representing about 3 percent of teaching positions. For months, teachers' unions nationwide had been warning that pandemic fatigue and political attacks were driving educators out of the profession at an unsustainable rate nationally—claims that some experts say were exaggerated. Nevertheless, there was no denying that the policies of the DeSantis administration, especially the new law focused on gender and sexual orientation, had some educators rethinking their role in the classroom, and their futures.

A nationwide survey of teachers by the RAND Corporation that year found that one in four teachers said they had revised their instructional materials or teaching practices to limit or exclude discussions of race and gender. The trend was especially true among teachers of color, teachers working in suburban school systems, and those employed in states such as Florida that had adopted laws restricting lessons on race, sexuality, and history. That same school year, just 13 percent of the nation's eighth graders were proficient in U.S. history, according to a national assessment, a five-point drop compared to five years earlier. Secretary of Education Miguel Cardona linked the poor performance to the "profound impact" of the pandemic and political attacks on educators. "Banning history books and censoring educators from teaching these important subjects does our students a disservice and will move America in the wrong direction," he said.

Meanwhile, a third of teachers said they soon planned to leave their jobs.

Michael Woods, a high school special education teacher in Palm Beach County, who recalled being bullied as a teenager for being gay, said he cried the night before the first day of school in August 2022. "As a gay teacher, as a queer male, it's been painful," said Woods, who'd proactively removed all books from his classroom library to avoid running afoul of what he viewed as vague and subjective content restrictions imposed by the state.

Books weren't the only things coming down in Florida classrooms.

Michael James, a special education teacher in Pensacola, resigned after a school district employee removed images of Black civil rights icons, including Martin Luther King Jr. and Harriet Tubman, from a bulletin board in James's class. The teacher had hung the images to inspire the mostly Black students he worked with each day. James said the district employee also removed an image of former president Barack Obama from his desk. "I've been teaching special education for fifteen years, and it just really floored me when she did that."

In some Florida districts, educators reported being told to purge their classrooms of any LGBTQ symbols. Pride flags were taken off walls. Tiny rainbow stickers, meant to signal support for marginalized queer students, were scraped off classroom windows. In Orange County, district lawyers initially told teachers they shouldn't display photos of same-sex spouses in their classrooms—guidance that was later reversed after the state made clear that the law did not prohibit educators from having family photos on their desks. But with the threat of having their teacher's licenses revoked should they ever discuss gender or sexual orientation with their students, some LGBTQ teachers weren't willing to risk it.

Others decided it was time to walk away.

Nicolette Solomon, a lesbian fourth-grade teacher in Miami–Dade County, worked in the same South Florida community where gay activists had spent years battling Anita Bryant for the right of LGBTQ teachers to work in classrooms as their authentic selves. Solomon told the *Washington Post* she now no longer believed that she could do both in the state of Florida.

Her students cried when she shared the news of her resignation. One child drew her a picture of hearts, along with a note that said: "I want you to stay." The sweet gesture made Solomon cry, but it did not change her mind.

Florida's elected leaders, she believed, had already delivered the opposite message.

Just a few days before DeSantis's landslide reelection victory that November, his campaign released a commercial that portrayed the governor and future presidential candidate as a man who'd been called on by a higher power.

By now, speculation about a 2024 DeSantis presidential run was dominating political news coverage, with some GOP donors pitching him with a simple three-word phrase: "Trump, but competent." His education policies in Florida and his so-called "war on wokeism" would serve as a road map for what he planned for America. To some—including, it seemed, his own campaign—DeSantis's rise to national power appeared almost preordained.

In the television commercial, black-and-white images of pristine Florida beaches and packed political rallies faded in and out on the screen as a baritone voice declared, "On the eighth day, God looked down on his planned paradise and said, 'I need a protector.'"

"So," the narrator said, as a picture of Ron DeSantis came into sharp focus, "God made a fighter."

14

I Lost My Son

THREE MONTHS AFTER PATRIOT Mobile went a perfect 11–0 in North Texas school board races in the spring of 2022, those newly installed board members began to deliver on their promises.

The Keller Independent School District made national headlines that August after rigid new content restrictions adopted by the school board led district employees to remove more than forty library books from shelves for review, including a graphic adaptation of Anne Frank's *The Diary of a Young Girl* and several LGBTQ-themed novels. Undeterred by the critical news coverage, Keller's Patriot Mobile–backed board majority went further, passing an additional policy to ban all books at every grade level that mentioned or depicted "gender fluidity." Calling the policy a flagrant attempt to "erase transgender and nonbinary" people, the ACLU of Texas called on the U.S. Department of Education to open a civil rights investigation.

In Southlake, Patriot Mobile donated framed posters depicting the national motto, "In God We Trust," to the Carroll school district, where conservatives aligned with the cell phone company and Southlake Families PAC now held all but two seats on the board of trustees. Under a new Texas law supposedly aimed at promoting patriotism in public schools, the district was required to accept the donation and to display the posters prominently at each of its campuses. But there was nothing in state law that said Carroll officials had to invite the leaders of Patriot Mobile to deliver the posters during a special presentation before the school board. In a photo of the ceremony shared on Carroll's social media pages, board member Michelle Moore could be seen standing off by herself behind the leaders of her husband's former company. Afterward—thirty years nearly to the month after a Carroll student sued to block school-sponsored prayers at Dragon pep rallies—Patriot Mobile celebrated the poster donation in a blog post titled "Putting God Back into Our Schools."

Progressives across the Dallas–Fort Worth suburbs were suddenly awakening to the idea that their public schools may have been hijacked by religious extremists, but Patriot Mobile appeared to welcome their attacks. "We have been called Christian nationalists by those who want to silence us, to break us, to make us stop," the company's CEO, Glenn Story, declared. "But we embrace the term Christian nationalist. We love our country and we love the Lord, and we strive to be light in the darkness."

No school board did more that fall to advance Patriot Mobile's vision for public education than the leaders of the Grapevine–Colleyville Independent School District, or GCISD. The suburban school system—much like Southlake, its neighbor to the west—had been reshaped by dramatic demographic changes in recent decades. In the early 1990s, the then overwhelmingly white school system briefly gained national notoriety after a string of reports about young neo-Nazis, including a recent GCISD graduate, terrorizing Black and Jewish teens at school and in the community. Over the next thirty years, as the community grew far more diverse—by 2022, only about half of the district's fourteen thousand students were white—officials had adopted policies aimed at making their increasingly multicultural schools more inclusive.

Now, on the evening of August 22, the new conservative board majority was prepared to offer its answer to those programs.

Seventy-two hours earlier, the board had unveiled a sweeping thirty-six-page plan that touched on virtually every aspect of the political battles over race, gender, and sexuality. The Patriot Mobile–backed board members claimed that the plan merely codified policies already adopted by Republican state lawmakers, but in fact, the GCISD proposal went much further. Under the plan, teachers would be prohibited from discussing any concepts related to critical race theory, or what the proposal referred to as "systemic discrimination ideologies"—

amounting to an explicit ban on teachers acknowledging the existence of systemic racism. In the name of religious freedom, the policy would give school employees the right to refer to transgender and nonbinary students by pronouns and names matching the ones they were assigned at birth—a practice known as misgendering or deadnaming—even if the student's parents supported their child's gender expression. (The "parents' rights" movement did not extend to *all* parents, it seemed.) As in Florida, GCISD teachers would be prohibited from discussing sexual orientation or gender in elementary school, and only in limited ways in later grades. The proposal also banned any reading materials and classroom discussions dealing with "gender fluidity," which the document incorrectly defined as any belief that "biological sex is merely a social construct." (Transgender rights advocates argue that gender, not sex, is a social construct.)

Unlike Carroll's Cultural Competence Action Plan, there had been no community meetings to discuss the need for such a plan, no special volunteer committee to write and refine the document. To protest, some GCISD parents came to the board meeting wearing custom T-shirts with the school district's name, GCISD, crossed out and replaced with the words "Patriot Mobile Action ISD."

"They bought four school boards, and now they're pulling the strings," Rachel Wall, the white mother of a biracial Grapevine-Colleyville student, said ahead of the meeting. "I'm a Christian by faith, but if I wanted my son to be in a religious school, I would pay for him to go to a private school."

The conservative board majority ultimately would do as promised that night, voting 4–3 to adopt the plan. Tammy Nakamura, one of the white board members backed by Patriot Mobile, who two years earlier had posed with a man displaying a Confederate flag at a rally against COVID restrictions, said the party-line vote fulfilled her campaign pledge "to put an end to adults pushing their worldviews, whims, and fantasies onto unsuspecting children." Another board member said they were executing the will of local voters.

But the public comments prior to the vote revealed a suburban community bitterly divided by the new direction of its prized school system.

Nearly two hundred people signed up to speak, a majority of whom said they opposed the policy changes. A high school student who identified as LGBTQ told the board she feared that the policy would make queer students feel even more alienated. "Help my friends," she said. "Don't tell them that they should be erased." One mother, a former teacher, turned to scripture to explain her opposition to Patriot Mobile's influence over her school system. Paraphrasing Jesus, she said, "They will know us by our love.

"When I read about the policies and I watch and attend school board meetings," the woman said, "I keep thinking, 'This is not love.'"

By far the loudest and most colorful comments came from parents and activists on the other side, several of whom had traveled from outside the district. Many had answered a call from the Patriot Mobile–aligned True Texas Project, a far-right organization that had been labeled as an anti-government extremist group by the Southern Poverty Law Center, and whose leaders had asked supporters across the region to pack GCISD's meeting and to turn it into a party celebrating the new policy. Dozens had arrived hours beforehand, setting up tents and firing up barbecue pits in the GCISD parking lot, tailgating outside a school board meeting as if it was a college football game or Trump rally. They were joined by another anti-LGBTQ activist group whose leader had been suspended from Twitter after writing, "Let's start rounding up people who participate in pride events."

Inside, a husky white man wearing an American flag hat and red polo shirt encouraged the conservative board majority to "fight like hell" and "hold the ground against the LGBT mafia and their dang pedo fans"—echoing the false claims painting queer educators as pedophiles. "And guess what," the man shouted into the microphone, "teachers shouldn't be forced to use your freakin' made-up fantasy pronouns!" He ended his remarks by screaming, "Wooooo! Get some!" and slamming his fist on the lectern.

Another resident who spoke in support of the policy said one of the things that made America great at its founding were "schools that taught kids to read and know the Bible, and recite the Constitution." She commended the school board for working to restore those ideals.

"Our kids have to be taught our foundation," she said. "Our foundation of God-given inalienable rights, religious freedoms, individualism, democracy, and a free market."

Toward the end of the meeting, a white mother with short blond hair and wire-framed glasses stepped forward and introduced herself as Sharla. Reading from prepared remarks, she told the board why she supported banning classroom discussions and books about transgender people. "The doctrine of gender fluidity brings disorder, chaos, anarchy, and confusion into our schools and classrooms."

For Sharla, this debate was not philosophical; it was personal. When her child started identifying as a girl, she told the board, a teacher at Grapevine High School had provided the student with information affirming that gender expression. "Certain staff were labeling him," Sharla said, "feeding him incorrect information, especially about his 'unaccepting mom.' They gave him and other students unsolicited harmful information from their personal libraries. In doing so, they exploited my son's gender dysphoria."

As a result, the mother told the board, choking up as a beeper signaled that her time had expired, "I lost my son."

That evening, I was listening to a live feed of GCISD's school board meeting through wireless earbuds while juggling my nightly parental duties. Washing dishes, brushing teeth. By the time Sharla spoke, I had just put my preschooler to bed, and as I listened in the dark, I knew instinctively that the mother's comments were significant. She was sharing her firsthand account of a teacher going behind her back and filling her vulnerable child's head with what she described as lies about gender and biology—the exact horror story that Republican politicians like Ron DeSantis had been warning about. As I watched my three-year-old drift to sleep that night, a thought entered my mind, a question that I would spend months trying to answer.

What book or lesson could possibly drive a permanent wedge between a parent and their child?

To understand what happened to Sharla and her family, you had to rewind two years, to the fall of 2020. A young teacher named Em

Ramser had just begun what she thought was her dream job, as an English teacher at GCISD's ASPIRE Academy, an accelerated program based at Grapevine High School for the district's brightest students. Ramser hadn't initially set out to become a teacher. She'd majored in English in college with the goal of becoming a writer, but ended up discovering a passion for education while working at a summer program where she taught literature and creative writing to high school students. She loved handing a kid a book and watching a new world open in front of them. In one of those summer classes, a student read one of her own poems aloud, and in the process revealed to the class that she was gay—the first time the teen had ever done so publicly. Afterward the girl was crying and upset, worried about how her peers might judge her, and what challenges her future might hold. Ramser, twenty at the time, recalled pulling the teen aside and telling her that she was queer, too. "As a way of saying, 'Look, you are going to survive. It is possible to be an adult and be queer. It's possible to grow up and have a life.'" At the end of the summer, the student wrote a thank-you note, comparing her encounter with Ramser—the first openly gay adult who the girl had ever known—to meeting Captain America.

That's when Ramser fully realized her purpose, not only to help young people cultivate a love of reading and writing, but to create a safe space for LGBTQ teens to flourish. Ramser never had anything like that at school growing up in North Carolina and California. She remembered a high school classmate shoving her to the ground and calling her an anti-LGBTQ slur once because she wore a rainbow ribbon on her backpack. Those years were lonely. Looking back, she realized that having just one openly queer teacher could have made a difference in her life.

Ramser felt as if she was fulfilling her calling that first year at GCISD. "I teach very rapidly, I do a lot with my students, and I get really good results," she said. To get the kids engaged in reading, Ramser set up a challenge: For every million words a student read, they would receive a prize. The kids were competitive, and books were flying off the shelves of Ramser's classroom library. One book in particular, *The Prince and the Dressmaker*, went through her class "like wildfire," Ramser said, "with kid after kid reading it and passing it to the next." The graphic novel told the story of a prince who liked to wear dresses. But, fearing rejection from his parents, the prince kept his fashion hobby hidden. When his secret was finally revealed, the prince ran away from home. He returned in the end to discover that his mother and father loved him, no matter how he dressed.

That fall, a freshman who'd asked Ramser to refer to them as Ren took *The Prince and the Dressmaker* home based on a recommendation from a classmate. Ren, the child of divorced parents, was one of Ramser's quieter kids. Throughout the school year, the student—listed as a boy on official school documents—had asked the teacher at various times to refer to them by gender-neutral or female pronouns. Other times, Ren said not to do that. Ramser didn't make a big deal about it, she said. "That was very much my mentality with teaching. I'm going to give you some space to figure yourself out."

Then, one day in January 2021, Ren, who has since come to identify as a transgender female, wasn't in school, and some of her friends were worried. Ramser went to a counselor and discovered that Ren was missing. Later, when Ramser learned that the student was safe, she was relieved. But then complaints started rolling in from the student's mother, Sharla. It seemed Sharla had found the copy of *The Prince and the Dressmaker* in her child's backpack and had come to believe that the book is what led Ren to think it was OK to identify as a girl, and worse, that the way to gain acceptance was to run away from her unsupportive mother.

Ramser was baffled. "To me," she said, "the book is very much about the message, 'Your parents will always support you. It's never right to run away from your responsibilities. You just have to talk to people. And friendship is good.'" Even so, Ramser got pulled into a meeting with her principal to discuss the books in her library. Ren's mother alleged that Ramser had been forcing her students to read *The Prince and the Dressmaker*, which the teacher said was untrue. The book, Ramser noted, was rated for children as young as twelve and contained no explicit passages. Her students were free to read—or not to read—any of the books in her class library. That made sense to Ramser's principal, and no action was taken. After her disappearance, Ren finished out the last half of her freshman year remotely, with her mother sometimes visible on the video feed during Ramser's advanced English class.

The teacher assumed she would never see her well-worn copy of *The Prince and the Dressmaker* again, which was fine. It wasn't one that she'd purchased with her own money; someone had donated it. Then, one day toward the end of the school year, Ramser stepped out of her classroom and looked down. The graphic novel was sitting on the floor outside her door. No note. No explanation. The teacher picked it up, flipped through the pages, then returned it to her bookshelf.

That, Ramser figured, would be the end of it.

The episode looked different from Ren's perspective. The student had gotten into an argument with her mother on the day she didn't show up for class in January 2021, which had been happening more often in the two years since the teen first told Sharla that she thought she might be a girl. Ren couldn't understand why her mother refused to accept her as a female; Sharla wished her "son" could see that his "gender confusion" was something that needed to be treated, not embraced. At fourteen, Ren was tired of suppressing her feelings. So instead of going to school that morning, she caught a ride to a bus station and purchased a ticket west. Ren's father, Rich, lived in Portland, Oregon, and had never hesitated to support his child's transgender identity. "Is that what you were so afraid to tell me?" Rich had said after Ren came out to him on a long car ride a couple of years earlier. "I love and support you no matter what gender you are." After running away, Ren had made it about three hundred miles to Lubbock before a police officer boarded the bus during a stop and returned her to her mother.

Ren didn't know initially that her mom had blamed her disappearance in part on *The Prince and the Dressmaker*—which Ren had checked out but never actually read—and on her teacher Ms. Ramser, whom Ren adored. The idea that a friendly teacher or a fairy tale had played a role in shaping Ren's transgender identity was "very much made up entirely," the teen said. She and Ramser had never directly discussed the subject, and Ren had been trying to tell her mother about her female identity for more than a year by then. Sharla, a devout Christian, had reacted then by enrolling Ren in a religious counseling program that promised to help children become "the person they were created to be."

Ren described her conversations with her mother about gender like "talking to a brick wall." No matter how she framed her feelings, Ren said Sharla would invariably reply by quoting scripture or saying that she loved her child "the way God made you."

The festering dispute between mother and child was emblematic of similar fights roiling families and educators all over the country. Although the overall population of transgender people was still small, in an era of increased LGBTQ acceptance among young people, the number of teens identifying as trans had, in the span of a few years, nearly doubled to 1.4 percent by the time Ren was entering high school. The growing embrace of alternative gender expressions had triggered a panic among some parents who claimed that teens were being pressured to change genders by peers and society, while raising new ethical questions for educators. Should teachers and guidance counselors be required to notify parents when a child asked to be called by different pronouns at school? What if sending a note home put a child at risk of emotional or physical abuse? On the other hand, others argued, shouldn't parents be involved with something so important?

For Ren, school was the one place where she felt completely free to be herself, thanks to teachers like Ramser and supportive friends. But after she attempted to run away and her mother pulled Ren out of in-person classes, the tension between the two tightened. The following school year Sharla found girls' clothing in Ren's room. Sharla texted the update to Ren's father, Rich, whom she blamed in part for their child's life choices: Their child needed "someone to help with gender dysphoria," she wrote, asking for help finding and paying for a provider. "P.S. It should be a male."

Rich, an electrical engineer and former teacher, responded by sending his ex-wife research documenting the harm of refusing to affirm transgender children, including the heightened risk for serious mental health disorders and suicide. "The American Psychological Association does not support any therapeutic treatment aimed at changing gender identity or trying to align birth gender with gender identity."

"I have read all about the secular definitions and I understand how the LBGQTX+ have corrupted biblical morality and thinking," Sharla texted back. "You are his father and should be guiding him in moral ways, not accepting whatever sexuality he wants to assign himself."

It was around that time that Ren started pleading with her father to seek full legal custody. Rich had grown increasingly concerned by his ex-wife's refusal to affirm their daughter's gender, but he didn't want to tear Ren away from her teachers and friends at Grapevine High School. He changed his mind in 2022, after Texas governor Greg Abbott directed the state's child welfare agency to open child abuse investigations against any parents who sought gender-affirming hormone treatments for their transgender children.

"[Ren] is at high risk of self-harm or running away because of her mother's reaction to her gender identity, and the dangerous political situation makes her feel even more unsafe in Texas," Rich wrote to a family lawyer in March of that year, beginning the process of seeking full custody. That summer, a judge in Oregon signaled her support for Ren's request to be with her father full-time, and on August 1, 2022, Sharla signed a consent decree granting her ex-husband sole legal custody.

That's what she meant when she went before the GCISD school board three weeks later and said, "I lost my son."

Even though her claim about GCISD teachers convincing her child to identify as a girl appeared to be unsupported, Sharla's public comments that night were just the start of a campaign to expose the teacher whom she believed had brainwashed her child. Afterward, the mother created a Facebook page titled *Woke Mama Bear: Gender Truth God's Way*, and filled the feed with photos of her newly estranged child, always referring to Ren by male pronouns and by the boy's name given to her at birth. Sharla posted links to a blog warning that cultural shifts in America signaled the coming end times, along with select Bible verses:

> God Created mankind in His own image, in the image of God He created them; male and female He created them.
>
> —GENESIS 1:27

Later, Sharla launched a YouTube channel and recorded a video of herself warning parents about the toxic ideology that she believed was poisoning children's minds and destroying families. "Let me be clear," Sharla said in the video, which was scored with a haunting piano track. "Transgender people exist, and they should be respected and loved like any other human beings." But nowadays, Sharla continued, "I think most transgender people are made, not born. They are made . . . by woke."

That August, Sharla shared her story with the *Dallas Express*, a far-right news source owned by a billionaire named Monty Bennett, a hotel magnate who'd been in Washington, D.C., to support Trump's bid to overturn American democracy on January 6. Bennett in recent years had taken a keen interest in two seemingly divergent but intertwined causes: bankrolling conservative school board candidates who promised to guard against liberal indoctrination in public schools, including in GCISD, while also giving to groups and politicians who were on a mission to divert public school funding to parents in the form of private school vouchers. Bennett's newspaper had become a vehicle for both of those causes, sowing distrust of public schools while simultaneously calling for their funding to be siphoned to private schools. The *Dallas Express* article about Sharla ran under the headline "Bombshell Claims of GCISD Teacher Misconduct," and quoted from an email that the mother had recently sent to the principal of Grapevine High School: "I hope and pray you will never have to feel the pain I have gone through," she wrote, "trying to talk to your child but he has been poisoned by those you trusted."

That same week, Sharla wrote a social media post detailing the custody battle with her ex-husband—going public with what until then had been a private family drama. She recalled flying to Oregon that summer, just weeks before she'd officially lost custody, and fighting to see her child. Ren had agreed to give her mother forty minutes.

"He was cold and hostile, saying that I needed to give his dad sole custody," Sharla wrote, continuing to use male pronouns despite her child's wishes. "He was not dressed as a female for my visit, but I did have to go into the lion's den (his dad's house)."

In what might have been her final meeting with her only child, Sharla issued a warning. "I told him he has made a tough decision, and he will have to pay the consequences. When he finds out the truth, he is always welcome home."

Until then, she wrote, "This momma's arms are open wide."

Ramser was at school when the *Dallas Express* published the article about Sharla and Ren. A colleague approached her in class and showed her the headline on her phone. Ramser felt light-headed as she read through the piece, which called her out by name and quoted Sharla saying that the English teacher had "infected" her child with toxic ideas.

"It felt like being plunged into an ice bath," Ramser said, "and you can't catch your breath."

The article noted that Ramser had been the faculty monitor for the district's Gay-Straight Alliance. Sharla claimed the student club was a conduit "to mold our teens not only to accept the LGBTQ+ agenda, but to indoctrinate and confuse their own gender identities." Distressed, Ramser left in the middle of the school day. She didn't come back the next day, or the day after that.

Even before the article, her life at GCISD had become difficult. Some parents had read through her lesson plans the previous spring and accused her on social media of pushing critical race theory and "woke" gender ideology in her reading assignments. That resulted in a wave of online harassment—including a Facebook post calling her a pedophile—but nothing compared to what followed the *Dallas Express* piece. Her social media accounts and email were being bombarded with messages accusing her of grooming and sexualizing children. Someone used her email account to sign up for several pornography sites, and now her inbox was filling up with links to nude images and videos. Later, the teacher would end up moving to a new address—one that she would keep secret even from her employer, out of fear that it might get leaked by a school employee or board member. (Ramser believed she had reason to worry: One GCISD board member, Tammy Nakamura, had said during an event hosted by the Republican National Committee that she had a list of educators who she believed were indoctrinating kids. "We cannot have teachers such as these in our schools," said Nakamura, who was joined at the event by Southlake school board member Hannah Smith, "because they are poison, and they are taking our schools down.")

Ramser's plight seemed to confirm Chris Rufo's hunch; the "reservoir of sentiment on the sexuality issue" ran deep, and the resulting backlash had blown its way through the English teacher's life with explosive force.

Initially, Ramser was leaning against returning to school at all after the article about Sharla's claims. She was disappointed that district leaders hadn't issued a public statement defending her and making clear that she'd done nothing wrong. Instead, a GCISD spokesperson sent out a couple of sentences saying the district couldn't comment on individual student or employee matters. But after a few days hiding out at home, Ramser caught word that some of her students were deeply worried about her. She didn't want them to think she had quit on them.

And so, she returned to finish out the 2022–23 school year, a shell of the teacher she once was. To avoid additional complaints from parents, she'd had to take down her entire classroom library and run every reading assignment by higher-ups for approval. It's difficult to inspire a love for reading without books, and even harder to create a safe space for queer teenagers when a school district imposes rules against discussing LGBTQ people. Ramser was not allowed to continue serving as the faculty sponsor for the Gay-Straight Alliance student club, a role she had cherished. Even as she suppressed her identity, she still endured ridicule; one student left an anonymous note on her desk with an antigay slur written on it.

As the school year progressed, Ramser sank into a deep depression but did her best to hide her sorrow from students. Her mother still noticed. "If you kill yourself," she told her daughter one night, "I'm going to sue that damn school."

When Ren and her father learned about what had happened to Ms. Ramser, they were outraged. The English teacher had done nothing but show Ren kindness during a difficult period in her life. "She was such a good teacher to me and my friends," Ren said, "and now she's being punished because of it."

In the fall of 2022, a little more than two months after Grapevine-Colleyville ISD adopted one of the most sweeping anti-LGBTQ, anti-CRT school board policies in the country—at a time when many parents and educators nationally had begun to lose hope that they would be able to stop conservative Christian groups from taking over their suburban schools—progressives saw a glint of sunshine poke through the darkened political clouds.

The glimmer had come from a fast-growing suburb north of Austin that until recently had been regarded as a Republican stronghold. Politically and demographically speaking, the Round Rock Independent School District looked a lot like the suburbs north of Fort Worth, which is perhaps why the Republican Party of Texas and a group called Round Rock One Family PAC, yet another political action committee explicitly modeled after Southlake Families, had made it their mission to win control of the school board there. Conservatives spent nearly $300,000 backing a slate of five candidates, including one whose slogan had been "Teach ABCs + 123s, Not CRTs & LGBTs." The conservative activists in Round Rock followed the Southlake Playbook at every stage. And yet, when all the votes had been counted on election night that November, all five of their candidates had lost by double digits.

The Round Rock election was marred by all the ugliness that had come to define school board politics during this period of American life. One incumbent school board member, a Black woman, had received harassing messages at her home, including a package that contained a dildo. Two other packages sent to a pair of Harrison's supporters contained used tampons. But the Round Rock election had something that had been missing from earlier school board elections in places like Southlake and Grapevine: a highly organized and well-funded opposition from liberals and moderate conservatives.

Krista Laine, a white mother of two, had closely followed events out of Southlake, and when she and her friends noticed some of the same political tactics being deployed in Round Rock, they knew they needed to act fast. They formed a political action committee of their own, Access Education RRISD, and set out to beat Round Rock One Family PAC at its own Southlake-inspired game. They worked to build a bipartisan coalition of Democrats and disaffected "regular" Republicans who were united in their opposition to Christian nationalism and the infusion of far-right politics in schools. They recruited their own slate of five candidates and spent $50,000 dollars on political mailers and yard signs. Although they were still out-funded, the Access Education PAC went on the offensive, attacking the conservative candidates as the "Hate Slate," and getting volunteers to stand outside polling sites to lobby voters.

"We would tell people, 'Look, we just want to make school boards boring again,'" Laine said. "And we proved that most people agreed with that message."

The Round Rock outcome embarrassed the state Republican Party, which had endorsed a total of eleven candidates in nonpartisan school board races across Texas that November and ended up losing all but two of them. Access Education's success cast doubt on an argument first espoused by Steve Bannon, which had become conventional wisdom among GOP strategists; school boards, it turns out, may not have held the key to reversing Republican losses in fast-diversifying suburbs.

Round Rock showed that when progressives and moderate parents organized, they could win, maybe not in overwhelmingly conservative towns like Southlake, but in lots of suburbs across the country. A group of parents in Grapevine and Colleyville were among those who'd taken note. With the Round Rock blueprint—the left's answer to the Southlake Playbook—they were going to try one more time to reverse Patriot Mobile's gains and, Lord willing, retake control of their children's schools.

15

The Holy Grail

ON THE FIRST DAY of the 2023 Texas legislative session, one of the state's newest lawmakers held up his cell phone inside the capitol rotunda in Austin and started filming himself. Representative Nate Schatzline, a youth pastor turned freshman Republican legislator, smiled into the camera. "We have an entire team of church coming together and worshiping right here, and we are singing and giving glory to God," Schatzline said to his followers watching on Instagram, before panning the camera to show dozens of fellow believers swaying and harmonizing with their hands raised. "There is nothing more important that we could be doing than this right here, worshiping and praying in the middle of the Capitol."

For the next twenty-five minutes, Schatzline and the other worshipers invited the Holy Spirit to reign over the statehouse, singing, "Let heaven come to earth; as it is in heaven, let heaven come." With a fast-paced drum beat echoing through the three-hundred-foot-tall rotunda, believers began to speak in tongues—the Pentecostal practice of uttering incomprehensible, speechlike sounds meant to represent a divine language unknown to the speaker. Schatzline prayed over the hum of voices, calling on his supporters to let the world know "that God is in authority over everything that goes on in this building." A moment later, a pastor named Landon Schott—a Fort Worth preacher whose mixing of far-right politics and religion had drawn national media attention—stepped forward and declared that Schatzline and other conservative Christian lawmakers had been elected, not because of a brilliant political strategy, but as ordained by "the spirit of God."

Schott may have been understating another, less mystical factor in Schatzline's recent election to the statehouse: His campaign had raked in a whopping $168,000 from Defend Texas Liberty, a far-right political action committee bankrolled by a pair of West Texas oil and gas billionaires, Farris Wilks and Tim Dunn, who have expressed the Christian nationalist view that government should be guided by biblical values and run exclusively by evangelicals. Schatzline had put the PAC's money to use, in part, to attack his Republican primary opponent, former Southlake mayor Laura Hill, whom he tagged—in an ironic twist—as a friend of Black Lives Matter. Hill, his campaign alleged, had opened the door to allow critical race theory in the Carroll school system by initially supporting the work of Carroll's District Diversity Council in 2019, even though she later came out against the diversity plan. The shrewd strategy of painting a fellow conservative as a woke liberal paid off, and now, at age thirty-one, Schatzline was part of a class of far-right Christian Republican lawmakers who were promising to pass laws to glorify God in Texas government—first and foremost through its education system.

Over the previous decade, Schatzline's primary benefactors, Wilks and Dunn, had put millions of dollars toward pushing Texas further to the right. This shift was significant, not only for the state's thirty million residents, but for the rest of America. Texas, like Florida under Ron DeSantis, had become a national laboratory for conservative governance. Wilks and Dunn had used their money and network of advocacy groups to advance several causes of the far right, helping win major victories to ban abortion and eliminate basic firearm restrictions. But until recently, their signature objective—public funding for private religious schooling, considered by many to be the holy grail of the far-right Christian movement in America—had been out of reach in Texas, blocked by an unlikely coalition of Democrats opposed to private school vouchers on ideological grounds and rural Republican lawmakers who worried that siphoning funding from public education would hurt cash-strapped, small-town school districts.

By 2023, two years into the national debate over racism and LGBTQ inclusion in education, the politics had shifted. Groups that had spent years fighting for school privatization, including a national political action committee founded and funded by Trump's former education secretary Betsy DeVos, seized on what some were calling a once-in-a-generation opportunity. In a fundraising email, the Texas Public Policy Foundation, a Heritage Foundation–style libertarian advocacy group based in Texas, told supporters that "the time is ripe to set Texas children free from enforced indoctrination and Big Government cronyism in our public schools."

Ahead of the 2023 legislative session, which began in January, Texas lieutenant governor Dan Patrick hosted a strategy call with conservative leaders and fifty Texas pastors. On the phone, Allan Parker, president of The Justice Foundation, a Texas nonprofit whose mission is to "restore proper respect for God's word and law to American jurisprudence," lamented what he viewed as the spread of liberal ideologies in public schools. "Now that abortion is illegal," Parker said, "I believe that the greatest injustice in Texas today is that we compel a family to pay taxes for the education of their children, to send them to a school that teaches them things that aren't in line with their family's values."

As school privatization efforts swept Republican state legislatures nationally, activist Chris Rufo once again appeared to give the game away, telling an audience at an event hosted by Hillsdale College in Michigan that, "To get universal school choice, you really need to operate from a premise of universal public school distrust." Now, having convinced many GOP voters that public schools were teaching white students to hate themselves and pressuring kindergartners to change genders, Schatzline and other Texas Republicans set out to rescue the state's schoolchildren from that alleged threat.

In the weeks after the rotunda worship gathering, they proposed a raft of bills to divert public school funding to private religious academies, to limit the rights of LGBTQ children in public schools, and to require districts to display Christian symbols inside classrooms. The centerpiece of the package, Senate Bill 8—dubbed the Texas Parental Bill of Rights by its authors—would give parents who wanted to pull their children out of public school $8,000 a year to cover homeschooling expenses or private school tuition, while giving those who chose to keep their children in public schools new oversight over what students were taught and what books they could access.

Joining forces with the Texas Public Policy Foundation—which also drew funding from billionaire Tim Dunn—Governor Greg Abbott hit the road that winter to sell voters on the idea. Speaking exclusively at private Christian academies that stood to benefit financially from his plan, Abbott pitched privatization as a necessary tool to defeat "the woke agenda that's being forced on children in their schools."

At one of Abbott's stops at Brazos Christian School in Bryan, a college town about an hour northwest of Houston, the school's headmaster, Jeffrey McMaster, made clear whom the voucher plan would help. Brazos Christian, McMaster told the audience, "isn't here to serve every family or every student." Instead, he said, the school was founded in 1981 "to serve specifically a small subset of families" who want children to learn "the Bible as our source and standard of truth."

McMaster had inadvertently highlighted a chief criticism of private school voucher schemes. Unlike federally funded public schools, which must accommodate all students, regardless of their race, religion, gender, sexual orientation, or learning ability, private schools are free to pick and choose which students are allowed to attend and cater only to families who share their values—a reality plainly visible in Brazos Christian's student demographics. Located in a zip code where more than half of the children were Black or Hispanic, more than 91 percent of the school's students were white. Those seeking to enroll at Brazos were required to meet three requirements: Children had to show evidence of a relationship with Jesus, verified through a pastor's reference. They were required to be on grade level academically. And they needed to have a "clean behavior record."

Abbott's plan would ensure that more families whose children matched that description could afford to leave public schools and find refuge in religious academies like Brazos Christian, where, McMaster said, his staff would train them "to impact the world for Jesus."

The first proposal in Texas to provide government funding for private school tuition emerged in 1956, when a legislative subcommittee floated the idea as a way of allowing white parents to opt out of sending their children to newly desegregated public schools. Republicans nationwide revived and rebranded the idea beginning about three decades later, pitching vouchers instead as a way to give students—especially low-income students—access to high-quality private schools.

The "high-quality" component of that proposition was debatable. A 2017 investigation by the *Orlando Sentinel* found that Florida's voucher program for low-income students had been used to pay tuition at private schools that taught students "that dinosaurs and humans lived together, that God's intervention prevented Catholics from dominating North America and that slaves who 'knew Christ' were better off than free men who did not." The newspaper also found that some state-supported private schools hired teachers who lacked professional training, while others threatened LGBTQ students with expulsion.

Today, a wide range of policies fall under the umbrella of what advocates call educational freedom, but each adheres to the same underlying principle: The state provides parents with the money that would have been spent to educate their child in public school to pay for private school tuition or other educational expenses. This can come in the form of direct payments, tax credits, government savings accounts, and scholarships. Sixteen states had adopted such programs by 2022, and that year Arizona became the first to approve "universal vouchers," providing about $7,000 per year per child to any parent, regardless of their income, who chose to homeschool their children or send them to a private school. Despite initial indications that the policy was draining public school coffers and primarily benefiting Arizona parents who'd already been sending their children to private schools, similar programs were swiftly adopted in Iowa and Utah. After Governor Ron DeSantis signed a law in early 2023 to expand Florida's education savings account program to all students, national school choice advocates turned their focus to Texas—the largest red state without an expansive voucher program.

In March, two months into the legislative session, the public got its first chance to weigh in on Governor Abbott's plan during a public hearing before the Senate education committee. Hundreds of educators, parents, school officials, and activists came to Austin to sound off on the bill, including Glennda Hardin. The seventy-three-year-old retired teacher awoke before sunrise to drive to the capital, her prepared speech folded neatly in her handbag. Hardin had never done anything like this before, but once she'd heard what Republicans had planned for the state's education system, she knew she had to come speak her mind. "I really believe the future of our schools is at stake," Hardin said.

"This isn't about helping public schools," she continued, her hands shaking as she waited in the back of the committee room for her turn to speak. "It's a program to give a break to affluent parents who want to send their children to private Christian schools. Period."

Hardin wasn't the only one pushed to political activism for the first time. The campaign for private school vouchers seemed to awaken a sleeping giant of opposition, made up of a broad coalition of traditional public school advocates—educators, teachers unions, local school superintendents—and those who opposed the plan for vastly different reasons. A Trump-voting Republican said the plan would hurt the public school district in his rural West Texas town, which happened to be the town's largest employer. A conservative homeschooling mother argued that the bill would give the government a dangerous foothold in regulating what she taught her children. And a group of faith leaders, Pastors for Texas Children, said their religious beliefs propelled them to speak out against any plan that diverted funding from public schools that serve vulnerable children.

The Reverend Holly Bandel, a pastor at First United Methodist Church in Dallas and a member of the pastors group, traveled to Austin because she worried the voucher plan chipped away at the separation of church and state, which she considered to be at the bedrock of what makes America great. "An essential part of providing equity in our nation," Bandel said, "is that we are not imposing beliefs on people."

Those supporting the voucher bill were just as passionate. Some came in matching shirts that read, "My school. My child. My choice," recasting the famous pro-abortion rights slogan in support of government funding for private schools. Vera Billingsley, wearing a red blazer over a "Parents Matter" T-shirt, a cross necklace around her neck, and a cherub angel pinned to her lapel, came to tell GOP legislators she supported their plans and hoped they went even further: Not only should parents be given money to send children to private Christian academies, she believed the same biblical values that guided curricula in those schools should be mandated in public school classrooms.

"We're forgetting our moral moorings," said Billingsley, a school board candidate from San Antonio who'd been running on a promise to slash local school funding, which she argued had grown out of control. Cutting the budget both at the state and local levels would have the added benefit of limiting the ability of public schools to indoctrinate students with liberal ideas, Billingsley said, and force schools "to get back to the basics." She recalled reciting a daily prayer and a Bible verse at school each morning as a child in Ohio in the early 1960s, back before, as Billingsley saw it, America lost its way. Now schools were becoming fortresses to protect against the ever-present threat of mass shootings, and children were struggling with soaring rates of depression.

To Billingsley and her allies, the solution to these problems was simple, and had nothing to do with gun control or increased funding for mental health services: "If they would bring the Proverbs every day into the school like I did with my kids at home, they would be fine."

A few weeks later, the Texas Senate voted along party lines to approve Senate Bill 8, sending the voucher package to the House of Representatives, where opponents still hoped they could convince enough rural Republican lawmakers to choose the interests of local public schools over the interests of their political party.

Far-right Christian activists had, in effect, opened a two-front battle in the war over education. While fighting to win public funding for private Christian schooling, they simultaneously pushed to impose conservative Christian values inside public school classrooms. In Alabama, a lawmaker introduced a bill to allow children to pray aloud over campus public address systems, essentially forcing schools to facilitate student-led prayer. In Oklahoma, Roman Catholic organizers pushed the state for approval to open the nation's first publicly funded Christian charter school, an audacious plan to bypass the voucher middleman and get the government into the business of directly paying for religious education. And, following Texas's lead, a lawmaker in Louisiana introduced a bill requiring public schools to display the national motto, "In God We Trust."

Republicans all over the country were suddenly attempting to do exactly what evangelicals had been demanding for decades: erasing the hard line between religion and public education. And they had reason to believe these plans would hold up in court.

A year earlier, the U.S. Supreme Court had ruled in favor of a Washington State high school football coach named Joseph Kennedy who'd argued that his religious rights were violated when his employer, a public school, sought to limit his practice of standing among a group of high school athletes and praying on the football field after games. In its 6–3 ruling in *Kennedy v. Bremerton School District*—handed down three days after the court overturned abortion rights in America—the court's conservative supermajority said the coach's prayers were protected by the First Amendment and rejected the school district's argument that allowing the prayers amounted to an official government endorsement of religion.

In her dissent, Justice Sonia Sotomayor argued that Kennedy had effectively coerced players who may have felt pressured to join their coach in prayer. "Students look up to their teachers and coaches as role models and seek their approval," she wrote. "Players recognize that gaining the coach's approval may pay dividends small and large, from extra playing time to a stronger letter of recommendation to additional support in college athletic recruiting." Writing for the majority, Justice Neil Gorsuch argued that the coach "was not instructing players, discussing strategy, encouraging better on-field performance or engaged in any other speech the district paid him to produce as a coach." Gorsuch and others in the majority rejected "the view that the only acceptable government role models for students are those who eschew any visible religious expression."

As recently as 2000, the court had ruled that organized prayers at high school football games, even when led by students, violated the

First Amendment's prohibition of government establishment of religion. Now the court, radically reshaped by Trump's three nominations, was scaling back such restrictions, overturning forty years of precedent guiding the court's handling of church-state separation.

To some lawmakers, it looked like a green light to begin pushing Christianity into schools.

Many of these legislative efforts were being steered and supported by the National Association of Christian Lawmakers, a group founded in 2019 with a mission to advance "biblical" laws in America's statehouses and "restore the Judeo-Christian foundation of our nation." The group—whose board of advisors included Texas lieutenant governor Dan Patrick; Patriot Mobile CEO Glenn Story; and Andrew Wommack, a celebrity pastor from Colorado and a leading promoter of the Seven Mountains Mandate—had produced several model bills aimed at glorifying Jesus in America's halls of power, and in its classrooms.

No state legislature went further in attempting to advance that vision than Texas. One bill introduced in 2023 required public schools to set aside time each day for students and teachers to pray and read their Bibles. Another mandated that the Ten Commandments—the King James version, specifically—be displayed in every public school classroom in the state. Yet another, which was swiftly approved by both legislative chambers, allowed public schools to replace mental health counselors and social workers with unlicensed Christian chaplains.

One of the advocacy groups pushing the chaplain bill, the National School Chaplains Association, revealed in a promotional video that its goal was to use America's public school system "to bring Jesus to an entire nation." Rocky Malloy, the association's leader, argued that public schools in America were already guided by a religion—secularism—and that installing Christian pastors on school payrolls would allow students to turn to faith leaders who he said were capable of sharing "absolute truth." Malloy then made clear whose truth he was talking about. "Right now it's all relative," he said. "Right now there's a big discussion like, what is a woman? Just a couple years ago that was pretty straightforward." In addition to correcting student's views on the existence of transgender people, Malloy later suggested that chaplains—he called them "campus youth pastors"—could be placed in charge of reviewing what books are allowed in school libraries.

The flurry of Christian nationalist legislation prompted a pair of *Dallas Morning News* reporters to imagine for their readers what early childhood education might soon look like in the state: "In kindergarten classrooms across Texas, five-year-olds coming to school for the first time could soon be greeted by picture books, colorful blocks and the words, 'Thou shalt not covet thy neighbor's wife.' As those children grow up in the state's public schools, they could get dedicated time in the day to read the Bible or pray. And if they are going through a hard time, they could turn to a chaplain—rather than a licensed school counselor—for help on campus."

To justify their attempts to exalt Jesus in the public education system, Republican lawmakers repeatedly cited and parroted the writings of one man in particular: the self-taught historian David Barton. "There is absolutely no separation of God and government, and that's what these bills are about," Texas state senator Mayes Middleton told the *Washington Post*. "When prayer was taken out of schools, things went downhill."

In a series of public hearings on the religion bills, legislators repeated Barton's claims about the "false doctrine" of church-state separation and blamed it for school shootings and the growing acceptance of LGBTQ people. Texas senator Donna Campbell praised one of Barton's discredited books while arguing in favor of posting the Ten Commandments in classrooms. At that same legislative hearing, Senator Phil King, the bill's author, invited Barton to testify as an "esteemed" expert witness.

"It's hard to say that anything is more traditional in American education than was the Ten Commandments," Barton told King and the other members of the Texas Senate Education Committee.

State lawmakers weren't the only officials now turning to Barton and his disputed take on American history to guide their decisions. That March, at an event sponsored by Patriot Mobile and hosted at a theater in Grapevine, Barton spoke onstage alongside several sitting school board members, including Cam Bryan, Carroll's school board president, and Shannon Braun, the board vice president at neighboring Grapevine-Colleyville.

Barton encouraged the school board members not to wait around for legislation from Austin, but to instead "go on the offensive" to restore biblical values in classrooms at the local level. Citing the Supreme Court's recent ruling in the Kennedy prayer case, Barton said public schools were now free to display Christian symbols in classrooms, pray at the beginning of school events, and have kids sing traditional Christian hymns during school performances.

"We can now go back to teaching things we haven't been able to teach in fifty years," Barton said, and then argued that public schools should present the biblical creation narrative as an alternative to the science of evolution. "Progressives took all this stuff out, we have an opportunity to put it back in."

Barton acknowledged that school leaders would face blowback for making these decisions. But that, too, it seemed, was part of God's plan. "Hopefully somebody will sue you if you do this," Barton said. "That's what we need. Because if they will sue you, these guys will take it to court, we can win at that, and the whole nation wins as a result."

That was the game plan, spelled out in public view: Use the power of local boards and state legislatures to force religion back into public schools, then hope for a legal challenge that might serve as a test case to get the Supreme Court to overturn the separation of church and state in America, once and for all.

As the 2023 Texas legislative session neared its end, it became clear that Governor Greg Abbott's signature policy objective—public funding for private schooling—was going to come up short in the state House of Representatives. Despite an unprecedented push by school choice advocates, the same surprising coalition that defeated the policy in years past had once again stood firm: Rural, Trump-voting Republicans, it turns out, loved their public schools just as much as suburban Democrats.

That didn't stop evangelicals from pressing forward on their parallel mission to infuse conservative Christian morality in the state's public schools. Lawmakers sent bills to Abbott's desk to allow schools to replace licensed therapists with pastors and to force publishers and school districts to apply age-appropriateness ratings to all children's books sold to public schools in the state—a law that opponents argued would be used by activists to purge school libraries of books depicting LGBTQ characters.

Before classes resumed in the fall, the state's teachers would once again be required to attend training sessions on how to comply with these new restrictions, taking time away from their primary task of educating children. But they and their schools wouldn't be getting any additional resources to manage this additional load. Because despite working with a record budget surplus, the bare-knuckled fight over school vouchers had gotten in the way of approving increases to school funding and teacher pay, with pro-voucher legislators refusing to consider those items without an agreement also to provide state funding for private schools.

"This was a lost session for public education," said Zeph Capo, president of the Texas American Federation of Teachers. "Texas legislators let a generational surplus slip through their fingers while ignoring the generational threat of teachers streaming out of classrooms. All to chase a voucher scam Texans did not want."

If public school boosters believed they'd won the war over vouchers, though, they needed only to study the fifty-year campaign to put prayer back in school and overturn abortion rights. Christian conservatives and their donors had gotten used to playing the long game.

As the 2023 legislative session ended, Abbott made his intentions plain, telling voucher supporters that he would "never relent."

He vowed to use his power as governor to order lawmakers back into session in the coming months. And if they once again failed to hammer out a deal to approve government funding of private schools, he was going to continue calling them back to Austin, month after month, until they bent to the will of his backers, and finally delivered Texas parents and their children from the tyranny of public education.

16

It Still Mattered

A LITTLE MORE THAN four years after a viral video of high school students chanting the N-word triggered a movement to confront racism in Southlake, the Carroll Independent School District's board of trustees met in December 2022 to consider a proposal to undo the last remaining vestige of that effort.

Once more, the district meeting room was filled with outraged parents.

"It is power that you desperately sought, and power that you now have," the ex–Dallas Cowboy and former District Diversity Council member Russell Maryland told the board during public comments ahead of the vote that night. "The question is, will you continue to be a detriment to our children of color in this district? Will you continue to not only ignore the cries and concerns of our LGBTQ students, but also try to deny their existence?"

After the racist video and subsequent outcry in 2018, Carroll administrators had moved quickly to update the student code of conduct, adding harsher penalties for students caught using racial slurs, and new language explicitly prohibiting discrimination on the basis of sexual orientation and gender. The changes were meant to send a signal to students and parents about what was acceptable at Carroll, and about who was welcome there. Now, with Southlake Families PAC–backed members holding all but two seats on the board, the district was about to send another message.

A new volunteer committee—this one loaded almost exclusively with residents who'd donated to Southlake Families PAC and its candidates—had spent months studying the student code of conduct and concluded that it should be simplified. It hadn't taken long for the community to notice a major change in the draft proposal: It omitted any reference to gender identity, sexual orientation, and religion from the district's nondiscrimination statement. The new version said only that Carroll would not "discriminate on the basis of race, color, national origin, sex, disability, or age." The phrase "sexual orientation" had appeared eighteen times in the existing code of conduct, but not once in the revised plan. Language addressing racial slurs also had been removed.

To members of the community who'd fought and failed to stop the Southlake Families takeover, the revised code of conduct seemed to put the finishing touches on what had been a two-year remaking of their local school district. A new model, perhaps, to be copied in suburbs across America.

Leaning down to speak into the microphone, Maryland accused members of the board majority of turning their back on their most vulnerable students. "It's time to stop defending the indefensible."

Some parents came wearing rainbow pride buttons. The father of an LGBTQ student accused the board of doing the bidding of "the billionaire funders of the Christian nationalism political movement." A mother read an anonymous statement from a closeted transgender high school student who said they struggled with depression and self-hatred because of their years at Carroll.

Angela Jones strained to keep composed as she approached the microphone. As one of the parents who'd filed federal civil rights complaints against the district, Jones said she was amazed by the brazenness of the board's plan. At the time of the meeting, the U.S. Department of Education's Office for Civil Rights was actively investigating six reports of discrimination at Carroll, including the complaint submitted by Jones. The number of investigations would grow to eight the following month as additional families came forward.

Jones was disappointed it was taking the agency so long to finish its work. Civil rights lawyers were now cautioning that, given the crush of discrimination complaints being handled by the federal agency, it might be well into the 2023–24 school year before the cases came to a resolution, which meant that Jones's youngest child would likely graduate before anything changed. Nevertheless, she hadn't given up on demanding reforms.

At the lectern, she reminded the trustees that they were under a national microscope. "Yet you are actually considering a student code of conduct that further erodes rights?" Jones said, an angry tremor in her voice. "You don't give a hoot about my son or any students that continue to be called racial slurs."

When the floor was opened for debate among members, trustee Eric Lannen justified his support for the changes by arguing they would have no material impact on the district's commitment to protecting students. The district wouldn't tolerate bullying of any kind, he said, and he saw no need to list additional categories. Otherwise, Lannen said, "Where do you stop?"

"I mean, how many protected classes should there be?"

As had become the norm that year, one board member, Michelle Moore, saw things differently. Even if Lannen's analysis was accurate—even if the changes didn't strip students of legal protections—Moore saw no upside to removing sexual orientation, gender, and religion from the code of conduct. Just cruelty.

"I think we can do better," Moore said.

In the end, the board approved the new student code of conduct by a vote of 5–1.

When it came time for school board candidates to submit paperwork for the spring 2023 elections, Moore didn't file to run against the Southlake Families PAC–endorsed candidate running for her seat—and neither did anyone else. The PAC had been so dominant in recent campaigns, nobody on the other side of the aisle was willing to put their name or reputation on the line—to subject themselves to accusations of grooming and indoctrinating children—just to lose by forty percentage points.

All over the country, longtime school board members were making similar calculations as bare-knuckle partisan politics—and all the ugliness that comes with it—became the norm in America's small towns and suburbs. Some members had endured threats of violence. In Brevard County, Florida, a school board member installed security cameras after she spotted someone come near her home brandishing a weapon. The daughter of a school board member in Loudoun County, Virginia, received a handwritten letter: "If [your mother] doesn't quit or resign before the end of the year, we will kill her, but first, we will kill you!" The school board president in Dublin, Ohio, got a letter warning that officials would "pay dearly" for supporting programs addressing racism. "You have become our enemies and you will be removed one way or the other."

Moore hadn't signed up to serve in an unpaid position to be someone's enemy. "I'm not sure who would want to serve on a school board at this point," she said.

After these elections, the takeover would be complete, with Southlake Families holding all seven seats on Carroll's board.

The diversity plan supporter Sheri Mills was technically still a member. Her seat, too, would go to an unopposed PAC candidate. But Mills hadn't attended a meeting in more than a year, perhaps recognizing the futility of her presence on a deliberative body controlled by people who seemed to despise her values.

Moore also had debated whether it made sense to continue showing up, month after month, to cast a lone vote against what she viewed as a destructive political agenda. Her husband suggested she resign. But she felt she still owed something to the parents and students who'd come to her four years earlier with dispiriting stories of discrimination on campus. She'd pledged to herself then: *This is not how it's going to be under my watch.*

Now her watch was coming to an end, and she didn't have much to show for the effort, other than a stack of legal bills. The legal bills, it turned out, may themselves have been only for show. Within days of her official departure from the board, Tarrant County's Republican district attorney would formally drop the criminal charges that had been filed against her and another board member two years earlier over their alleged violation of the state's Open Meetings Act. The timing made sense to Moore and her lawyer. The charges, they believed, had always seemed intended to push her off the board.

At one of her final meetings as a trustee, a gay Carroll graduate named Carson Henderson came forward to thank Moore for continuing to fight for "scared and lonely" kids like him, even when it seemed hopeless.

"To all listening," Henderson said, "God does not leave us in darkness, and neither should our public schools. To Ms. Moore, it's in the darkness that light shines the brightest. So thank you for shining bright."

As a timer beeped to signal that his time was up, Henderson approached the dais and presented Moore with his Carroll Dragons letterman's jacket, as a token of his thanks, and as a reminder to the rest of the trustees that their decisions would impact real students. As he handed her the coat, tears streamed down Moore's cheeks.

"Even when my vote no longer mattered," she said afterward, "it still mattered. Showing up mattered."

Parents in a neighboring school district, meanwhile, were staging a counteroffensive. Following the model set in Round Rock, a coalition of progressive parents and disillusioned conservatives were on a mission to retake control of the Grapevine-Colleyville Independent School District.

Unlike Southlake, the twin communities of Grapevine and Colleyville were more diverse, its electorate more evenly divided between Democrats and Republicans. In that way, the May 2023 school board contest would be a test with national implications. Would the community continue to support school board candidates backed by groups seeking to impose their version of biblical morality in public schools, or would it reverse course?

In contrast to a year prior, when Patriot Mobile Action's candidates were swept into office with little organized opposition, Grapevine-Colleyville parents who opposed the company's openly Christian nationalist agenda had deployed a political action committee of their own, the Texas Nonpartisan PAC. They raised more than $30,000 to support candidates who promised to move the district in a different direction. That was a drop in the bucket compared to the $130,000 spent by Patriot Mobile, but the opposition faction believed they had momentum on their side. That winter, after the school board enacted a sweeping policy banning lessons on racism and LGBTQ inclusion, a survey conducted by a consulting firm found that 65 percent of parents believed GCISD was heading in the wrong direction.

But unlike Patriot Mobile, which once again endorsed a single candidate in each of the three open board seats while clearing the field of any far-right challengers who might split the vote, the loose coalition of Democrats and moderate Republicans struggled to agree on a single slate. The disarray had, in effect, divided the community in three. There was a slate of school board candidates backed by Patriot Mobile, another group supported by Texas Nonpartisan PAC, and a third slate of moderate conservatives who said they opposed the influence of PACs of any kind in local elections.

Even still, the nonpartisan group felt they were on a path to victory.

While greeting voters on the morning of the election, Kimberly Phoenix, a Grapevine-Colleyville parent who was running with the nonpartisan PAC's support, warned that the current board was driving teachers out of the district and cutting academic programs while their benefactors were pushing divisive religious values. "I believe in the separation of church and state," said Phoenix, a white Christian who had primarily voted for Republicans in past elections. "Everyone deserves to come to a public school and feel safe and feel like they fit in."

In response to that stance, a voter had recently accused Phoenix on social media of supporting "gay porn in our school libraries" and "counselors convincing our kids" to change genders.

"It's gotten ugly," Phoenix said.

At a series of candidate forums ahead of the election, the debate over religion and education rarely came up, with candidates instead focused on recent teacher departures, shoring up the budget, and changes to the district's advanced academic programs.

Patriot Mobile and its surrogates, in contrast, set the election's stakes in starkly religious terms. During a sermon that spring at Patriot Mobile's corporate office in Grapevine, the pastor Rafael Cruz warned that "our children are being destroyed" by "an evil agenda" in public schools. "It's gotten to the point that they are telling girls you're not really a girl, you're a boy," Cruz said. In another sermon, Cruz took the scaremongering to a new level, falsely claiming that children were receiving gender reassignment surgeries "in our public schools."

"We are the only thing that stands," he said, "between the destruction of America or the revival of America."

The hyperbolic messaging, meant to instill fear, appeared to be turning some conservative Christian voters against the group. Kim Slater, the parent of a middle school–age student, said she'd voted for all the Patriot Mobile–backed candidates a year earlier. But Slater, a white Christian, was bothered by the group's increasing emphasis on imposing their version of religious morality, which she believed had led to a decline in academic rigor. She'd heard reports that teachers were pulling down entire classroom libraries to comply with board policies, and Slater said she had to give consent in writing any time her child asked to read a book above grade level.

"I can tell you flat-out that I will not vote for a single candidate that is aligned with Patriot Mobile," Slater said. "I do not think they are serving an agenda that serves the kids in our school district."

Those types of comments gave Phoenix hope that her community, and America, might be ready to move on from the unpleasantness of the past few years.

The tumult overtaking school boards had also seemed to awaken a generation of young people.

With seven minutes to spare before the polls closed on election night, a pair of transgender seniors at Grapevine High School, Teddy and June, arrived at a voting site, one in a black dress, the other in a stylish suit. They were on their way to prom—but first June needed to cast her ballot. Teddy had voted earlier. Both students, having just turned eighteen, said they were determined to vote because they didn't want students who followed them to suffer the type of bullying they'd endured in Grapevine.

"That gives me hope," Phoenix said a moment later. "The kids give me a lot of hope."

Three years into the new fight for the soul of America's public schools, as more groups formed to counter the far-right movement taking control of school boards, and as the consequences of classroom restrictions and book bans were increasingly laid bare, Phoenix and the parents who'd sacrificed money and time with their families to try and get her elected said they were confident that change was on the way.

But it wasn't yet coming to Grapevine and Colleyville.

When the votes were tallied that night, Patriot Mobile had expanded its majority on the board, winning two out of three seats. That meant the group's candidates would be in control of setting policy in the district for at least another two years.

Parents like Phoenix, who cried over the outcome, nonetheless saw reason for optimism in the results. None of the three Patriot Mobile candidates had managed to win more than 50 percent of the vote. They won only because the vote had been split among three candidates, and because the current Patriot Mobile–backed board majority had voted to change the rules ahead of the election, allowing the races to be decided by a plurality and negating the need for a runoff.

Despite the outcome, a majority in the community had now signaled that they were ready to move in a different direction, Phoenix said. They just needed to get on the same page before the next election. "Change is coming," another of the losing candidates said that night, as if willing it to be true. "It's gonna happen."

Two weeks later, Grapevine High School English teacher Em Ramser was invited to attend a GCISD school board meeting. Earlier that month, a statewide organization had named her one of the twelve best humanities teachers in Texas. Now the GCISD board of trustees was planning to formally celebrate her achievement—the same trustees who'd adopted policies forcing Ramser to remove books from her classroom, and who'd refused to defend her when a mother accused her of "infecting" her transgender child with an evil ideology.

Ramser felt as if her voice and identity had been stripped from her that school year. To protect against additional attacks, the principal at Grapevine High School had advised Ramser to remove the rainbow pride stickers that she'd placed on her classroom nameplate, erasing what she'd intended as a symbol of her love for all students. The principal also told her not to take it personally when residents went on social media to accuse her of being a pedophile, or to wish for her to contract monkeypox and die.

"What you're going to realize about people, if you haven't already, is that they don't all love people," the principal told Ramser, before suggesting that such harassment was now an unfortunate but unavoidable part of being a public educator in America.

With each new controversy and baseless accusation, Ramser pleaded with the district to put out statements to defend her, to confirm publicly what administrators repeatedly told her in private: that she was a great teacher, and she'd done nothing wrong. But district officials never spoke up, and they told her to stay quiet, too. *Just keep your head down*, they'd say. *Let the storm pass.*

But the storm didn't pass, and she was done being muzzled.

Moments after a member of the school board presented Ramser with her statewide honor and posed for photos with her, the English teacher stood up during public comments and approached the lectern. She told the board she'd come to set the record straight.

"This community has continuously harassed me for the past few years, getting up at this podium, on Facebook and elsewhere online, and lying about me, my personhood, my curriculum, and my teaching." The harassment was so relentless, and so vile, Ramser said, her voice cracking, "that there were days I didn't even want to be alive anymore, much less be a teacher."

Ramser was speaking for herself, but also giving voice to a sentiment shared by many of her colleagues. That spring, GCISD hired Gallup to survey educators on their satisfaction with the district. The 1,500 responses were largely negative:

How could GCISD have made this year better?
"If the school board policies were less racist, homophobic and transphobic."

Which initiatives, programs, or changes have been especially successful this year?
"None. The majority of board members have embarrassed our district and . . . created a hostile work environment."

What has been the best part of your experience at GCISD this year?
"The days I don't want to leave crying are good days."

Some teachers used their anonymized responses to explain why they planned to resign at the end of the school year. And although Ramser had skipped the survey, she was among those now heading for the exit. In four days, she would be leaving the school system that she'd once regarded as her dream job—part of a national wave of young educators exiting the profession.

For a while, it seemed Christina McGuirk might have been on a similar path. After being pressured into resigning by Southlake's superintendent, the fourth-grade teacher who'd helped blow the whistle on an administrator's instruction to present both sides of the Holocaust hadn't been sure if she would ever return to the classroom. Like Ramser, her final year at Carroll had diminished her passion for the vocation she'd built her life around. She eventually found reason for hope, though. After taking a year off to care for her baby, McGuirk landed an interview with a nearby public school system that, despite some parent complaints, had remained firm in its commitment to fostering diversity, equity, and inclusion. Not every district in the fast-diversifying suburbs outside Dallas and Fort Worth had been taken over by far-right political action committees, and now one of them was offering to hire both McGuirk and her best friend, Rickie Farah, even though each had been publicly attacked by parents in Southlake. "I'm really excited," McGuirk said, sounding every bit as giddy as she did on her first day at Carroll five years earlier. "I can't wait to get in and get my classroom set up and to be able to do what I know how to do, and to do it well, without all the other stuff getting in the way."

Ramser, at age twenty-seven, saw no such future for herself in public education. At least not in Texas. That fall, she'd be starting at an area private school that had expressed a commitment to fostering equity and inclusion. She hated the thought of leaving public schools for a system that was out of reach for the most at-risk children, but what choice did she have?

Leaning down to the microphone, she told GCISD's school board majority that they and their supporters had sent a clear message. It didn't matter how many awards she won, or how well her students scored on their Advanced Placement exams.

"Y'all don't want people like me, people who might be gay, to teach here."

The English teacher ended by turning toward the audience. Some of her students had gathered to show support. She wished she could shield them from the ugliness and divisiveness that had rippled across the country and was now driving her out of their classroom. She wished she could just tell them everything would be OK. But she couldn't. "I want you to know that you did *nothing* wrong, and I am so incredibly proud of each and every one of you," Ramser told the teens, and in the process, offered up one final lesson before ending her brief career as a public educator.

She'd always told her students that their voices mattered.

Now, she was reclaiming her own.

Epilogue

ON A FRIDAY EVENING in May 2023, Southlake's Dragon Stadium was packed with thousands of spectators. As the sun sank behind a scoreboard, casting a heavenly orange glow across the football field, the marching band struck up "Pomp and Circumstance," and more than seven hundred high school seniors in green caps and gowns began to file into rows of folding chairs that stretched from end zone to end zone.

"There's Roman," Amy Rolle said, pointing to one of the few Black boys in the procession.

Seventeen years after taking her three children on a road trip in search of a great public school system, Rolle was about to watch the youngest of them graduate. Sitting in the bleachers, she reflected on the consequences of that cross-country move. Southlake had, in many ways, delivered on its promise, said Rolle, who'd since divorced Reggie. Their children excelled academically at Carroll, opening college and career opportunities that might not have come otherwise. But the community had also shaped and injured them in ways that she hadn't anticipated. It had taught them hard and sometimes painful lessons about racism, politics, and the backlash that always seems to follow progress.

Knowing all that she knew now, Rolle said she probably wouldn't make the same decision today as she'd made in 2006.

"I wouldn't have come," she said. "I think I would have found someplace different."

The calculations that parents make when deciding where to send their children to school have always been fraught—especially for parents raising students of color. But the past few years have added new layers to agonize over. What do you do when the local district with the best academic record is led by school board members who won't let teachers counsel children about the evils of racism, but are OK with them praying aloud after the morning bell? What do you do as the parent of a gender-nonconforming child when you love your neighborhood school, but your state legislature has passed laws banning teachers from pulling out a picture book to teach classmates how to show him kindness?

For Amy, this night was, in some ways, a moment of relief as much as celebration. "I'm just glad my kids are done and out before whatever comes next," she said, expressing a sentiment shared by many parents of high school graduates across the country that spring.

After three years of bitter fights over race, identity, and inclusion, America and its public schools were nearing a crossroads. Two days earlier, Ron DeSantis formally announced his candidacy for president, promising if elected to nationalize the education policies that he'd enacted in Florida. That agenda had included eliminating school diversity training programs, elevating the perspectives of Christian conservatives in social studies curriculum, downplaying the legacy of racism, and banning teachers from discussing the existence of people who don't conform to traditional gender norms. DeSantis launched his presidential campaign under the slogan "Make America Florida," but to Raven Rolle, it felt as if he and his criminally indicted rival Donald Trump were effectively promising to "Make America Southlake."

The GOP frontrunners seemed to be caught in an escalating campaign to prove which would take a harsher stance against "liberal indoctrination" in schools. In a speech in North Carolina that spring, Trump promised he would "immediately sign a new executive order" to take federal funding away from schools that teach children about critical race theory and what he called "transgender insanity." He paused as his supporters got on their feet and cheered, marveling at the power of the hottest new wedge issue. "It's amazing how strongly people feel about that. You see I'm talking about cutting taxes, people go like that," said Trump, mimicking a half-hearted golf clap. "I talk about transgender, everyone goes crazy. Who would have thought? Five years ago, you didn't know what the hell it was."

The question of who would occupy the Oval Office in 2025 mattered a lot in conservative suburbs like Southlake, where parents of Black and LGBTQ students increasingly looked to the Biden administration to force local schools to adopt more inclusive policies. While the U.S. Education Department was continuing its investigations into alleged civil rights violations at the Carroll school district that spring, both Trump and DeSantis revealed plans to abolish the federal agency and its mission.

As her little brother found his seat near the thirty-yard line, Raven made note of a massive banner stretching above the visitor bleachers at Dragon Stadium, emblazoned with the words "Tradition Never Graduates." It was a riff on the district's "Protect the Tradition" motto, a way of suggesting that Carroll graduates would always be shaped by their experiences attending Southlake schools.

Raven—who still dwelled on the time she'd had to debate the meaning of the N-word with a white classmate in the principal's office—was proof of that concept.

Two weeks earlier, she'd graduated from the University of Kentucky with a degree in journalism. Despite having pledged to get as far away as possible from Southlake after high school, she'd spent much of the past four years obsessively following and documenting her hometown's school board battles from afar. She ran the Southlake Anti-Racism Coalition's social media accounts, which often involved watching a live feed of Carroll's board meetings from her dorm room, and then posting videos of outrageous parent comments. She'd become known on campus as the college kid who was hyper-engaged in the activities of a school board nine hundred miles away. Her capstone student journalism project, a requirement of graduation, documented the entire Southlake saga from the perspective of the ousted school board president Michelle Moore.

"It's honestly become my identity in some ways," Raven said of her town's school board drama. She was part of a generation of students who'd found their voice, not by protesting police violence or foreign wars, but through local school board activism. She and her peers had also learned a thing or two about losing, as evidenced by the people now seated next to the graduation stage.

All seven chairs set out for members of the school board were filled by trustees backed by Southlake Families PAC and Patriot Mobile. One of those members, though, would soon be stepping down. A few months later, after just two years on the board, Hannah Smith would surprise supporters and adversaries alike by announcing plans to resign from her elected post and leave Southlake. The religious liberty lawyer and CPAC darling was returning home to Utah, where she'd accepted a job as associate director of the International Center for Law and Religion Studies at her alma mater Brigham Young University. Before departing, Smith would write a final message to supporters, declaring that she'd "accomplished all that I said I would" during her brief and consequential tenure. Above all else, Smith had strived to deliver changes that she said reflected "the community's values."

But the board members' all-white faces did not reflect the diversity of students staring back at them that evening at Dragon Stadium. An older white couple seated near the Rolles appeared to notice the multitude of cultures represented on the field and in the names listed in the graduation program. The wife grumbled about the number of South Asian surnames among the class of 2023's top ten students. Her husband complained under his breath, but still loud enough for others to hear, about the valedictorian's Chinese accent: "I can't understand a word she's saying."

Amy and Raven didn't appear to notice the comment, and soon it was Roman's turn to cross the stage. After the announcer called his name, his mother and sister jumped to their feet and cheered. The youngest Rolle child shook superintendent Lane Ledbetter's hand and strode past board members who'd voted to kill a diversity plan meant to teach students how to be kind to people who looked like him. Then he headed for his seat, diploma in hand.

"That's done," Amy Rolle said afterward, sounding like a weight had been lifted.

Her children's journey through Southlake's public school system was finished. The last several years had been a brutal reminder that the district would not be embracing change. Now Rolle and her family were considering some changes of their own. She planned to soon put her house on the market and leave Southlake. In the fall, Roman would be attending college in Los Angeles, returning to the city of his birth in pursuit of a less restrictive educational environment, one in which Black students were not on the margins. Raven, meanwhile, was still sorting out her next move. She was leaning toward going to grad school to continue studying journalism, or enrolling in a prelaw program.

One way or another, this Southlake product was going to stay involved in the fight to make public schools more welcoming and inclusive—even if that battle appeared all but settled in her hometown.

Acknowledgments

I'm grateful to all the people who contributed to this project, and none more so than the parents, students, and teachers who welcomed me into their homes and helped me understand what's happening inside public schools during this era of backlash.

This book builds on three years of reporting for NBC News, much of it done in collaboration with my friend and colleague Antonia Hylton. Her insights and perspective helped shape every chapter, and this book would have never been published without her partnership. Many other NBC News colleagues have guided and improved my writing on this subject, especially Julie Shapiro, Susan Carroll, Reid Cherlin, Frannie Kelley, Michelle Garcia, and Tyler Kingkade.

Thank you to Deanne Urmy, my editor at Mariner, who saw the potential for what this book could become before I fully did. Her feedback and revisions have made it worthy of your time. Hilary McClellen's meticulous fact-checking saved me from embarrassment, and thanks to Karen Richardson's diligent copy edits, I'm not nervous for my high school English teachers—Steven Howell and Steve Wyllie—to read what I've written. Generous financial support from Columbia Journalism School and the Nieman Foundation for Journalism at Harvard got me across the finish line.

My career path has been paved by editors and mentors who believed in me, fought for my ideas, and taught me the craft of journalism. There are too many to name here, but they include: Maria Carrillo, Charles Ornstein, Roger DiPaolo, Jeff Herrin, Gene Metrick, Greg

Barnes, Steve Riley, Kate Wiltrout, Vernon Loeb, David Firestone, and Tom Namako.

I'm indebted to all the education journalists whose reporting in recent years has revealed the breathtaking scope and toll of the new classroom wars in the lives of students and educators. Many of their bylines can be found in the source notes of this book, including those of Talia Richman, Hannah Natanson, Erica L. Green, Ana Ceballos, Sommer Brugal, Ana Goñi-Lessan, Nicole Carr, and Brian Lopez. Thanks also to Jeremy Schwartz and the team at ProPublica and the *Texas Tribune*, who collaborated with me to report and publish articles cited in this book, and to Bud Kennedy of the *Fort Worth Star-Telegram*, for unearthing a fascinating detail about Southlake's history in his newspaper's archives.

As a first-generation college graduate and the son of a pair of retired warehouse laborers, I must acknowledge the sacrifices my parents made to make this dream I'm living a possibility. They worked grueling, backbreaking jobs so that I could write and talk to people for a living. Mom, Dad, look how far we've come.

When my agent, Lauren Sharp, first emailed me with the idea to write this book, my instinct was to tell her no, thank you. It's not that I didn't believe in Lauren's vision. She was right; this book needed to be written. I just didn't know whether I should have been the one to write it.

But when I told my spouse about the pitch and my hesitation, she set me straight, like she always does. Even though it would require me to spend more time on the road and more weekends holed up in my office—even though *she* would be the one picking up the slack at home and solo parenting our four young children—my wife and best friend told me, without hesitation, that I should go for it.

Bethany, thank you for believing in me, for encouraging me, and for teaching me to see the world from a perspective other than my own. For all that you've done over the years to make this book possible, your name ought to be on the cover, right next to mine.

Notes

PROLOGUE

1 *those of 2024*: William H. Frey, "Today's suburbs are symbolic of America's rising diversity," Brookings, June 5, 2022.

1 *white nationalist extremist groups pivoted*: Tom Schuba and Nader Issa, "Proud Boys join effort to ban 'Gender Queer' book from school library—rattling students in suburban Chicago," *Chicago Sun-Times*, November 21, 2021, and Madeleine List, "Proud Boys enter library during LGBTQ story time, NC parents say. 'I felt unsafe,'" *Charlotte Observer*, June 24, 2022.

3 *depending on which cable news network*: David Broockman and Joshua Kalla, *The impacts of selective partisan media exposure: A field experiment with Fox News viewers,* OSF Preprints, April 1, 2022.

3 *a viral conspiracy theory*: Brandy Zadrozny and Ben Collins, "Antifa rumors spread on local social media with no evidence," NBC News, June 2, 2020.

4 *Trump's campaign sent a text*: Andrew Solender, "'They'll Attack Your Homes': Trump Campaign Sends 'Antifa Alert' to Supporters," *Forbes*, September 13, 2020.

5 *acts of anti–Black Lives Matter aggression*: A search of LexisNexis news archives turns up more than 2,700 newspaper articles about vandalism of Black Lives Matter signs and murals between June 1 and December 1, 2020.

5 *a white man in a Detroit suburb*: "Man sentenced for attacking Black neighbors' Michigan home," *Associated Press*, August 17, 2021.

6 *I turned it into a journalism project*: Mike Hixenbaugh, "'Not just politics': How the 2020 campaign is dividing Houston's booming suburbs," NBC News, October 9, 2020.

6 *a false statistic*: When I asked West for evidence to support the claim, a Texas GOP spokesman sent articles from 2017 and 2018, published years before the protests for racial justice, showing that more women of all races, and more Black people overall, had been applying for concealed handgun permits.

CHAPTER 1: PERFECT CITY, U.S.A.

12 *metrics that tend to measure student demographics*: Matt Barnum and Gabrielle LaMarr LeMee, "Looking for a home? You've seen GreatSchools ratings. Here's how they nudge families toward schools with fewer black and Hispanic students," *Chalkbeat*, December 5, 2019.

14 *good enough to get most students into top-tier universities*: Carroll's average SAT score in 2021, 1259, was high enough to gain admittance to the University of Texas.

14 *a few dozen people filtered through the Carroll Hill School*: "Southlake incorporates; Elects officials," *Grapevine Sun*, October 19, 1956.

14 *pay twenty-five cents*: According to announcements published in the *Grapevine Sun* between 1947 and 1962, community groups periodically staged Negro minstrel performances at Carroll Hill, including a script titled "Lady Minstrels of Dixie" that called for white actors in blackface.

14 *White settlers had begun arriving*: The Southlake Historical Society has compiled a comprehensive accounting of the community's history.

14 *ties to the Ku Klux Klan*: B. E. Carroll's affiliation with the Ku Klux Klan is noted in a July 9, 1922, *Fort Worth Star-Telegram* article and in a political advertisement published in the newspaper on July 21, 1922, but this fact appears to have been lost to history. Nobody I spoke to in Southlake was aware that the namesake of the Carroll Independent School District was, at one time, an endorsed candidate of a white supremacy terrorist group.

15 *Hurst was planning to annex*: Tony Slaughter, "3 Cities Work on Points of Boundary Conflicts," *Fort Worth Star-Telegram*, February 24, 1957.

15 *a conservative campaign to expand the influence of Christianity*: Kevin M. Kruse, *One Nation Under God: How Corporate America Invented Christian America* (Basic Books, 2016), xiv–xvi.

15 *legislation to pay private school tuition*: Sam Kinch, "Plan Submitted to Legislature to Maintain School Segregation," *Fort Worth Star-Telegram*, September 28, 1956.

15 *an ugly and widely publicized showdown*: "Mansfield school takes no negros," *Dallas Morning News*, September 1, 1956.

16 *a prime target for developers*: Jim W. Jones, "Ex-Pilot Mayor Confident Southlake Has Big Future," *Fort Worth Star-Telegram*, September 10, 1966.

16 *In the years after the civil rights movement*: William A. Fischel, "An Economic History of Zoning and a Cure for Its Exclusionary Effects," *Urban Studies,* 41, no. 2 (2004).

17 *a Southlake resident complained*: "2.7 Homes OK for 1-Acre Lot," *Fort Worth Star-Telegram*, June 16, 1971.

17 *a litmus test*: "Candidates back rural atmosphere," *Fort Worth Star-Telegram*, March 31, 1978, and Louis Porter II, "Growth atmosphere at stake in election," *Fort Worth Star-Telegram*, March 30, 1983.

17 *Latta told the newspaper*: Rhonda Glenn, "Southlake's country air here to stay," *Fort Worth Star-Telegram*, March 6, 1985.

17 *city attorney warned town leaders*: Judy Putnam, "Public debate on Southlake issues planned," *Fort Worth Star-Telegram,* January 19, 1989, and Julie Herrick, "Southlake to address weak links in zoning," *Grapevine Sun*, January 29, 1989.

18 *a councilman once bluntly confided*: Thomas Korosec, "Sunnyvale: The Whitest Town in North Texas," *D Magazine*, February 22, 2012.

18 *The outrage would be so severe*: Julie Herrick, "Southlake to address weak links in zoning," *Grapevine Sun*, January, 29 1989.

18 *a lesser-known U.S. Supreme Court decision*: To place *Milliken v Bradley* in historical context, I drew from a conversation with University of Michigan law school professor Michelle Adams, who has written extensively about the case.

18 *a regime of de facto segregation*: Frank I. Goodman, "De Facto School Segregation: A Constitutional and Empirical Analysis," *Faculty Scholarship at Penn Law* (1972).

18 *the Supreme Court had an opportunity*: Elissa Nadworny and Cory Turner, "This Supreme Court Case Made School District Lines a Tool for Segregation," NPR, July 25, 2019.

19 *had written a memo only a few years earlier*: Howard Kurtz, "Rehnquist Wrote School Segregation Memo," *Washington Post*, September 7, 1986.

20 *waving signs with handwritten messages*: "Boston Desegregation Controversy," *Evening Compass*, WGBH-TV, 1974.

20 *pelted with rocks*: John Kifner, "Boston School Buses Stoned a 2d Day, but City Is Mostly Calm," *New York Times*, September 14, 1974.

20 *One anti-busing mother warned*: Kathleen Banks Nutter, "'Militant mothers': Boston, busing, and the bicentennial of 1976," *Historical Journal of Massachusetts*, 38, no. 2 (2010).

20 *hundreds of irate white parents*: James T. Wooten, "Philadelphia Scraps a Plan for Busing," *New York Times*, June 8, 1975.

20 *segregation academies flourished*: Kathryn J. Edin, H. Luke Shaefer, and Timothy Nelson, *The Injustice of Place: Uncovering the Legacy of Poverty in America*, Mariner (2023).

20 *In a 1983 newspaper interview*: Louis Porter II and Barbara Holsomback, "SAT scores high in Carroll district," *Fort Worth Star-Telegram*, November 13, 1983.

21 *a new niche field of study*: Kimberle Crenshaw, "Twenty Years of Critical Race Theory: Looking back to Move Forward Commentary," *Connecticut Law Review*, 117 (2011).

21 *Black families had begun*: David J. Dent, "The New Black Suburbs," *New York Times*, June 14, 1992.

22 *"the city of the 90s"*: Monticello Reality advertisement, *Fort Worth Star-Telegram*, October 27, 1991.

23 *on a warm Saturday afternoon*: Yamil Berard and Rick Herrin, "Student suspended over racial sign," *Fort Worth Star-Telegram*, October 21, 1996.

23 *students had also dangled a dummy*: Jack Brewer, "Putting Nooses Around Our Own Necks," *Newsmax*, March 5, 2019.

23 *a wake-up call for the city*: Laurie Wilson, "Carroll trustees call for tolerance," *Dallas Morning News*, November 2, 1996.

24 *a special school board meeting*: Yamil Berard, "Carroll faces tolerance issue," *Fort Worth Star-Telegram,* November 5, 1996, and Laurie Wilson, "Carroll board, parents talk about racism," *Dallas Morning News*, November 8, 1996.

24 *the Carroll school board directed*: Teri Bishop, "Officials: We can work out differences," *Grapevine Sun*, November 7, 1996.

24 *after a Southlake mother complained*: Holly Jo Linzay, "Parents ask CISD to draft policy on discrimination," *Grapevine Sun*, January 9, 1994.

24 *it would take a few years*: Yamil Berard, "Race issue shadows Carroll," *Fort Worth Star-Telegram*, October 10, 1997, and Carol Lewis, "In search of familiar faces," *Fort Worth Star-Telegram*, February 28, 1999.

24 *the principal credited the town's traditional values*: Courtney Denby, "Top 10 public high schools," *D Magazine*, May 1, 1998.

25 *The magazine article caused an uproar*: Tim Rogers, "Former Southlake Mayor Calls for Apology," *D Magazine*, August 29, 2007.

27 *a Black Southlake resident reported*: Nicholas Sakelaris, "Obama Sign Burned," *Fort Worth Star-Telegram*, October 24, 2008.

27 *bowing to pressure*: Letters to the editor, *Fort Worth Star-Telegram*, September 16, 2009.

CHAPTER 2: YOU'VE GOT TO CHANGE

31 *white hip-hop fans*: Baylor University, a private Christian college in Waco, Texas, later banned "Mo Bamba" from campus after white sorority members recorded themselves singing the song, including the N-word—one of several such incidents involving the song to make the news nationally.

32 *falsely accusing the DJ*: A white mother who was not at the dance alleged at a Carroll school board meeting that the DJ "was provoking the crowd to shout that N-word over and over," a claim refuted by interviews with seven students and one adult who were in attendance.

33 *a profound impact inside America's public schools*: Maureen Costello, "The Trump Effect: The impact of the presidential election on our nation's schools," Southern Poverty Law Center, November 28, 2016.

33 *in the mostly white Detroit suburb*: James David Dickson and Candice Williams, "Royal Oak Middle School students chant 'Build that wall,'" *Detroit News*, November 10, 2016.

33 *someone vandalized a bathroom stall*: "Maple Grove School Investigating Racist, Pro-Trump Graffiti," CBS News, November 9, 2016.

33 *a student at Shasta High School:* Alayna Shulman, "Shasta High student gives 'deportation' notices to other kids," *Redding Record Searchlight,* November 10, 2016.

33 *a suburban high school outside of Tampa*: Jeffrey S. Solochek, "Pasco investigates Wesley Chapel High teacher for Trump-related racial comment," *Tampa Bay Times*, November 10, 2016.

34 *a doubling of hate crimes*: "Students' Experiences with Bullying, Hate Speech, Hate Crimes, and Victimization in Schools," Government Accountability Office, November 2021.

34 *a growing body of research*: Yvonne Lei, Vivek Shah, Christopher Biely, et al., "Discrimination and Subsequent Mental Health, Substance Use, and Well-being in Young Adults," *Pediatrics* (2021).

34 *the group Teaching Tolerance*: The group changed its name to Learning for Justice in 2021.

34 *In October 2017 alone*: Maureen Costello, "Hate at School: October 2017," Teaching Tolerance, November 3, 2017.

38 *Sheri Mills called the meeting to order*: All Carroll ISD school board meetings are recorded and archived at www.southlakecarroll.edu.

CHAPTER 3: NOT JUST A WORD

42 *Trump infamously denounced immigrants*: Ali Vitali, Kasie Hunt, and Frank Thorp V, "Trump referred to Haiti and African nations as 'shithole' countries," NBC News, January 11, 2018.

42 *Mayor Laura Hill*: Hill declined interview requests, writing in an email, "I have moved on."

42 *elected Southlake's first female mayor*: Sherelle Black, "Southlake chooses first female mayor," *Community Impact*, May 20, 2015.

44 *a weeks-long blitz*: Hanaa' Tameez and Elizabeth Campbell, "Standing-room only crowd in this city vow to fight racism, bullying," *Fort Worth Star-Telegram*, November 15, 2018, and Alice Barr, "Southlake Dads Discuss Healing Racial Divides Over a Beer and a Handshake," KXAS, November 27, 2018.

45 *an open call for volunteers*: "Carroll ISD Launches Work of District Diversity Council," *My Southlake News*, January 31, 2019.

46 *a white real estate investor*: "Bryant Wins CISD Board Seat," *My Southlake News*, May 6, 2018.

46 *According to Maryland's retelling*: Bryant did not respond to interview requests.

47 *Trump's election emboldened*: Simon Clark, "How White Supremacy Returned to Mainstream Politics," Center for American Progress, July 2020.

47 *after a gym teacher*: Debbie Truong, "'Slavery is not a game': Virginia school apologizes over Black History Month exercise," *Washington Post*, February 21, 2019.

47 *to study the racial climate at its schools*: Debbie Truong, "'Growing sense of despair': A wealthy, diversifying school system in suburban D.C. confronts racism and hate in schools," *Washington Post*, September 8, 2019.

47 *It was a similar story*: Elizabeth Miller, "After Portland High School Hate Incidents, Community Wants Better Response," *Roseburg News-Review*, July 26, 2019.

47 *a school system in Cheyenne, Wyoming*: Mead Gruver, "Racist, anti-gay student flyers challenge Cheyenne school district," *Associated Press*, July 30, 2019.

48 *a suburb outside Atlanta*: Kristal Dixon, "Group wants Cobb schools to address racism, bias in classroom," *Atlanta Journal-Constitution*, August 2, 2019.

48 *the Chicago suburb of Naperville*: Susie An, "Naperville Schools Try to Rebuild Trust After Incident Exposes Persistent Race Issues," WBEZ, December 10, 2019.

49 *could be found in textbooks*: Brian Lyman, "Southern schools' history textbooks: A long history of deception, and what the future holds," *Montgomery Advertiser*, December 2, 2020.

50 *the conservative Fordham Institute think tank*: Jeremy A. Stern and Sheldon M. Stern, "The State of State U.S. History Standards," Fordham Institute, February 16, 2011.

51 *another video of Carroll students*: Diane Smith and Elizabeth Campbell, "Video with Southlake Carroll student in it includes repeated use of the n-word," *Fort Worth Star-Telegram*, February 7, 2019.

53 *secretly hit record on her cell phone*: Duhon and the white student declined to speak with me about the meeting with Raven.

CHAPTER 4: EVERYTHING IMPLODED

58 *the evening of March 11*: Laurel Wamsley, "March 11, 2020: The Day Everything Changed," NPR, March 11, 2021.

58 *Abbott made the decision*: Patrick Svitek, "Gov. Greg Abbott closes bars, restaurants and schools as he anticipates tens of thousands could test positive for coronavirus," *Texas Tribune*, March 19, 2020.

59 *yet another viral video*: "Video appears to show black man forced to the ground as he says 'I can't breathe,'" CNN, May 26, 2020.

59 *a forty-six-year-old Black man*: "George Floyd's America," *Washington Post*, October 26, 2020.

59 *Louisville police had shot and killed*: Minyvonne Burke, "Breonna Taylor police shooting: What we know about the Kentucky woman's death," NBC News, May 15, 2020.

59 *murdered by three white men*: Richard Fausset, "Two Weapons, a Chase, a Killing and No Charges," *New York Times*, April 26, 2020.

60 *unlike anything the nation had seen*: Larry Buchanan, Quoctrung Bui, and Jugal K. Patel, "Black Lives Matter May Be the Largest Movement in U.S. History," *New York Times*, July 3, 2020.

60 *most protests that spring had been peaceful*: Sanya Mansoor, "93% of Black Lives Matter Protests Have Been Peaceful, New Report Finds," *Time*, September 5, 2020.

60 *a speech from the Rose Garden*: Katie Rogers. "Protesters Dispersed with Tear Gas So Trump Could Pose at Church," *New York Times*, June 1, 2020.

62 *the morning of the protest*: Gavin Pugh, "Peaceful march for racial equality held at Southlake Town Square," *Community Impact*, June 6, 2020.

62 *Nikki grabbed a bullhorn*: The student's speech, like much of the rally, was captured on videos posted online.

65 *armed school resource officers*: The Carroll school district partnered with Southlake's police department to place an officer at every district campus in 2013, a program that conservative activist Leigh Wambsganss lobbied for after the 2012 mass shooting at Sandy Hook Elementary School in Newtown, Connecticut.

67 *Moore's phone vibrated*: Text messages sent and received by members of the Carroll school board during that period were later filed with a Tarrant County district court as part of a lawsuit against the district. Ronnell Smith declined to be interviewed.

68 *first speaker was Andrew Yeager*: At the time, Yeager worked in regional ad sales for local stations owned by NBCUniversal, the parent company of my employer, NBC News.

CHAPTER 5: COMING TO A TOWN NEAR YOU

73 *false conspiracy theories and outright lies*: Nicholas Riccardi, "How Trump ignored advisers, spread election lies," *Associated Press*, December 21, 2022.

75 *At the urging of their president*: Michael Kunzelman, "Trial: Trump tweet about 'wild' protest energized extremists," *Associated Press*, October 13, 2022.

75 *white supremacist extremist groups*: Spencer S. Hsu, Rachel Weiner, and Tom Jackman, "Proud Boys led Jan. 6 riot to keep Trump in office, U.S. says at trial," *Washington Post*, January 12, 2023.

75 *A realtor from a wealthy Dallas suburb*: Teresa Gubbins, "Frisco real estate agent who stormed Capitol is going to jail after all," *CultureMap Dallas*, November 4, 2021.

75 *A West Virginia state lawmaker*: Maggie Astor, "Derrick Evans, a West Virginia legislator who stormed the Capitol, has resigned," *New York Times*, January 9, 2021.

75 *A retired New York City police officer*: Ryan J. Reilly. "Ex-NYPD officer who assaulted D.C. officer on Jan. 6 gets record 10-year sentence," NBC News, September 1, 2022.

75 *a construction worker from Delaware*: Holmes Lybrand, "Man who carried Confederate flag in US Capitol and son found guilty of felonies," CNN, June 15, 2022.

76 *a once-fringe belief*: Nicholas Confessore and Karen Yourish, "A Fringe Conspiracy Theory, Fostered Online, Is Refashioned by the G.O.P.," *New York Times*, May 15, 2022.

76 *Southlake Families PAC*: Despite numerous requests, nobody from the PAC has ever agreed to speak with me.

76 *a long-dormant group*: Jasmin Brown, "Liquor stores kept out of Southlake," *Southlake Times*, May 17, 2011.

76 *where he'd made national headlines*: Gretel C. Kovach, "Voters in Dallas Suburb Back Limit on Renting to Illegal Immigrants," *New York Times*, May 13, 2007.

76 *later deemed unconstitutional*: Elvia Limón, "Farmers Branch still trying to move forward from shadow of controversial rental ordinance," *Dallas Morning News*, August 26, 2016.

76 *O'Hare had said at the time*: Brantley Hargrove, "Farmers Branch Has Spent Five Years and Millions of Dollars Trying to Keep Out Mexicans. Is It Time for a Truce?" *Dallas Observer*, June 21, 2012.

81 *a typical Black family*: Kriston McIntosh, Emily Moss, Ryan Nunn, and Jay Shambaugh, "Examining the Black-white wealth gap," Brookings, February 27, 2020.

83 *studies have shown*: Naiqi G. Xiao, Paul C. Quinn, Shaoying Liu, Liezhong Ge, Olivier Pascalis, and Kang Lee, "Older but not younger infants associate own race faces with happy music and other-race faces with sad music," *Developmental Science*, 21 (2018), and Naiqi G. Xiao, Rachel Wu, Paul C. Quinn, Shaoying Liu, Kristen S. Tummeltshammer, Natasha Z. Kirkham, Liezhong Ge, Olivier Pascalis, and Kang Lee, "Infants Rely More on Gaze Cues From Own-Race Than Other-Race Adults for Learning Under Uncertainty," *Child Development*, 89 (2018).

84 *a post he'd seen on social media*: I was never able to find the video, but lots of Southlake parents were talking about it that fall, including in public social media comments.

85 *a powerful Tea Party–aligned advocacy group*: Casey Tolan, Matthew Reynard, Will

Simon, and Ed Lavandera, "How two Texas megadonors have turbocharged the state's far-right shift," CNN, July 24, 2022.

86 *famous for appearing in short NRA promos*: Amanda Holpuch, "'We're coming for you': NRA attacks *New York Times* in provocative video," *The Guardian*, August 11, 2017.

86 *In a profile later published in the* Washington Post: Manuel Roig-Franzia, "Former NRA spokeswoman Dana Loesch, a rising right-wing radio star, doesn't care if you call her a murderer," *Washington Post*, August 30, 2021.

87 *"twenty-seven days of building an army"*: Rich Lowry, "How Southlake, Texas, Won Its Battle against Critical Race Theory," *National Review*, June 3, 2021.

87 *From the pulpit at Grapevine Baptist*: Multiple videos of the event were posted on YouTube.

89 *Among those standing to cheer was John Huffman:* Huffman, later elected Southlake's mayor, did not respond to interview requests.

CHAPTER 6: EXISTENTIAL THREAT

90 *Carlson told his four million nightly viewers*: *Tucker Carlson Tonight*, Fox News, September 1, 2020.

90 *a* New York Times *analysis*: Nicholas Confessore, "How Tucker Carlson Stoked White Fear to Conquer Cable," *New York Times*, April 30, 2022.

91 *Rufo had been writing articles*: Christopher F. Rufo, "Cult Programming in Seattle," *City Journal*, July 8, 2020, and Christopher F. Rufo, "'White Fragility' Comes to Washington," *City Journal*, July 18, 2020.

93 *carefully rehearsed remarks*: Benjamin Wallace-Wells, "How a Conservative Activist Invented the Conflict Over Critical Race Theory," *New Yorker*, June 18, 2021.

93 *Rufo later acknowledged*: Rufo was responding to an email I'd sent requesting comment.

94 *a false conspiracy theory*: Calvin Woodward and David Klepper, "Trump seeds race animus with COVID falsehood," *Associated Press*, January 16, 2022.

95 *Hill wrote a letter*: Robert Montoya, "Mayor Sides with Citizens Against School Board on Divisive, Pro-LGBTQ+ Culture Plan," *Texas Scorecard*, September 17, 2020.

96 *critical race theory had now become a stand-in*: Stephen Sawchuk, "What Is Critical Race Theory, and Why Is It Under Attack?" *Education Week*, May 18, 2021.

97 *a high school English class*: Aimee Cho, "'Privilege Bingo' in Fairfax Co. Class Meets Controversy for Including Being a Military Kid," WRC-TV, January 20, 2022.

97 *a teacher in Cupertino, California*: Christopher F. Rufo, "Woke Elementary," *City Journal*, January 13, 2021.

97 *It became popular to argue*: Jesse Singal, "What if Diversity Training Is Doing More Harm Than Good?" *New York Times*, January 17, 2023.

97 *researchers at Stanford University*: Li Lucy, Dorottya Demszky, Patricia Bromley, and Dan Jurafsky, "Content Analysis of Textbooks via Natural Language Processing: Findings on Gender, Race, and Ethnicity in Texas U.S. History Textbooks," *AERA Open*, 6, no. 3 (2020).

98 *surveys showed that nearly half of all Americans*: Russell Heilmlich, "What Caused the Civil War?" Pew Research Center, May 18, 2011, and "A Nation Still Divided: The Confederate Flag," Marist College Institute for Public Opinion, August 6, 2015, and Emily Guskin, Scott Clement, and Joe Heim, "Americans show spotty knowledge about the history of slavery but acknowledge its enduring effects," *Washington Post*, August 28, 2019.

98 *Carroll's interim superintendent*: Talia Richman, "Judge halts Carroll ISD's diversity plan after opponents win temporary restraining order," *Dallas Morning News*, December 4, 2020.

98 *In one session that August*: Southlake resident Guy Midkiff obtained secretly recorded audio of the diversity training and published it on his podcast, *Wise Guy Talks*.

99 *In another district-wide training*: Joy Pullman, "Parents Revolt After Texas's No. 1 School District Tries to Institutionalize Racism," *The Federalist*, April 27, 2021.

99 *a nationally recognized religious liberty lawyer*: Smith's biography can be found on the website of the Federalist Society for Law and Public Policy Studies, where she is listed as a contributor.

99 *in the hopes of raising her kids*: Virginia Allen, "She Won Her School Board Race by Opposing Critical Race Theory," *Daily Signal*, June 10, 2021.

99 *helped chip away at the contraceptive mandate*: Hannah C. Smith, "Beyond Hobby Lobby, the government's war on nuns rages," *Deseret News*, July 2, 2014.

100 *a* New York Times *article*: Dena Kleiman, "Parents' Groups Purging Schools of 'Humanist' Books and Classes," *New York Times*, May 17, 1981.

101 *activists demanded that educators*: Joan DelFattore, *What Johnny Shouldn't Read: Textbook Censorship in America* (Yale University Press, 1992), 31–38.

102 *fundamentalists waged a years-long crusade*: Jill Lepore, "Why the School Wars Still Rage," *New Yorker*, March 14, 2022.

102 *campaign against popular social studies textbooks*: Ronald Evans, "This Happened in America: Harold Rugg and the Censure of Social Studies," *Curriculum History* (2006).

102 *a direct forebearer of the anti-secularism movement*: Meagan Day, "This violent 1974 clash over textbooks in West Virginia prepped the nation for a New Right movement," *Timeline*, January 24, 2017, and Sarah Posner, "Debate over teaching books by Black authors has roots in violent 1974 clash in West Virginia," *Washington Post*, October 29, 2021.

103 *a 1988 list of demands*: Joan DelFattore, *What Johnny Shouldn't Read: Textbook Censorship in America* (Yale University Press, 1992), 146–47.

103 *passed a law in 1984*: Judy Mann, "What's Secular Humanism?" *Washington Post*, January 30, 1985.

104 *one liberal critic said at the time*: "Secular Humanism: Meaning Varies with Political Stance," *New York Times*, February 28, 1986.

104 *In Burlington, Wisconsin*: Tyler Kingkade, "How one teacher's Black Lives Matter lesson divided a small Wisconsin town," NBC News, October 24, 2020.

105 *In rural Tennessee*: Hannah Natanson, "A White teacher taught White students about White privilege. It cost him his job," *Washington Post*, December 6, 2021.

105 *An art teacher*: Zack Briggs and Adam Pyle, "Former charter school teacher fired

after declining to stop wearing Black Lives Matter mask," KENS-TV, September 21, 2020.

105 *a suburb outside Columbus*: Alissa Widman Neese, "Dublin educators' T-shirts ignite controversy, conversations about racism," *Columbus Dispatch*, September 20, 2020.

CHAPTER 7: ONE ELECTION AWAY

108 *"I get the easy question"*: The Southlake Families PAC candidate interviews were conducted in private. This account is based on a secret recording of one of the sessions and an interview with one of the participants.

110 *its slate of five candidates*: None of the candidates responded to interview requests.

111 *efforts to make the school culture more welcoming*: "MISD Board Names Chalisa Fain As District's Director of Diversity, Equity and Inclusion," *Focus Daily News*, August 17, 2020.

112 *a cease-and-desist letter*: No lawsuit was ever filed. In a statement, members of SARC defended the video, writing, "If any of these individuals are ashamed of their statements or how they may be perceived by the public, then they should reconsider why they felt justified making these statements in front of the school board."

112 *a twenty-seven-year-old news article*: "Bank Plot Leads to Prison," *South Florida Sun-Sentinel*, November 14, 1994.

112 *The uglier the fighting got*: At one point the Tarrant County Democratic Party posted and then deleted an image on social media showing photos of all the Southlake Families candidates, including Smith and Bryan, and labeling all of them as "racist." Meanwhile, the PAC blanketed the city with glossy political flyers accusing each of the pro–diversity plan candidates of pushing for radical socialism in Southlake.

114 *Wilson denied the allegation*: A spokeswoman for Wilson issued a statement defending the charges: "The Texas Open Meetings Act embodies the most basic values of democracy. Its requirements ensure that the citizens of Texas can stay informed about and participate in their local government."

114 *The PAC had spent a few thousand dollars*: Details about Southlake Families PAC's fundraising and spending can be found in financial disclosures filed with the Texas Ethics Commission.

116 *"He can't choose what his name is"*: Smith's opponents seized on this line, which they said seemed to suggest there was something wrong with the bullied child's name.

117 *Four boys in her grade had created a private chat*: I reviewed copies of the Instagram messages and records detailing the district's investigations in the matter.

118 *both female and gender-neutral pronouns*: With Mia's permission, this book refers to her by female pronouns.

121 *an era of broadening acceptance*: Dante Chinni, "1 in 5 adult members of Gen Z self-identify as LGBTQ," NBC News, July 3, 2022.

121 *backlash from conservatives*: Judith Butler, "Why is the idea of 'gender' provoking backlash the world over?" *The Guardian*, October 23, 2021.

121 *wasn't up for debate*: Later that spring, the U.S. Department of Education would formally weigh in with official guidance. Federal civil rights laws meant to protect students from discrimination on the basis of sex, the agency advised, also extended to transgender and nonbinary students like Mia.

CHAPTER 8: BLOWOUT

125 *I'd published a written article*: Mike Hixenbaugh, "A viral video forced a wealthy Texas suburb to confront racism. A 'silent majority' fought back," NBC News, January 22, 2021.

125 *Antonia brought that story*: *NBC Nightly News with Lester Holt*, "Texas town in spotlight after parents push back against diversity plan," NBC News, February 24, 2021.

126 *inflamed anti-media animosity*: Michael M. Grynbaum, "Trump Calls the News Media the 'Enemy of the American People,'" *New York Times*, February 17, 2017.

126 *published a series of articles*: Joy Pullman, "Parents Revolt After Texas's No. 1 School District Tries to Institutionalize Racism," *The Federalist*, April 27, 2021, and Joy Pullman, "Agitators Get Dirty to Push Institutional Racism in Texas's No. 1 School District," *The Federalist*, April 29, 2021, and Auguste Meyrat, "The Southlake Schools Uproar Shows Parents Need to Speak Up About Their Kids' Schools," *The Federalist*, April 30, 2021.

126 *a segment about the Southlake controversy*: *The Story with Martha MacCallum*, Fox News, April 28, 2021.

126 *a segment on his primetime broadcast*: *Tucker Carlson Tonight*, Fox News, April 27, 2021.

128 *CCAP opponents had raised nearly twenty times more*: Hernandez raised only about $4,500 for his campaign against Smith, whose campaign brought in more than $67,000 and received significant support from Southlake Families PAC.

129 *mayor-elect John Huffman grabbed a microphone*: Videos of the Southlake Families PAC victory party were posted on social media.

130 *having changed his position*: Ronnell Smith, who declined to be interviewed, said in social media posts that his opposition to the CCAP was the result of conversations with voters.

CHAPTER 9: THE SOUTHLAKE PLAYBOOK

132 *The* Federalist *compared the conservative uprising*: Tristan Justice, "It's Time for a New Cultural Tea Party to Offer Its Vision for America," *The Federalist*, May 07, 2021.

132 *The* Wall Street Journal *editorial board*: "Southlake Says No to Woke Education," *Wall Street Journal*, May 7, 2021.

132 *Laura Ingraham opened her nightly Fox News broadcast*: *The Ingraham Angle*, Fox News, May 3, 2021.

133 *a dark vision of America*: Tim Dickinson, "How Roger Ailes Built the Fox News Fear Factory," *Rolling Stone*, May 25, 2011.

133 *Steve Bannon declared*: Tyler Kingkade, Brandy Zadrozny, and Ben Collins, "Critical race theory battle invades school boards—with help from conservative groups," NBC News, June 15, 2021.

133 *Southlake Families threw themselves a victory party*: Video of the event was posted to YouTube by the Republican Party of Texas.

134 *in a darkened parking lot*: "Outraged protesters harass parents outside school board mask vote," CNN, August 12, 2021.

135 *Similar scenes had played out in Loudoun County, Virginia*: Tyler Kingkade, "In wealthy Loudoun County, Virginia, parents face threats in battle over equity in schools," NBC News, June 1, 2021.

135 *and in Rockwood, Missouri*: *NBC Nightly News*, "Educators under pressure from parents amid critical race theory debate," NBC News, September 3, 2021.

135 *School board meetings grew so volatile*: ProPublica identified fifty-nine people arrested or charged over an eighteen-month period because of turmoil at school board meetings across the country.

135 *wrote a letter to President Joe Biden*: Following intense backlash, the National School Board Association later apologized for the letter, writing, "there was no justification for some of the language included" in it.

135 *sending a memo to the FBI*: Gary Fields, "Garland says authorities will target school board threats," *Associated Press*, October 5, 2021.

135 *Conservative activists seized on the missive*: Daniel Dale, "Fact check: Kevin McCarthy keeps repeating false claim that attorney general called parents 'terrorists' for wanting to attend school board meetings," CNN, April 26, 2022.

135 *and Moms for Liberty*: A year later, in June 2023, the Southern Poverty Law Center declared Moms for Liberty as an anti-government extremist group. The designation drew condemnation from Republicans.

135 *Robin Steenman had launched*: Julie Carr, "Moms for Liberty Member and Retired Air Force Major Robin Steenman: 'Now It's Time to Be Awake and to Understand Who the True Conservatives Are Because the Stakes Are High,'" *Tennessee Star*, May 4, 2022, and Paige Williams, "The right-wing mothers fueling the school-board wars: Moms for Liberty claims that teachers are indoctrinating students with dangerous ideologies. But is the group's aim protecting kids—or scaring parents?" *New Yorker*, October 31, 2022.

136 *an eleven-page letter*: Gabriella Borter, "'Critical race theory' roils a Tennessee school district," *Reuters*, September 21, 2021.

136 *she admired Martin Luther King Jr.'s call*: It became popular that summer for anti-CRT activists to present themselves as the true defenders of Martin Luther King Jr.'s dream for a society where children are not judged by the color of their skin, but these parents rarely quoted King's other speeches or writings calling for structural reforms to undo the deep and lasting racial disparities created by slavery and Jim Crow. "It is a cruel jest," King once said, "to say to a bootless man that he ought to lift himself by his own bootstraps."

136 *refused to remove the books*: Jo Napolitano, "After Losing High-Profile Book Battle, Conservative Moms for Liberty Turns to Critical Tennessee School Board Race," *The 74*, March 23, 2022.

137 *Leigh Wambsganss reported receiving*: *America First News with Grant Stinchfield*, March 30, 2023.

138 *a barometer of the American conservative movement*: Matthew Brown, "What is CPAC? A brief history of the conservative movement's most influential gathering," *USA Today*, February 26, 2021.

138 *keynote address filled with grievances and lies*: Aaron Rupar, "Trump will never stop lying about the 2020 election. His CPAC speech proved it," *Vox*, February 28, 2021.

138 *Smith spoke from the same stage*: "Conservative Political Action Conference Discussion on Critical Race Theory," C-SPAN, July 11, 2021.

139 *In the affluent majority-white suburbs west of St. Louis*: The Francis Howell school district's ugly 2014 battle over integration was famously chronicled in a two-part special series on *This American Life*, the public radio program produced by WBEZ. The episodes, titled "The Problem We All Live With," were reported by 1619 Project creator Nikole Hannah-Jones.

139 *in the Dallas–Fort Worth suburbs alone*: Talia Richman and Corbett Smith, "Bolstered by CRT, book fights, conservative PACs aim to 'take back' Texas school boards," *Dallas Morning News*, March 3, 2022.

139 *a liberal Fort Worth newspaper coined the phrase*: "The Southlake Playbook," *Fort Worth Weekly*, October 6, 2021.

139 *contemplating whether to discipline a Black high school principal*: Antonia Hylton, Emily Berk, and Alicia Victoria Lozano, "Texas principal forced to resign over critical race theory," NBC News, November 9, 2021.

CHAPTER 10: THE PARENTS ARE OUR CLIENTS

140 *"morals and faith"*: Muns, who did not respond to interview requests, wrote about the episode on social media.

141 *was largely symbolic*: Three months later, the board reversed its decision to reprimand Farah after the teacher challenged the legality of the punishment. Along with approving a confidential settlement with Farah, the board adopted a mea culpa resolution acknowledging that the authority to discipline and reprimand employees at the campus level rested with district administrators, not the school board.

142 *One educator sent me a copy of a rubric*: Mike Hixenbaugh, "Southlake, Texas, schools restrict classroom libraries after backlash over anti-racist book," NBC News, October 8, 2021.

146 *One of them was McGuirk*: The teacher agreed to reveal her identity in this book.

147 *nearly every major news outlet*: Eric Kleefeld, "After Texas teachers were told to give 'other perspectives' on the Holocaust, Fox News is quiet about a 'critical race theory' story," *Media Matters*, October 15, 2021.

147 *including the* New York Times, Washington Post, *and* USA Today: Johnny Diaz, "Texas Superintendent Apologizes After Official's Holocaust Remarks," *New York Times,* October 15, 2021, and Meryl Kornfield and Timothy Bella, "Texas school official tells teachers that Holocaust books should be countered with 'opposing' views," *Washington Post*, October 15, 2021, and Scott Gleeson, "Texas school leader tells teachers to balance Holocaust books with 'opposing' views," *USA Today*, October 15, 2021.

147 *Jewish authors and descendants of Holocaust survivors*: Fern Schumer Chapman, "School administrator's compassionless comments on Holocaust invalidate pain of generations," *USA Today*, October 18, 2021, and *New Day*, CNN, October 15, 2022.

147 *came forward to defend her*: Mike Hixenbaugh, "Jewish Southlake residents on Holocaust remark: 'There are not two sides,'" NBC News, October 18, 2021.

148 *mayor John Huffman issued a statement*: Anna Caplan, "Southlake mayor responds to Holocaust comments, says NBC reporting aims to 'tear down' families," *Dallas Morning News*, October 18, 2021.

150 *accused of pushing "pornography"*: Elizabeth A. Harris and Alexandra Alter, "With Rising Book Bans, Librarians Have Come Under Attack," *New York Times*, July 6, 2022.

150 *a nationwide movement to diversify*: Kathy Ishizuka, "Can Diverse Books Save Us? In a divided world, librarians are on a mission," *School Library Journal,* October 21, 2018.

150 *call for criminal charges*: Cassandra Pollock and Jolie McCullough, "Gov. Greg Abbott calls for criminal investigation into availability of 'pornographic books' in public schools," *Texas Tribune*, November 10, 2021.

150 *a list of 850 titles*: Brian Lopez, "Texas House committee to investigate school districts' books on race and sexuality," *Texas Tribune*, October 26, 2021.

150 *The free speech advocacy group PEN America*: "Banned in the USA: The Growing Movement to Censor Books in Schools," PEN America, September 19, 2022.

151 *a Virginia school district's fight*: Hannah Natanson, "A mom wrongly said the book showed pedophilia. School libraries banned it," *Washington Post*, December 22, 2022.

151 *made national headlines that fall*: David K. Li, "Texas school district pulls books by acclaimed Black author amid critical race theory claims," NBC News, October 6, 2021.

153 *"OK, groomer"*: Io Dodds and Alex Woodward, "GOP 'groomer' smears are sparking a new wave of anti-LGBT+ violence," *The Independent*, April 14, 2022.

153 *I'd written a story about the growing campaign*: Mike Hixenbaugh, "Banned: Books on race and sexuality are disappearing from Texas schools in record numbers," NBC News, February 1, 2022.

155 *a school board policy meant to prevent censorship*: Later, the Carroll school board would rewrite its library policy, giving residents more power to have books removed.

155 *who'd gone on Fox News*: "Critical race theory harmful, American children in 'dangerous' position: Karith Foster," Fox News, July 8, 2021.

155 *Smith told a reporter*: Virginia Allen, "She Won Her School Board Race by Opposing Critical Race Theory," *Daily Signal*, June 10, 2021.

156 *The school board voted that winter*: Sandra Sadek, "Carroll ISD employees now prohibited from secretly recording meetings following policy change," *Community Impact*, December 13, 2021.

CHAPTER 11: CHRISTIANITY WILL HAVE POWER

159 *"the reservoir of sentiment"*: Trip Gabriel, "He Fuels the Right's Cultural Fires (and Spreads Them to Florida)," *New York Times*, April 24, 2022.

159 *sentiment on the sexuality issue*: Although Rufo said "sexuality," most of the examples he provided dealt with gender.

159 *took that message onto* Tucker Carlson Tonight: Tucker Carlson calls for teachers who discuss LGBTQ identity in schools to 'get hurt,'" Media Matters, July 22, 2022.

160 *the original sin that triggered what they viewed as this country's moral decline*: David Barton, *America: To Pray or Not to Pray* (WallBuilder Press, 1994), 130–131.

160 *did not blossom into a full-fledged national coalition*: Martin King, "Another New Day for the woman who started the religious right," *Baptist Press,* August 3, 2001.

161 *Bryant told a reporter*: Broadcast news report, WFOR-TV (1977).

161 *"will hear what the people have said"*: B. Drummond Ayres Jr., "Miami Votes 2 to 1 to Repeal Law Barring Bias Against Homosexuals," *New York Times*, June 8, 1977.

161 *helped give rise to Jerry Falwell's Moral Majority*: Chris Bull and John Gallagher, *Perfect Enemies: The Religious Right, the Gay Movement, and the Politics of the 1990s* (Crown 1996), 16–17.

161 *"Here's one for Anita!"*: "Bryant Sued by Mother of Slain Gay," *Associated Press*, July 2, 1977.

161 *For her follow-up act*: "Bryant wants prayer back in schools," *Orlando Sentinel*, November 9, 1977.

161 *repeatedly failed to achieve that goal*: Joan Biskupic, "Federal Court Rejects Prayer at Graduation," *Washington Post*, November 19, 1994.

161 *In one case from 1992*: Terry Lee Goodrich, "Carroll High student protests prayers at pep rallies," *Fort Worth Star-Telegram*, November 11, 1992, and Jim Jones, "Another fight over school prayer," *Fort Worth Star-Telegram*, November 14, 1992.

161 *A Southlake mother*: Karen Lincoln Michel, "Prayer backers rally," *Dallas Morning News*, December 6, 1992.

162 *the Carroll school board settled the case*: Karen Lincoln Michel, "Carroll schools OK prayer settlement," *Dallas Morning News*, January 26, 1993.

162 *shocked the conscience of evangelical Christians*: "Attitudes on Same-Sex Marriage," Pew Research, May 14, 2019.

162 *Donald Trump gave a speech*: Colin Campbell, "TRUMP: If I'm president, 'Christianity will have power' in the US," *Business Insider*, January 23, 2016.

163 *From the stage of a conference center in Dallas*: Barton's comments were recorded and later broadcast in a December 30, 2021, episode of the *WallBuilders Live!* podcast and radio show.

163 *For more than three decades*: David D. Kirkpatrick, "Putting God Back into American History," *New York Times*, February 27, 2005.

164 *After touring the site of Nazi atrocities in Poland*: Barton, who did not respond to interview requests, made the comments on an April 13, 2017, episode of the *WallBuilders Live!* podcast and radio show.

164 *Barton's pseudo-history provided the philosophical underpinnings*: Tara Isabella Burton, "Understanding the fake historian behind America's religious right," Vox, January 25, 2018.

165 *filed a police report*: Brown and the other mother, Karen Lowery, later told reporters at KXAS-TV that the constable recruited them to file the charges after hearing a presentation they gave on library content: "Constable London asked

if we would be the complainant on the original report," Lowery wrote. "Monica and I agreed to do so believing we should support law enforcement."

166 *Brown's adult son, Weston, came forward*: I wrote an August 11, 2022, article for NBC News about Brown's fractured relationship with her son under the headline "A mom's campaign to ban library books divided a Texas town—and her own family." In a series of email exchanges, Brown initially invited me to interview her over dinner at her home in Granbury, but in a subsequent message, she said her husband would not allow the meeting, adding, "I have been advised to not speak with you at all."

167 *"a large millstone hung around your neck"*: The retributive Bible verse was also the inspiration behind an Oklahoma lawmaker's bill to ban medical care for transgender children, which he titled the "Millstone Act."

167 *a secret recording surfaced*: Mike Hixenbaugh and Jeremy Schwartz, "Texas superintendent tells librarians to pull books on sexuality, transgender people," NBC News, ProPublica, and *Texas Tribune*, March 23, 2022.

167 *a book of Christian devotionals*: Kerry Roberts, Pauline Sampson, and Jeremy Glenn, *Daily Devotions for Superintendents* (Stephen F. Austin State University Press, 2014). Glenn said he couldn't recall whether he or one of his coauthors wrote the passages likening LGBTQ acceptance to Nazi indoctrination, but he acknowledged coauthoring the book, adding, "It's fair to say I am aware of its content."

168 *According to one national survey*: Rina Torchinsky, "Nearly half of LGBTQ youth seriously considered suicide, survey finds," NPR, May 5, 2022.

170 *more than double the total from the previous year*: Erica L. Green, "Strife in the Schools: Education Dept. Logs Record Number of Discrimination Complaints," *New York Times*, January 1, 2023.

CHAPTER 12: SEVEN MOUNTAINS

172 *an ascendant figure in far-right Republican politics*: Steve Karnowski, "MyPillow Guy among the Trump acolytes picking up the torch," *Associated Press*, January 23, 2021.

172 *a coded phrase*: Colleen Long, "How 'Let's Go Brandon' became code for insulting Joe Biden," *Associated Press*, October 30, 2021.

173 *now a regular on the CPAC stage*: In a twist of irony, Smith was joined on the panel by Jack Brewer, a Black former NFL wide receiver who'd been the target of a white Carroll student's racist "T.A.N.H.O." sign when Brewer was a star football player at Grapevine High School in 1996. Since then, Brewer, who'd once supported Obama for president, had gained a national following in conservative circles following his endorsement of Trump, later calling him the nation's "first Black president."

174 *Southlake Families PAC cofounder, Leigh Wambsganss*: I approached Wambsganss for an interview at CPAC, but she declined.

174 *which rented space on T-Mobile's cellular network*: Shelly Hagan, Scott Moritz, and Todd Shields, "T-Mobile Faces Backlash on Ties to Conservative Carrier in Texas," *Bloomberg*, October 14, 2022.

175 *The company's transformation*: Mike Hixenbaugh, "How a far-right, Christian cellphone company 'took over' four Texas school boards," NBC News, August 25, 2022.

175 *the Seven Mountains Mandate*: Katherine Stewart, "Christian Nationalists Are Excited About What Comes Next," *New York Times*, July 5, 2022.

176 *rife with dominionist talking points*: Conrad Swanson, "Lauren Boebert is part of a dangerous religious movement that threatens democracy, experts say," *Denver Post*, September 14, 2022.

176 *spent years studying*: For more on the GOP's recent embrace of Christian dominionism, read Fea's 2018 book, *Believe Me: The Evangelical Road to Donald Trump*. Eerdmans.

176 *famously misnamed a book of the Bible*: Jessica Taylor, "Citing 'Two Corinthians,' Trump Struggles to Make The Sale to Evangelicals," NPR, January 18, 2016.

176 *a larger share of white evangelical voters*: Eugene Scott, "More white evangelical voters back Trump than Romney," CNN, July 15, 2016.

177 *invited them directly into the fold*: Elle Hardy, "The 'modern apostles' who want to reshape America ahead of the end times," *The Outline*, March 19, 2020.

177 *one of the leading proponents of the Seven Mountains*: Keri Ladner, "The quiet rise of Christian dominionism," *Christian Century*, September 22, 2022.

179 *Patriot Mobile blasted out fliers*: Mike Hixenbaugh, "After a Texas school shooting, conservatives blamed 'woke' programs once approved by Republicans," NBC News, July 18, 2022.

179 *an extra boost from the pulpit*: A video of Morris's sermon was posted on Gateway's website.

182 *"you are actually advertising suicide"*: Tyler Kingkade and Mike Hixenbaugh, "Parents protesting 'critical race theory' identify another target: Mental health programs," NBC News, November 15, 2021.

183 *who'd spoken anonymously to CNN*: "Texas teacher says 'fear and ignorance' are driving school policy," CNN, October 16, 2021.

CHAPTER 13: THE FLORIDA BLUEPRINT

185 *blossomed into a powerful force*: Tyler Kingkade, "Moms for Liberty's conservative activists are planning their next move: Taking over school boards," NBC News, July 17, 2022.

185 *written as a tribute to DeSantis*: Tom Szaroleta, "Lynyrd Skynyrd, .38 Special's Van Zant brothers write 'Sweet Florida' tribute song for DeSantis," *Florida Times-Union*, April 7, 2022.

185 *"This is called a Rudis"*: In the case of gladiators—many of whom were forced to battle as slaves of the Roman Empire—the freedom they fought for was their own.

186 *candidate to supplant Donald Trump*: Dexter Filkins, "Can Ron DeSantis Displace Donald Trump as the G.O.P.'s Combatant-in-Chief?" *New Yorker*, June 20, 2022.

187 *scrapped diversity and inclusion training programs*: "College halts diversity training to comply with DeSantis law," *Associated Press*, January 27, 2023.

187 *the state cited the law*: Patricia Mazzei and Anemona Hartocollis, "Florida Rejects A.P. African American Studies Class," *New York Times*, January 19, 2023.

187 *an alternative college aptitude test*: Ana Ceballos and Sommer Brugal, "Florida is considering a 'classical and Christian' alternative to the SAT," *Miami Herald* and *Tampa Bay Times*, February 17, 2023.

187 *Florida's "Don't Say Gay" law*: Anthony Izaguirre, "'Don't Say Gay' bill signed by Florida Gov. Ron DeSantis," *Associated Press*, March 28, 2022.

188 *In one high-profile case*: Leyla Santiago, "Fact check: Emails show one of DeSantis' stories backing the rationale for so-called 'Don't Say Gay' law didn't happen as the governor says," CNN, April 6, 2022.

188 *a genuine and complicated debate*: Katie J. M. Baker, "When Students Change Gender Identity, and Parents Don't Know," *New York Times*, January 22, 2023.

188 *a rare politician with the courage*: Douglas Blair, "Gov. Ron DeSantis Proves Conservatives Can Beat LGBT-Obsessed Left," *Daily Signal*, March 08, 2022.

188 *joined onstage by anti-CRT activist*: Sommer Brugal, "DeSantis signs 'stop woke' act, Disney bills next to a stage full of supporters," *Miami Herald*, April 23, 2022.

188 *the goal of purging the school of progressive pedagogy*: Michelle Goldberg, "DeSantis Allies Plot the Hostile Takeover of a Liberal College," *New York Times*, Jan. 9, 2023.

189 *accused it of pushing sexuality*: Fatma Khaled, "Bugs Bunny's Controversial History Revisited After Ron DeSantis' Comments," *Newsweek*, April 29, 2022.

189 *elevated fringe medical experts*: Eric Hananoki, "Key Ron DeSantis medical ally: 'Fauci should face a firing squad,'" Media Matters, January 31, 2023.

189 *directed someone in his office*: Loren Cecil, "Libs of TikTok Creator Chaya Raichik Called Ron DeSantis 'Incredible' for Offering Her Refuge in Florida Governor's Mansion," *BuzzFeed*, December 27, 2022.

189 *For his part, DeSantis*: The governor's press team did not respond to interview requests.

189 *a group of social studies teachers*: Ana Ceballos and Sommer Brugal, "Teachers alarmed by state's infusing religion, downplaying race in civics training," *Miami Herald* and *Tampa Bay Times*, June 29, 2022.

190 *the administration appointed Larry Arnn*: Daniel Payne, "Trump ally Hillsdale College pitches 1619 Project counterweight," *Politico*, July 21, 2021.

191 *minimized the role of slavery*: Derrick Clifton, "How the Trump administration's '1776 Report' warps the history of racism and slavery," NBC News, January 20, 2021.

191 *In secretly recorded remarks*: Phil Williams, "REVEALED: Teachers come from 'dumbest parts of dumbest colleges,' Tenn. governor's education advisor tells him," WTVF-TV, July 12, 2022.

191 *DeSantis echoed those remarks*: Steven Lemongello and Leslie Postal, "DeSantis wants retired police, firefighters, EMTs to be teachers," *Orlando Sentinel*, August 17, 2022.

192 *DeSantis's chief of staff told the* National Review: Caroline Downey, "DeSantis Shakes Up Leadership of Woke Florida College, Appoints Conservative," *National Review*, January 6, 2023.

192 *created the 1836 Project*: Heidi Pérez-Moreno, "Texas' 1836 Project aims to promote 'patriotic education,' but critics worry it will gloss over state's history of racism," *Texas Tribune*, June 9, 2021.

192 *PEN America tracked three hundred state bills*: Jonathan Friedman, Jeffrey Sachs, Jeremy C. Young, and Samantha LaFrance, "Educational censorship continues: The 2023 legislative sessions so far," PEN America, February 16, 2023.

192 *Writing for the* Guardian: Jason Stanley, "Banning ideas and authors is not a 'culture war'—it's fascism," *The Guardian*, February 14, 2023.

193 *likened the policies favored by DeSantis*: Timothy Snyder, "The War on History Is a War on Democracy," *New York Times Magazine*, June 29, 2021.

193 *popular among some mainstream conservatives*: Will Carless, "Month before Buffalo shooting, poll finds, 7 in 10 Republicans believed in 'great replacement' ideas," *USA Today*, June 1, 2022.

193 *who famously embraced the QAnon*: After her election to Congress, Green disavowed the conspiracy theory.

194 *educators nationwide were once again grappling*: Mike Hixenbaugh, "Laws restricting lessons on racism are making it hard for teachers to discuss the massacre in Buffalo," NBC News, May 18, 2022.

195 *who'd claimed on Fox News*: Justin Baragona, "Texas Lt. Guv Spews Racist 'Great Replacement' Theory on Fox: 'A Revolution Has Begun,'" *Daily Beast*, September 17, 2021.

195 *reported more than five thousand vacancies*: Sam Sachs, "Florida education report forecasts which areas may have teacher shortages as school starts," WFLA-TV, August 29, 2022.

195 *A nationwide survey of teachers*: Ashley Woo, Sabrina Lee, Andrea Prado Tuma, Julia H. Kaufman, Rebecca Ann Lawrence, and Nastassia Reed, "Walking on Eggshells—Teachers' Responses to Classroom Limitations on Race- or Gender-Related Topics" (Rand 2022).

195 *just 13 percent of the nation's eighth graders*: Donna St. George, "Students' understanding of history and civics is worsening," *Washington Post*, May 3, 2023.

196 *planned to leave their jobs*: Elizabeth D. Steiner, Sy Doan, Ashley Woo, Allyson D. Gittens, Rebecca Ann Lawrence, Lisa Berdie, Rebecca L. Wolfe, Lucas Greer, and Heather L. Schwartz, "Restoring Teacher and Principal Well-Being Is an Essential Step for Rebuilding Schools" (Rand 2022).

196 *a high school special education teacher*: Michael Sainato, "'It's had a chilling effect': Florida teachers anxious about 'don't say gay' bill," *The Guardian*, August 31, 2022.

196 *a special education teacher in Pensacola*: Pocharapon Neammanee, "A Florida elementary school teacher resigned after a district employee took down posters of prominent Black figures like Harriett Tubman in his classroom, saying 'it was not age appropriate,'" *Business Insider*, August 13, 2022.

196 *purge their classrooms*: Matt Lavietes, "As Florida's 'Don't Say Gay' law takes effect, schools roll out LGBTQ restrictions," NBC News, June 30, 2022.

196 *district lawyers initially told teachers*: Katie Anthony, "A Florida school district now says LGBTQ teachers can put photos on their desk of their partners and

talk about them in class as DeSantis' restrictions on teaching causes confusion," *Business Insider*, August 1, 2022.

196 *a lesbian fourth-grade teacher*: Hannah Natanson, "This Florida teacher married a woman. Now she's not a teacher anymore," *Washington Post*, May 19, 2022.

CHAPTER 14: I LOST MY SON

198 *made national headlines*: María Luisa Paúl, "Anne Frank adaptation, 40 more books pulled from Texas school district," *Washington Post*, August 18, 2022.

199 *reports about young neo-Nazis*: Karen Lincoln Michel, "Diverse Tensions; Grapevine's changes may be fueling racial incidents," *Dallas Morning News*, October 23, 1993.

200 *posed with a man displaying a Confederate flag*: Mark Dent, "Fort Worth–area councilwoman poses with Confederate flag even as protests convulse Texas," *Fort Worth Star-Telegram*, June 10, 2020.

201 *labeled as an anti-government extremist group*: Emily Brindley, "Tarrant County–based True Texas Project added to national list of extremist groups," *Fort Worth Star-Telegram*, March 25, 2022.

202 *introduced herself as Sharla*: To protect the identity of her child, I'm not publishing Sharla's last name.

206 *the number of teens identifying as trans*: Azeen Ghorayshi, "Report Reveals Sharp Rise in Transgender Young People in the U.S.," *New York Times*, June 10, 2022.

206 *a panic among some parents*: Maggie Astor, "Transgender Americans Feel Under Siege as Political Vitriol Rises," *New York Times*, December 10, 2022.

206 *research documenting the harm*: Anna Forsythe, Casey Pick, Gabriel Tremblay, et al., "Humanistic and Economic Burden of Conversion Therapy Among LGBTQ Youths in the United States," *JAMA Pediatrics* (2022).

207 *directed the state's child welfare agency*: Chuck Lindell, "Texas Gov. Greg Abbott orders state agency to treat gender-affirming care as child abuse," *Austin American-Statesman*, February 23, 2022.

208 *Sharla shared her story*: Eric Geist, "Bombshell Claims of GCISD Teacher Misconduct," *Dallas Express*, August 26, 2022.

211 *followed the Southlake Playbook at every stage*: Brant Bingamon, "Has Round Rock ISD Hit Rock Bottom?" *Austin Chronicle*, November 4, 2022.

CHAPTER 15: THE HOLY GRAIL

213 *had drawn national media attention*: Stephanie McCrummen, "An American Kingdom," *Washington Post*, July 11, 2021.

214 *$168,000 from Defend Texas Liberty*: Mike Hixenbaugh and Kate Martin, "Texas politicians rake in millions from far-right Christian megadonors pushing private school vouchers," NBC News, November 6, 2022.

214 *government should be guided by biblical values*: Michelle Conlin, "Special Report: Touting morality, billionaire Texas brothers top 2016 donor list," Reuters, September 11, 2015.

214 *run exclusively by evangelicals*: R. G. Ratcliffe, "The Power Issue: Tim Dunn Is Pushing the Republican Party into the Arms of God," *Texas Monthly*, December 2018.

214 *a friend of Black Lives Matter*: Schatzline made the claim in a campaign video posted on May 14, 2022 that was captioned "EXPOSING THE LIES OF Laura Hill."

214 *pushing Texas further to the right*: Ed Lavandera, "CNN Special Report: Deep in the Pockets of Texas," CNN, June 24, 2022.

214 *out of reach in Texas*: Mike Hixenbaugh, "Inside the rural Texas resistance to the GOP's private school choice plan," NBC News, March 21, 2023.

215 *a national political action committee*: Tyler Kingkade, "A Betsy DeVos–backed group helps fuel a rapid expansion of public money for private schools," NBC News, March 30, 2023.

215 *hosted a strategy call*: Meghan Mangrum, "Lt. Gov. Dan Patrick, Texas pastors gearing up for school voucher fight," *Dallas Morning News*, September 7, 2022.

215 *at an event hosted by Hillsdale College*: Rufo later disputed accusations that he was calling on activists to create distrust in public schools, but instead meant that teachers unions and pandemic closures had caused people to distrust schools, paving the way for school choice.

216 *drew funding from billionaire Tim Dunn*: Although nonprofit donor lists are not public, the *Texas Observer* obtained and published a copy of TPPF's 2010 donor list, showing $43,000 from Dunn, who also served on the foundation's board of directors.

216 *exclusively at private Christian academies*: Forrest Wilder, "Preaching to the Choir: Greg Abbott Tours Private Christian Schools (Exclusively) to Make the Case for Vouchers," *Texas Monthly*, March 16, 2023.

217 *A 2017 investigation by the* Orlando Sentinel: "Schools Without Rules: An *Orlando Sentinel* Investigation," *Orlando Sentinel,* October 18, 2017.

217 *Despite initial indications*: Howard Fischer, "Most applying for Arizona vouchers already go to private schools," *Arizona Star*, September 8, 2022.

219 *In Alabama*: Trisha Powell Crain, "Alabama bill would protect student-led school prayer, PA broadcasts of prayer," *AL.com*, March 2, 2023.

219 *In Oklahoma*: John Kruzel, "Oklahoma eyes first US religious charter school after Supreme Court rulings, *Reuters*, April 6, 2023.

220 *following Texas's lead*: Greg Hilburn, "Representative Dodie Horton wants In God We Trust displayed in every Louisiana classroom," *Lafayette Daily Advertiser*, January 19, 2023.

220 *ruled in favor of a Washington state high school football*: Robert Barnes, "Supreme Court rules for high school football coach who prayed at midfield," *Washington Post*, June 27, 2022.

221 *the National Association of Christian Lawmakers*: Tim Dickinson, "The Christian Nationalist Machine Turning Hate into Law," *Rolling Stone*, February 23, 2023.

221 *No state legislature went further*: Michelle Boorstein, "Texas pushes church into state with bills on school chaplains, Ten Commandments," *Washington Post*, May 24, 2023.

221 *"to bring Jesus to an entire nation"*: Malloy made a different argument while testifying in support of the bill, telling lawmakers chaplains would not be "working to convert people to religion."

222 *to imagine for their readers*: Talia Richman and Allie Morris, "Texas plan to put chaplains in public schools is latest move to inject Christianity," *Dallas Morning News*, May 10, 2023.

222 *at an event sponsored by Patriot Mobile*: Reporters were not permitted at the event, which Patriot Mobile filmed and posted on YouTube.

223 *come up short in the state House of Representatives*: Patrick Svitek, "After House vote signaling opposition to school choice, Gov. Greg Abbott says the fight isn't over," *Texas Tribune*, April 7, 2023.

224 *"This was a lost session for public education"*: Brian Lopez, "Time runs out for taxpayer-funded private school tuition bill as special session looms," *Texas Tribune*, May 20, 2023.

CHAPTER 16: IT STILL MATTERED

225 *residents who'd donated to Southlake Families PAC*: A review of campaign finance reports showed at least seven of the ten committee volunteers had donated to Southlake Families or publicly endorsed the PAC. School board member Hannah Smith also served on the committee.

228 *endured threats of violence*: Gabriella Borter, Joseph Ax, and Joseph Tanfani, "School boards get death threats amid rage over race, gender, mask policies," Reuters, February 15, 2022.

228 *perhaps recognizing*: Mills did not respond to interview requests.

229 *a political action committee of their own*: Mike Hixenbaugh and Antonia Hylton, "Christian activists are fighting to glorify God in a suburban Texas school district," NBC News, May 2, 2023.

231 *had also seemed to awaken*: Michelle Pitcher, "Students Taking Back 'Ownership' of Education," *Texas Observer*, January 5, 2023.

233 *had advised Ramser*: Ramser recorded the conversation and shared it with me. The principal did not respond to interview requests.

EPILOGUE

238 *continuing its investigations*: As of this writing in September 2023, seven of those federal civil rights investigations remained unresolved, including those involving complaints filed on behalf of Mia Mariani and Angela Jones's son. An eighth case was dismissed in August.

238 *revealed plans to abolish the federal agency*: DeSantis went on to say that if he failed to abolish the Education Department, he would instead harness its powers to attack "woke ideology" in schools. Another GOP candidate, Vivek Ramaswamy, promised to take $80 billion saved by shuttering the federal education agency and give it to parents to pay for their children's private school tuition.

Index

ABOUT

MARINER BOOKS

MARINER BOOKS traces its beginnings to 1832 when William Ticknor co-founded the Old Corner Bookstore in Boston, from which he would run the legendary firm Ticknor and Fields, publisher of Ralph Waldo Emerson, Harriet Beecher Stowe, Nathaniel Hawthorne, and Henry David Thoreau. Following Ticknor's death, Henry Oscar Houghton acquired Ticknor and Fields and, in 1880, formed Houghton Mifflin, which later merged with venerable Harcourt Publishing to form Houghton Mifflin Harcourt. HarperCollins purchased HMH's trade publishing business in 2021 and reestablished their storied lists and editorial team under the name Mariner Books.

Uniting the legacies of Houghton Mifflin, Harcourt Brace, and Ticknor and Fields, Mariner Books continues one of the great traditions in American bookselling. Our imprints have introduced an incomparable roster of enduring classics, including Hawthorne's *The Scarlet Letter,* Thoreau's *Walden,* Willa Cather's *O Pioneers!,* Virginia Woolf's *To the Lighthouse,* W.E.B. Du Bois's *Black Reconstruction,* J.R.R. Tolkien's *The Lord of the Rings,* Carson McCullers's *The Heart Is a Lonely Hunter,* Ann Petry's *The Narrows,* George Orwell's *Animal Farm* and *Nineteen Eighty-Four,* Rachel Carson's *Silent Spring,* Margaret Walker's *Jubilee,* Italo Calvino's *Invisible Cities,* Alice Walker's *The Color Purple,* Margaret Atwood's *The Handmaid's Tale,* Tim O'Brien's *The Things They Carried,* Philip Roth's *The Plot Against America,* Jhumpa Lahiri's *Interpreter of Maladies,* and many others. Today Mariner Books remains proudly committed to the craft of fine publishing established nearly two centuries ago at the Old Corner Bookstore.